Calculations for the Electrical Exam
By Tom Henry

While every precaution has been taken in the preparation of this book, the author and publisher assumes no responsibility for errors or omissions. Neither is any liability assumed from the use of the information contained herein.

National Electrical Code® and NEC® are Registered Trademarks of the National Fire Protection Association, Inc., Quincy, MA.

Based on the 2005 NEC®   Seventh Printing July 2007

ENRY PUBLICATIONS SINCE 1985

ISBN 0- 945495 -62-5

DEFINITIONS...

Calculate: To determine by mathematical processes.

To design or adapt for a purpose.

Calculating: Marked by prudent and deliberate analysis or by shrewd consideration of self-interest.

Calculation: Studied care in analyzing or planning.

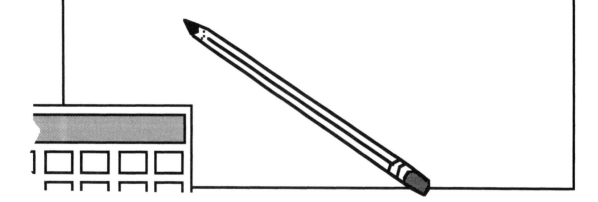

Preface

The writing of this book is an accumulation of over 48 years electrical experience working as an apprentice electrician, journeyman electrician, industrial electrician, construction electrician, master electrician, electrical inspector, author of 30 books, and the past 25 years as an electrical instructor preparing over 25,000 electricians throughout the U.S.A. for their electrical license examination.

I have learned how broad the term "electrician" can be in the specialized world we work in today.

I consider myself very fortunate to have been able to work in several of the "electrician" categories. Starting in 1956 as an apprentice electrician on diesel locomotives I learned the DC theory, generation, and horsepower. Later I worked as a railway signalman, a job that involves the climbing of poles and maintenance of cross-arms, towers, and gates. In the automated industry you are the "control electrician", the troubleshooter and maintainer. As a construction electrician you are the installer. At Disney World, I was a monorail electrician working on everything from the sophisticated control systems to the traction motors. As a master electrician, I was the electrical contractor involved with the electrical permits, design and running the job. As an electrical inspector you become the authority on the rules. As the electrical instructor and author, you never stop learning or studying and researching the exceptions and the fine print notes.

My objective in writing this book is to make the electrical exam calculations easier for the "electrician".

The electrical examination is something that will follow some electricians throughout their career.

An electrical license is required by most cities, counties, and states (which generally do not reciprocate). This requires taking electrical exams in different areas as you travel in your electrical work.

I have found in my experiences that test-taking by the electrician is difficult for the simple reason that an electrician is working from a blueprint where the calculations were performed by an electrical designer. Often in the field we use a slide for determining how many conductors can be installed in a certain size conduit or what size overloads are required for a motor, etc. The electrical exam requires the electrician, with the Code Book, to determine the maximum fill permitted in the conduit, the minimum size overloads, and to design the electrical system to the Code minimum requirements, which requires applying all the rules and demand factors that apply.

For some contractors, it has been twenty years or more since they have used math formulas, theory, and calculations. For most, the last time was an apprenticeship class. Now, for the exam, we are required to be an expert in the reading of the Code and in applying all of the tables and demand factors to the calculations.

In the exam preparation classes that I teach, I'm continually mentioning the "careful reading of each word" in the exam calculation question. You must first understand what the question is asking before you can accurately solve the calculation.

If I had to select one key word, it would be the word **minimum**. Keep in mind that the Code is the minimum requirement. In reality, we often exceed the Code minimum requirements as we design for the future and a more economical and efficient electrical system. Exam calculations will require determining the minimum conductor size, minimum size service, etc. To find the minimum, we must apply each demand factor and Code rule that is applicable.

As you read the exam question, circle key words such as: copper or aluminum, single-phase or three-phase, branch-circuit or feeder, minimum or maximum, grounded or ungrounded conductor, fuse or circuit breaker, metallic or nonmetallic, neutral or ungrounded conductor, demand load or connected load, continuous load or noncontinuous load, THW or THHN insulation type, RHH with an outer cover or without an outer cover, dwelling or nondwelling occupancy, general or optional method of calculation. As you can see, the changing of **one word** in a question can change the answer. As you study from the book, learn to circle each key word in the calculation question. Never memorize answers! Learn from this book the proper way to prepare for your electrical examination.

You can't just read the Code book, it must be taught.

"This book is written for an electrician by an electrician".

CONTENT

This book "Calculations For The Electrical Exam" is based on exam calculations asked from the Code book.

I have written other books which cover the exam calculations that are not found in the Code book.

Other books that are required to complete the exam calculations preparation are:

"CALCULATIONS II WORKBOOK"

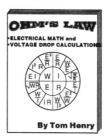

"OHMS LAW, ELECTRICAL MATH, and VOLTAGE DROP CALCULATIONS"

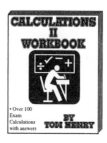

"TRANSFORMER EXAM CALCULATIONS"

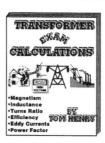

"CONTROL CIRCUITS"

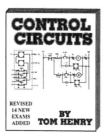

CHAPTER 1

BRANCH CIRCUIT

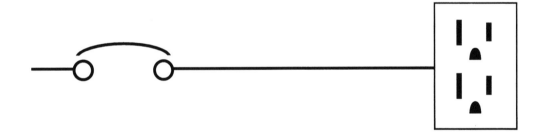

Defintion: **The circuit conductors between the final overcurrent device protecting the circuit and the outlet(s).**

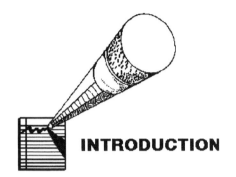

INTRODUCTION

The branch circuit is the final wiring after the fuse or circuit breaker.

This Chapter will start the student off on the right foot in the proper calculations and sizing of various branch circuits.

There are different Code rules for a circuit that supplies only one load compared to a circuit that supplies several loads. There are different rules for plug and cord connected than if the loads are hard wired.

You will learn how branch circuits are sized larger for continuous loads.

The basic beginning of installing wiring begins with following the Code rules for branch circuits.

•Note: Before using this book to prepare for your exam, make sure your Code book is tabbed using *Tom Henry's* 68 tabs **designed for exam calculations!**

Tom Henry's 68 CODE TABS
THE ELECTRICIAN'S TABS!

---

*Tom Henry's unique format saves you time & helps you avoid costly errors. Have all the **KEY** Code references at your fingertips!*

A special row of Service Calculation tabs for both Residential & Commercial Service Sizing to remind you of all the demand factors that can be applied to sizing the service conductor.

6 Motor Calculation tabs to size the wire, heaters, breakers, feeders, etc. to motors.

A ROW OF TABS FOR INDEXING QUICKLY! The toughest part of an electrical exam is trying to find the answer in the Code book in the allowed time. **14 tabs** let you use the "INDEX" faster - saving valuable test time.

• **KEY** tabs for standard size fuses & breakers, sizing equipment grounding conductors, grounding electrode conductors, multi-family optional calculation, burial depths, pools, Class 1, 2 & 3 circuits, signs, welders, hazardous locations, and much more. *A TOTAL OF 68 TABS!*

*These tabs are designed for **EVERYONE** that uses the Code book - Inspectors, Designers, Engineers, Electricians, Apprentices, Instructors, Helpers, Etc....*

DISTRIBUTION OF ELECTRICAL POWER

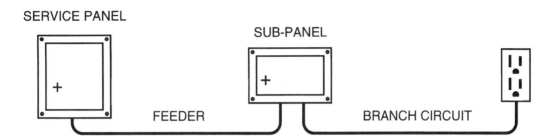

Definition of a branch circuit: The circuit conductors between the **final** over**current** device protecting the circuit and the outlet(s).

Over**current** device is a fuse or circuit breaker. Do not confuse over**current** device with over**load** device.

An over**load** device is a thermal protector that protects the motor against dangerous overheating. Sometimes referred to as the **heater**.

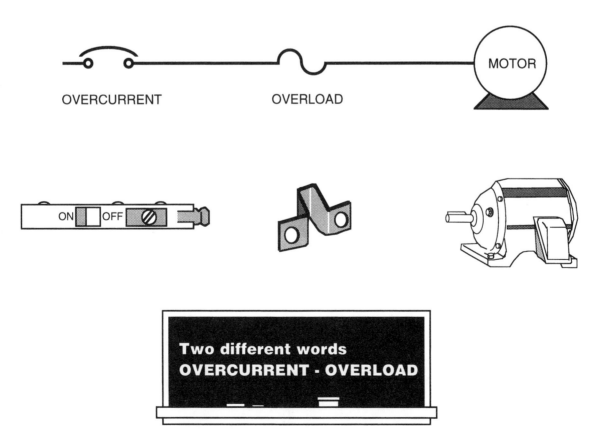

Most residential dwellings do not have feeders as the branch circuits originate at the service panel.

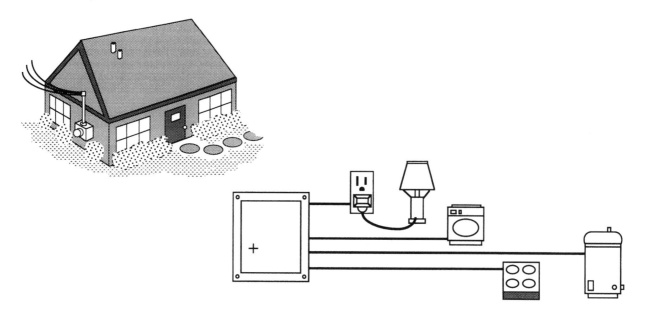

There are two types of branch circuits:

I.   A single-individual load.

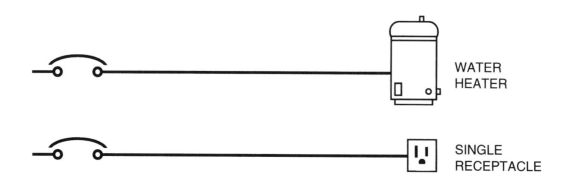

WATER HEATER

SINGLE RECEPTACLE

II. Two or more outlets.

MULTI-OUTLET DUPLEX RECEPTACLE

THE RATING OF A BRANCH CIRCUIT

The **rating** of a branch circuit is determined by the overcurrent device (fuse or circuit breaker).

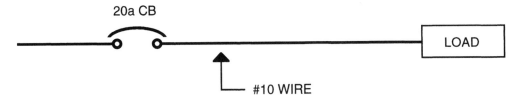

The branch circuit is **rated** 20 amps because the circuit breaker is 20 amps. The #10 wire may have been selected for voltage drop or for mechanical strength in an overhead circuit. The wire size does **not** determine the rating of a branch circuit.

It is very important in the designing of branch circuits and conductors to understand the rating of the branch circuit. Section 210.20(A) states the rating of the overcurrent device shall not be less than the noncontinuous load plus 125% of the continuous load. Or a 20 amp CB x 80% = 16 amp maximum continuous load.

CLASSIFICATIONS OF BRANCH CIRCUITS

Section 210.3. The classification for **other than individual** branch circuits shall be: 15, 20, 30, 40, and 50 amperes.

An **individual** branch circuit (to one load) can be any size. An example would be a water heater with a 25 amp overcurrent device. But branch circuits supplying **more than one load** are rated at 15, 20, 30, 40, and 50 amperes only.

15 and 20 amp branch circuits are used in residential dwellings for lighting and receptacle loads. Section 210.23(A,B,C) states that 30, 40, and 50 amp multi-outlet branch circuits are not permitted in a dwelling for lights and receptacle branch circuits. Section 210.21a states: lampholders used in branch circuits in **excess of 20 amps** shall be not less than 660 watts heavy-duty type which would not be used in a dwelling residence.

In a dwelling 30, 40, and 50 amp rated branch circuits are used for a **single** load such as a clothes dryer, range, water heater, etc.

30, 40, and 50 amp **multi-outlet** branch circuits would be found in **non-dwelling** occupancies supplying heavy-duty lampholders, infrared heating units or other utilization equipment. Welders in an industrial building would be a good example of a multi-outlet branch circuit.

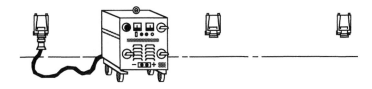

Table 210.21(B2) shows a **single** 20 amp rated receptacle can only be loaded to 16 amps. But, a 20 amp rated **duplex** receptacle can be loaded to 20 amps per Table 210.24.

KEY WORD IS "RECEPTACLE" WHICH MEANS ONE

Table 210.21(B2)
Maximum Cord and Plug Connected Load to Receptacle

Circuit Rating Amperes	Receptacle Rating Amperes	Maximum Load Amperes
15 or 20	15	12
20	20	16
30	30	24

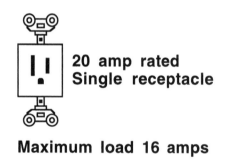

20 amp rated
Single receptacle

Maximum load 16 amps

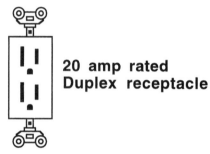

20 amp rated
Duplex receptacle

Maximum load 20 amps

CORD and PLUG CONNECTED LOADS

Single receptacle only 80%
Circuit can be loaded 100%

MAXIMUM LOADING OF BRANCH CIRCUITS

Section 210.23 and Table 210.24 list the maximum load permitted on each branch circuit.

Table 210.24
Summary of Branch Circuit Requirements

CIRCUIT RATING	15 Amp	20 Amp	30 Amp	40 Amp	50 Amp
CONDUCTORS (Min. Size)					
Circuit Wires*	14	12	10	8	6
Taps	14	14	14	12	12
Fixture Wires and Cords			Refer to Section 240.5		
OVERCURRENT PROTECTION	15 Amp	20 Amp	30 Amp	40 Amp	50 Amp
OUTLET DEVICES:					
Lampholders Permitted	Any Type	Any Type	Heavy Duty	Heavy Duty	Heavy Duty
Receptacle Rating**	15 Max. Amp	15 or 20 Amp	30 Amp	40 or 50 Amp	50 Amp
MAXIMUM LOAD	15 Amp	20 Amp	30 Amp	40 Amp	50 Amp
PERMISSIBLE LOAD	Refer to Section 210.23(A)	Refer to Section 210.23(A)	Refer to Section 210.23(B)	Refer to Section 210.23(C)	Refer to Section 210.23(C)

As shown in Table 210.24 a 20 amp circuit can be loaded to a maximum of 20 amps. An example would be a 20 amp receptacle circuit in a residential dwelling. Receptacles are not considered a continuous load. Limiting the load to 80% of the rating of the branch circuit applies to a **continuous load**.

Section 210.23(A1). The rating of any **one** cord-and plug-connected utilization equipment shall not exceed 80% of the branch circuit rating.

Example shows a cord and plug connected refrigerator on a 20 amp rated branch circuit. The refrigerator load could not exceed 16 amps which is 80% of 20 amps. But the 20 amp circuit could be loaded another 4 amps by another load which would reach the maximum load permitted of 20 amps.

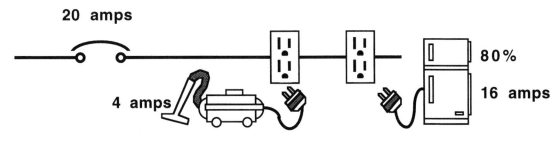

Section 210.23(A2) also states: The total rating of utilization equipment **fastened in place** shall not exceed 50% of the branch-circuit rating. Fastened in place (fixed) not portable appliances.

The following example shows a wall mounted air conditioning unit 120 volt cord and plug connected to an existing 15 amp rated branch circuit. 210.23(A2) states the maximum load for this fastened in place unit would be 50% of the 15 amp rated branch circuit = 7.5 amps.

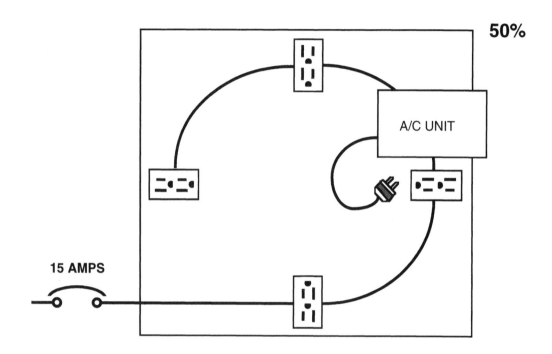

CONDUCTORS - MINIMUM SIZE AMPACITY

To properly solve branch-circuit sizing calculations you must meet the conductor ampacity requirements.

Section 210.19(A). Branch-circuit conductors shall have an ampacity not less than the maximum load to be served. Where a branch circuit supplies continuous loads or any combination of continuous and noncontinuous loads, the minimum branch-circuit conductor size, before the application of any adjustment or correction factors, shall have an allowable ampacity equal to or greater than the noncontinuous load plus **125% of the continuous load**.

210.19(A2). Conductors of **multioutlet** branch circuits supplying **receptacles** for **cord-and plug-connected** portable loads shall have an ampacity of not less than the **rating** of the branch circuit.

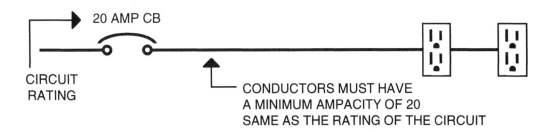

A #14 TW conductor has an **ampacity** of 20, but the * asterisk Table 310.16 states a #14 conductor can only be fused at a maximum of 15 amps. A #12 TW with an ampacity of 25 and protected at 20 amps would be the correct selection of conductor for this receptacle circuit.

What is the maximum size circuit breaker permitted for the following **multioutlet receptacle** branch circuit?

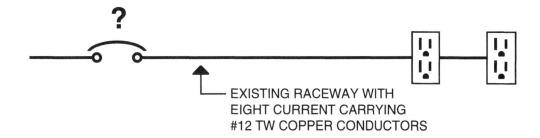

Section 310.15(B2a) requires an ampacity adjustment factor for more than three current carrying conductors, for **eight** current carrying conductors a reduction in ampacity of 70% is required.

310.15(B2a). Ampacity Adjustment Factors.
(a) More than Three Conductors in a Raceway or Cable. Where the number of conductors in a raceway or cable exceeds three, the ampacities shall be reduced as shown in the following table:

Number of Conductors	Percent of Values in Tables as Adjusted for Ambient Temperature if Necessary
4 through 6	80
7 through 9	70
10 through 20	50
21 through 30	45
31 through 40	40
41 through 60	35

Table 310.16: A #12 TW has an ampacity of 25. The 310.15(B2a) factor requires the 25 ampacity to be reduced 70%. 25 x 70% = 17.5 ampacity and maximum load permitted on this conductor.

Section 240.4(B2) states the next **higher** size overcurrent protective device can be used where the ampacity of the conductor does not correspond with the standard size overcurrent device.

The reduced ampacity is 17.5 amps which is not a standard size fuse or breaker. The next higher standard size from Section 240.6 is 20 amps. If the conductor is **not** part of a **multioutlet branch circuit supplying receptacles for cord and plug connected portable loads**, then 20 amps is permitted per Section 240.4(B1).

Since this example shows the branch circuit supplying receptacles the maximum size overcurrent device would be 15 amp. A 15 amp overcurrent device would protect the conductors at 15 amp. **If** a 20 amp overcurrent device was installed, loads could be plugged into the receptacles loading the circuit to the maximum rating of 20 amp. This would be in **excess** of the 17.5 ampacity or maximum loading which would result in exceeding the insulation rating of the conductor. This will be explained in full detail in Chapter 2.

If the loads on this branch circuit were **hard wired** instead of plug and cord connected receptacles, then the next higher overcurrent device 20 amp is permitted.

The electrical designer or electrician designing a lighting branch circuit could encounter this very same example.

A raceway containing eight #12 TW current carrying conductors to light fixtures. The reduced ampacity and maximum load permitted on these conductors is 17.5 amps. If each light fixture has a load of 2 amps, 17.5/2 = 8.75 or a maximum of 8 lights at 2 amps each = 16 amps which would not exceed the maximum load permitted of 17.5.

If eight light fixtures at 2 amps each (known loads) are **hard wired** to the branch circuit the next higher standard size 20 amp overcurrent device is permitted per Section 240.4(B2)

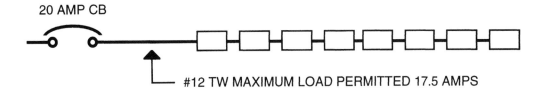

20 AMP CB

#12 TW MAXIMUM LOAD PERMITTED 17.5 AMPS

The designer of this circuit must limit the connected load to 17.5 amps or less.

As an electrical inspector this is what I would explain to the electrician in the field when he said "I'm only adding **one** light to the existing circuit". As you can see in the example **one** more light would exceed the maximum load permitted on the existing conductors.

CONTINUOUS LOAD

Article 100 - Definition of Continuous Load: A load where the maximum current is expected to continue for **three** hours or more.

Article 100 - Definition of Ampacity: The current in amperes a conductor can carry **continuously** under the conditions of use without exceeding its temperature rating.

Section 210.20(A). The rating of the branch-circuit overcurrent device serving continuous loads shall not be less than the noncontinuous load plus 125% of the continuous load. The minimum branch-circuit conductor size, without the application of any adjustment or correction factors, shall have an allowable **ampacity equal to or greater than** the noncontinuous load plus 125% of the continuous load.

Continuous loads shall not exceed 80% of the **rating** of the branch circuit. The reason for limiting the load to 80% is **not** that the conductors can't carry the continuous load. The 80% is a current limitation on the **overcurrent device** to limit the **heat**. Remember, the overcurrent device **not** the conductors.

The 80% limitation is based on the **inability** of the overcurrent device itself to handle continuous load without overheating.

Neutral conductor loads would **not** be calculated at continuous. The neutral conductor that is not connected to an overcurrent device has **no heating effect to the overcurrent device**. Same with service conductors. The **line** side service conductors are not calculated at continuous, they don't connect to overcurrent devices so there is no heating effect.

Good judgement and common sense will answer most of the exam questions on continuous loading.

Table 220.12. Dwelling occupancies and motel **rooms** are about the only occupancies **not** considered continuous lighting loads due to the small loading. Most of our travels throughout the day are in continuous type loading areas such as stores, schools, offices, banks, restaurants, churches, barber shops, industrial buildings and parking lots. These all have lighting loads recognized as continuous.

Receptacle loads are **not** considered continuous. If a receptacle is a continuous load, it would be identified as such in the calculation question. Going back to the definition of a continuous load will help when it comes to a receptacle being continuous. "A load where the **maximum** current is expected to continue for three hours or more". Most receptacles are normally lightly loaded. This is also why dwelling loads are considered noncontinuous. Although Section 424.3(B) and 422.13 requires the **branch circuit** for electric heat and 120 gallon or less water heater to be calculated at continuous.

A good example would be a hotel or motel. The motel room where you sleep would be the same as a dwelling **not** considered to be a continuous load. **But**, when you step out of your motel sleeping room into the hallway, the hallway lights would be a continuous load as these lights burn for more than three hours continuously. The rest of the loads at the motel or hotel such as parking lot lights, restaurant, meeting rooms, etc. would be considered continuous lighting loads.

Determining the Minimum Number of Lighting Branch Circuits

$$\text{Number of Branch Circuits} = \frac{\text{Lighting Load}}{\text{Circuit Capacity}}$$

Table 220.12. Lighting load = unit va per square foot x total square footage

Circuit capacity (noncontinuous)	= branch circuit rating x 120 volts
Circuit capacity (continuous)	= branch circuit rating x 120 volts x 80%
Example: (noncontinuous)	15 amp CB x 120 volts = 1800va circuit capacity
	20 amp CB x 120 volts = 2400va circuit capacity
(continuous)	15 amp CB x 120v x 80% = 1440va circuit capacity
	20 amp CB x 120v x 80% = 1920va circuit capacity

Noncontinuous Example:

A 1500 square foot dwelling would require how many 15 amp lighting circuits?

Table 220.12 $\dfrac{3va \ x \ 1500 \ sq.ft. = 4500va}{15a \ CB \ x \ 120v \ = 1800va}$ = 2.5 or 3 circuits required

Section 220.42 states the demand factors from Table 220.42 shall **not** apply when determining the number of branch circuits for general illumination.

Continuous Example:

A 6000 square foot restaurant would require how many 20 amp lighting circuits?

Table 220.12 $\dfrac{2va \ x \ 6000 \ sq.ft. = \ \ \ \ \ 12000va}{20a \ CB \ x \ 120v \ x \ 80\% \ = \ 1920va}$ = 6.25 or 7 circuits required

Show Window Example:

How many 20 amp branch circuits are required for 80 linear feet of show window lighting?

Section 220.14(G2) $\dfrac{200va \ x \ 80 \ feet \ = \ \ \ \ \ 16,000va}{20a \ x \ 120v \ x \ 80\% \ = \ 1920va}$ = 8.3 or 9 circuits

Noncontinuous Example:

An office has 100 general purpose receptacles. How many 20 amp circuits are required?

Section 220.14(I) $\dfrac{180va \ x \ 100 \ = 18,000va}{20a \ x \ 120v \ = 2400va}$ = 7.5 or 8 circuits

Note: The 180va per receptacle is for **other** than a dwelling unit. The demand factor Table 220.44 is for **feeders** not branch circuits. Receptacles are **not** a continuous load.

Office Example:

How many 20 amp lighting circuits are required for a 600 square foot office?

Table 220.12 $\dfrac{3.5va \ x \ 600 \ sq.ft. \ = 2100va}{20a \ CB \ x \ 120v \ x \ 80\% \ = 1920va}$ = 1.09 or 2 circuits

Table 220.12 is the **minimum** lighting load permitted. If a known lighting load is calculated to be larger than the Table 220.12 minimum it must be used as the Code states conductors shall have an ampacity not less than the **maximum** load to be served.

Example:

If the same 600 square foot office had a **known** lighting load of 25 fixtures @ 160w each, what is the required number of 20 amp lighting circuits?

$$\frac{25 \text{ fixtures } \times 160 \text{ watts}}{20a \times 120v \times 80\%} \quad \frac{= 4000va}{= 1920va} = 2.08 \text{ or } 3 \text{ circuits}$$

Section 220.18(B). If the lighting is flourescent, use the ampere rating of the unit instead of the wattage of the lamps.

Office Receptacle Load:

Table 220.12   1va x 600 sq.ft. = $\dfrac{600va}{180va}$ = 3.3 or 3 receptacles

Section 220.14(I)   180va   =

The 1 volt-amp per square foot from Table 220.12 for offices and banks would provide capacity for three receptacles in the office. If a known receptacle load of more than 600va is provided, then use the **largest** receptacle load.

> In general, receptacles are **not** considered to be a continuous load.

**Continuous load =
3 hours or more**

SUMMARY CONTINUOUS LOAD

An overcurrent device such as a circuit breaker does not trip on **current** alone. Example; an amp clamp clamped on a conductor could read 17 amperes and a 20 amp rated circuit breaker could trip.

20 amp rated

Amp clamp reads 17 amps

The current carrying conductor produces heat but so does the **ambient temperature**. This is the temperature surrounding the conductor or equipment (circuit breaker).

Ambient temperature is the temperature surrounding the conductor or equipment

The circuit breaker has a bimetallic element that trips on the amount of **heat.** The conductor and the ambient temperature combined with heat determines when it trips.

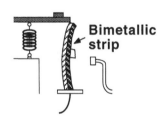

Bimetallic strip

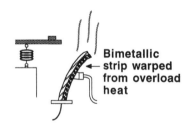

Bimetallic strip warped from overload heat

The reason for the 80% current limitation on the circuit breaker is when several circuits containing continuous loads such as lighting are contained in the same panelboard and with the cover enclosed **heat** is entrapped which has a definite affect on the tripping of the circuit breaker.

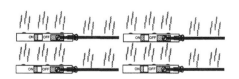

Even though only 17 amps of current is flowing through the circuit, this combined with the added ambient heat from the other circuits with continuous loads raises the heat thus tripping the circuit breaker.

SIZING OF INDIVIDUAL LOADS

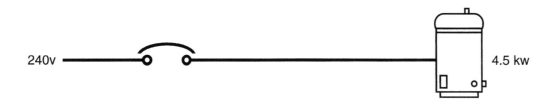

4.5 kw **water heater** 40 gallon 240v single-phase

Section 422.13. A branch circuit supplying a fixed storage-type water heater having a capacity of 120 gallons **or less** shall have a **rating** not less than 125% of the nameplate rating of the water heater.

$$\frac{4500w}{240v} = 18.75 \text{ amps} \times 125\% = 23.43 \text{ amps}$$

Section 422.11(E3). If the branch circuit supplies a single **nonmotor**-operated appliance, the overcurrent device rating shall not exceed a protective device rating marked on the appliance or, if there is no marking, the value specified as follows:
Appliance rating greater than 13.3 amperes = **150% of appliance rating**.

18.75 amps x 150% = 28.125 amps 422.11(E3) Use 30 amp circuit breaker #10 copper conductor.

SIZING OF FIXED ELECTRIC SPACE HEATING

Section 424.3(A). **Individual** branch circuits shall be permitted to supply **any size** fixed electric space heating equipment.

Branch circuits supplying **two or more** outlets for fixed electric space heating equipment shall be rated 15, 20, or 30 amperes. Exception: In other than residential occupancies, fixed **infrared** heating equipment shall be permitted to be supplied from branch circuits rated not over 50 amperes.

Section 424.3(B). The ampacity of the branch-circuit conductors and the rating or setting of overcurrent protective devices supplying fixed electric space heating equipment consisting of resistance elements with or without a motor shall not be less than 125% of the total load of the motors and the heaters.

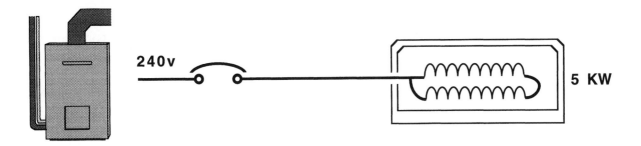

The 5 kw space heat unit shown above would calculate:

5000w/240v = 20.83 amps x 125% = 26 amps   Use 30 amp CB and #10 TW copper

SIZING FOR AIR CONDITIONING EQUIPMENT

Room air conditioning units and refrigerators are usually cord and plug connected to a general purpose branch circuit following the 80% for cord and plug connected and the 50% for fastened in place appliances in **Section 210.23(A1,2)**.

The rules are different for an A/C unit that has an hermetic refrigerant motor-compressor than a unit that does not.

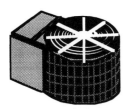

Section 440.2. Definition of Hermetic refrigerant motor-compressor: A combination consisting of a compressor and motor, **both** of which are enclosed in the same housing with no external shaft or shaft seals, **the motor operating in the refrigerant**.

Section 440.3(B). Examples of equipment which are **not** hermetic, would be refrigeration compressors driven by conventional motors, furnaces with air conditioning evaporator coils installed, fan-coil units, remote forced air-cooled condensers, remote commercial refrigerators, etc.

Branch circuit sizing for motors and cooking equipment have different rules and will be covered in following chapters of this book.

Appliance, fixed: An appliance which is fastened or otherwise secured at a specific location.

Appliance, portable: An appliance which is actually moved or can easily be moved from one place to another in normal use.

Appliance, stationary: An appliance which is not easily moved from one place to another in normal use.

Branch circuit, appliance: A branch circuit supplying energy to one or more outlets to which appliances are to be connected; such circuits to have no permanently connected lighting fixtures not part of an appliance.

Branch circuit, general purpose: A branch circuit that supplies a number of outlets for lighting and appliances.

Branch circuit, individual: A branch circuit that supplies only one utilization equipment.

Equipment: A general term including material, fittings, devices, appliances, fixtures, apparatus, and the like used as a part of, or in connection with, an electrical installation.

Lighting outlet: An outlet intended for the direct connection of a lampholder, a lighting fixture, or a pendant cord terminating in a lampholder.

Outlet: A point on the wiring system at which current is taken to supply utilization equipment.

Receptacle: A receptacle is a contact device installed at the outlet for the connection of a single attachment plug. (FPN): A **single** receptacle is a single contact device with no other contact device on the same yoke. A **multiple** receptacle is a single device containing two or more receptacles.

Receptacle outlet: An outlet where one or more receptacles are installed.

The Code uses two classifications for the wiring of appliances: Cord and plug connected or permanently connected (hard-wired).

Cord and plug connected appliances would include irons, toasters, mixers, coffee makers, vacuum cleaners, etc. Permanently connected is all appliances not cord and plug connected. Example would be a water heater as it is hard-wired.

Fastened in place appliances would include garbage disposers, dryers, cooking equipment, etc. These appliances can **not** be easily moved due to plumbing connections or are built into the counter-top, etc. These appliances might be cord and plug connected for convenience in servicing the unit.

CHAPTER 1   TEST 1   BRANCH CIRCUITS

1. Appliance outlets installed in a residence for a specific appliance, such as a washing machine, shall be installed within ____ feet of the intended location of the appliance.

(a) 2   (b) 4   (c) 6   (d) 8

2. Direct grade level access is defined as being located not more than ____ above grade level and being readily accessible.

(a) 6' 3"   (b) 6' 6"   (c) 7'   (d) 8'

3. Show windows require that one receptacle outlet be installed for each ____ linear feet of show window.

(a) 6   (b) 8   (c) 10   (d) 12

4. A receptacle is a contact device installed at the outlet for the connection of a ____.

(a) light   (b) single contact device   (c) two attachment plugs   (d) device

5. In a dwelling, a 40 or 50 amp branch circuit is permitted to supply ____.

I.   only fastened in place cooking appliances
II. infrared heating equipment
III. fixed lighting units with heavy-duty lampholders

(a) I only   (b) II only   (c) III only   (d) I, II and III

6. Equipment grounding conductors of different branch circuits that are installed in the same raceway must be ____.

I.   differentiated by having one with a green color and the others green with a colored stripe
II. differentiated by having one with a green color stripe and the others with a yellow stripe
III. color coded green, green with a yellow stripe, or bare

(a) I only   (b) II only   (c) III only   (d) none of these

CHAPTER 1   TEST 2   BRANCH CIRCUITS

1. A branch circuit conductor shall have an ampacity equal to or greater than the noncontinuous load plus ____ percent of the continuous load.

(a) 75   (b) 80   (c) 115   (d) 125

2. A 20 amp rated branch circuit with #12 wire supplying a duplex receptacle can be loaded to a maximum of ____ amps.

(a) 12   (b) 15   (c) 16   (d) 20

3. Which of the following is an overcurrent device?

I. circuit breaker   II. thermal overload   III. time-delay fuse

(a) I only   (b) I and II only   (c) I and III only   (d) I, II and III

4. A 20 amp rated branch circuit with a #12 wire supplying a fastened in place wall air conditioner can be loaded to a maximum of ____ amps.

(a) 10   (b) 15   (c) 16   (d) 20

5. Which of the following would violate the branch circuit loading rules?

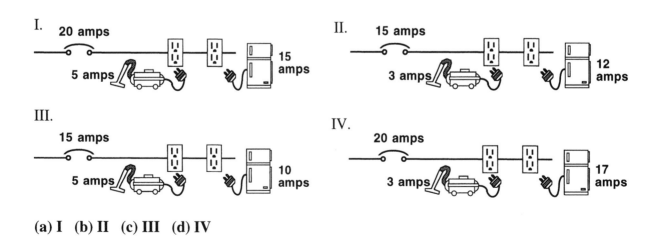

(a) I   (b) II   (c) III   (d) IV

CHAPTER 2

AMPACITY

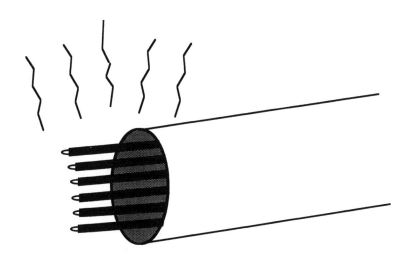

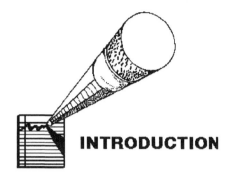

INTRODUCTION

This Chapter explains how the Table of Ampacity 310.16 is to be used per the Code. This is a very misused table.

The student will learn from Chapter 2:

•The definition of the insulation rating of a conductor

•As more conductors are added to the circuit the load on the conductors must be reduced

•Nonlinear loads add heat to the neutral

•The utility company can install a smaller wire as the conductors are in free air per Table 310.17

•Equipment and conductors must be terminated as listed per section 110.14(C)

Prepare for the exam properly with *Tom Henry's* personally hi-lited looseleaf Code book "The Ultimate".

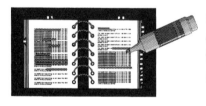

Over 1500 of the most frequent referenced areas of the Code are hi-lited for quick reference!

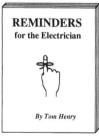

KEY WORD INDEX 2005

REMINDERS for the Electrician

By Tom Henry

68 TABS ARE INSTALLED FOR YOU!

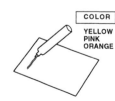

COLOR
YELLOW = JOURNEYMAN
PINK = MASTER
ORANGE = BOTH Journeyman & Master

PERSONALLY HI-LITED!

Even if the electrician does not use the Code often, at one time or another you have referred to the table of ampacity to determine how many amps a certain size wire can carry. Table 310.16 lists these ampacities for conductors.

This is probably the most misused table in the Code book as the ampacities listed in Table 310.16 are generally **never** correct. This is a very important table that you must learn to use correctly.

Table 310.16. Allowable Ampacities of Insulated Conductors
Rated 0-2000 Volts, 60°to 90°C (140°to 194°F)
Not More Than Three Conductors in Raceway or Cable or Earth
(Directly Buried), Based on Ambient Temperature of 30°C (86°F).

Size	Temperature Rating of Conductor. See Table 310.13.						Size
	60°C (140°F)	75°C (167°F)	90°C (194°F)	60°C (140°F)	75°C (167°F)	90°C (194°F)	
AWG kcmil	TYPES TW, UF	TYPES RHW, THHW, THW, THWN, XHHW, USE, ZW	TYPES TBS,SA, SIS, FEP, FEPB, MI, RHH, RHW-2, THHN, THHW, THW-2, THWN-2 USE-2, XHH XHHW, XHHW-2 ZW-2	TYPES TW, UF	TYPES RHW, THHW, THW, THWN, XHHW, USE	TYPES TBS, SA, SIS, THHN, THHW, THW-2, THWN-2, RHH, RHW-2, USE-2, XHH, XHHW, XHHW-2, ZW-2	AWG kcmil
	COPPER			ALUMINUM OR COPPER-CLAD ALUMINUM			
18	....	....	14	....	....	....	....
16	....	....	18	....	....	....	....
14*	20	20	25	....	....	....	....
12*	25	25	30	20	20	25	12*
10*	30	35	40	25	30	35	10*
8	40	50	55	30	40	45	8
6	55	65	75	40	50	60	6
4	70	85	95	55	65	75	4
3	85	100	110	65	75	85	3
2	95	115	130	75	90	100	2
1	110	130	150	85	100	115	1
1/0	125	150	170	100	120	135	1/0
2/0	145	175	195	115	135	150	2/0
3/0	165	200	225	130	155	175	3/0
4/0	195	230	260	150	180	205	4/0
250	215	255	290	170	205	230	250
300	240	285	320	190	230	255	300
350	260	310	350	210	250	280	350
400	280	335	380	225	270	305	400
500	320	380	430	260	310	350	500
600	355	420	475	285	340	385	600
700	385	460	520	310	375	420	700
750	400	475	535	320	385	435	750
800	410	490	555	330	395	450	800
900	435	520	585	355	425	480	900
1000	455	545	615	375	445	500	1000
1250	495	590	665	405	485	545	1250
1500	520	625	705	435	520	585	1500
1750	545	650	735	455	545	615	1750
2000	560	665	750	470	560	630	2000

CORRECTION FACTORS

Ambient Temp. °C	For ambient temperatures other than 30°C (86°F), multiply the ampacities shown above by the appropritate factor shown below.						Ambient Temp. °F
21-25	1.08	1.05	1.04	1.08	1.05	1.04	70-77
26-30	1.00	1.00	1.00	1.00	1.00	1.00	78-86
31-35	.91	.94	.96	.91	.94	.96	87-95
36-40	.82	.88	.91	.82	.88	.91	96-104
41-45	.71	.82	.87	.71	.82	.87	105-113
46-50	.58	.75	.82	.58	.75	.82	114-122
51-55	.41	.67	.76	.41	.67	.76	123-131
56-60	....	.58	.71	....	.58	.71	132-140
61-70	....	.33	.58	....	.33	.58	141-158
71-80	....	....	.41	....	....	.41	159-176

* See Section 240.4(D)

The reason for the misuse of the table comes from not reading the heading which states the ampacities shown for the various conductors are correct if you don't: (1) install over three current carrying conductors in a raceway or cable (2) exceed 30°C or 86°F in ambient temperature.

(1)

Table 310.16. Ampacities of Insulated Conductors Rated 0-2000 Volts,
60° to 90°C (140° to 194°F) **Not more Than** Three **Conductors in Raceway or Cable or Earth** (Directly Buried), **Based on Ambient Air Temperature of** 30°C (86°F).

(2)

Common sense would remind you that normally you are installing more than three conductors in a conduit and also the surrounding temperature of these conductors would be above 86°F. The **normal** ampacities listed in the table must be corrected if either condition (1) or (2) is present.

The conductor ampacity is the current carried **continuously** without increasing the temperature of its insulation beyond the danger point. The conductor ampacity varies with the type of insulation and the method of installation.

Except for mechanical abuse, the greatest hazard that conductors must endure is **heat**. Conductor insulation can be damaged by excessive heat in various ways, depending on the type of insulation and the degree of overheating. Continued exposure to excessive heat causes insulation to become soft, perhaps to melt, and in extreme cases to burn.

This heat comes from two sources: From the ambient air surrounding the conductors or from the current the conductors must carry. There is a point where an increase in current causes excessive heat even though conducting materials such as copper or aluminum have a low resistivity.

For many years natural rubber was used to insulate conductors, but age along with heat caused such rubber insulation to dry out, to crack, and to become brittle. Today we have better quality rubber and thermoplastic materials that not only permit thinner insulation on conductors but also withstand temperature better resulting in higher ampacities of conductors.

The maximum temperature permitted for conductor insulation is called the **temperature rating** of the conductor. **Table 310.13** shows the **maximum** temperature that the insulation type is permitted to reach. That maximum temperature will be reached when a conductor is loaded to its full ampacity in an ambient temperature of 30 degrees C or 86 degrees F.

The type letter on the insulation indicates its insulation, maximum operating temperature, and application provisions.

RHW insulation, the "R" indicates rubber insulation. The "H" indicates 75°C - 167°F maximum operating temperature (insulation rating). The "W" indicates moisture resistant.

THHN insulation, the "T" indicates thermoplastic insulation. The "HH" indicates 90°C - 194°F maximum operating temperature (insulation rating). The "N" indicates nylon covering.

The #10 THW has a maximum operating temperature of 75°C which is 167°F.

The #10 THHN has a maximum operating temperature of 90°C which is 194°F. A "HH" rated insulation will allow more heat to be dissipated faster than an "H" rated insulation thus raising the ampacity (the current the conductor can carry safely without damage).

The maximum operating temperature is the insulation rating of the conductor and must not be exceeded. Proper designing is a very important factor.

You must first understand what words mean; such as ampacity, ambient temperature, insulation rating, etc.

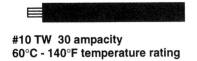

**#10 TW 30 ampacity
60°C - 140°F temperature rating**

A #10 TW conductor has an ampacity of 30 amperes. The insulation rating is 60°C or 140°F.
This does *not* mean that a TW insulation can be installed where the ambient temperature reaches 140°F.

What this means is: If a #10 TW conductor is loaded to the allowable ampacity, 30 amperes in an ambient that has a temperature of 30°C or 86°F, the temperature of the *insulation* will reach 60°C or 140°F.

Table 310.16 the table of ampacity is aimed at designating a level of current that will permit the conductor to reach its thermal limit, but not exceed it.

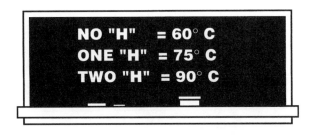

NO "H"   = 60° C
ONE "H" = 75° C
TWO "H" = 90° C

**#10 TW   30 amps
of current flowing**

The 30 amps of current flowing produces heat in the conductor which must dissipate through the insulation to the ambient.

With the ambient temperature at 86°F and with 30 amperes of current flowing through the conductor, a thermometer placed on the *insulation* would read 140°F which is maximum operating temperature for this type insulation (TW).

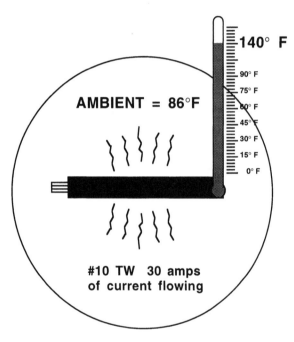

AMBIENT = 86°F

140° F

90° F
75° F
60° F
45° F
30° F
15° F
0° F

**#10 TW   30 amps
of current flowing**

For a #10 TW conductor, any current above 30 amps or any ambient temperature above 86°F will cause insulation damage, as you will exceed the maximum operating temperature of the conductor; 140°F.

Maximum operating temperature = Full ampacity at 86°F.

140°F - 86°F = 54°F for the 30 amperes of current flow in the #10 TW conductor.

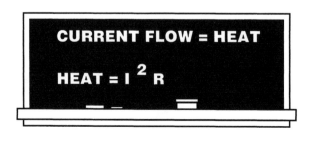

CURRENT FLOW = HEAT

HEAT = $I^2 R$

ADJUSTMENT FACTORS

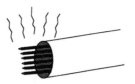

When there are more than three current-carrying conductors in a raceway or cable, the ampacity of each conductor must be reduced as indicated in Table 310.15(B2a) to compensate for heating effects and reduced heat dissipation due to reduced ventilation of individual conductors.

Table 310.15(B2a). Adjustment Factors.
  (a) More than Three Conductors in a Raceway or Cable. Where the number of conductors in a raceway or cable exceeds three, the ampacities shall be reduced as shown in the following table:

Number of Conductors	Percent of Values in Tables as Adjusted for Ambient Temperature if Necessary
4 through 6	80
7 through 9	70
10 through 20	50
21 through 30	45
31 through 40	40
41 and above	35

Example: A conduit contains six #8 TW current carrying conductors. The normal ampacity is 40 amps x 80% from note 8 = 32. The maximum current that can be passed through the #8 TW conductor without subjecting it to insulation damage is 32 amps.

Adjustment factors also apply when paralleling conductors per Section 310.4.

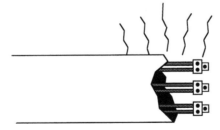

It is wrong to think since you connected two conductors in parallel on one lug that you now only have one conductor. Heat is measured by $W = I^2R$. In parallel you have **two** conductors carrying current producing heat.

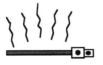

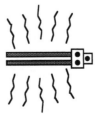

It is wrong to think that by using a larger size conduit than required would satisfy the adjustment factor required for the reduction of ampacity. The larger conduit would have more volume area, but it's like heating a rock, it may take a little longer but it will still reach the same temperature.

To avoid applying the adjustment factors of 310.15(B2a) you can install two separate conduits as shown below. Now you only have 3 current carrying conductors in each conduit.

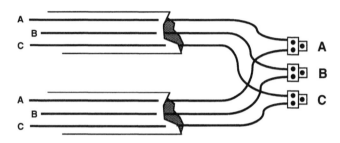

*Some conductors are **not** counted when applying 310.15(B2a):*

310.15(B2) ex. 1   Conductors of different systems
310.15(B2) ex. 2   Cable trays
310.15(B2) ex. 3   Nipples
310.15(B2) ex. 4   Outdoor trench
310.15(B4a)   The neutral conductor in a normally balanced circuit is **not** counted

But, 310.15(B4b) states: The neutral conductor is **counted** in a 3-wire circuit consisting of 2-phase wires of a 3-phase wye system.

310.15(B4c) states: The neutral is considered a **current carrying** conductor in nonlinear loads. Circuits such as discharge lighting (fluorescent, mercury, sodium) data processing, or similar equipment. The Harmonic currents in the nonlinear loads can cause the neutral currents to rise a little higher than the line current.

310.15(B5) states: A grounding or bonding conductor shall **not** be counted when applying the provisions of Table 310.15(B2a). The grounding conductor (green or bare wire) only carries fault current to trip the overcurrent device. This is **not** a heat factor.

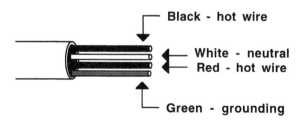

Summary of 310.15(B4) on when to count the neutral as current carrying:

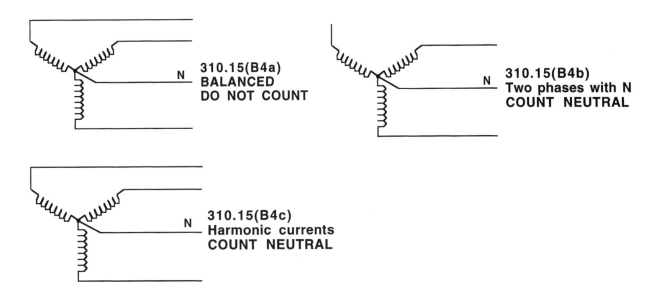

310.15(B4a)
BALANCED
DO NOT COUNT

310.15(B4b)
Two phases with N
COUNT NEUTRAL

310.15(B4c)
Harmonic currents
COUNT NEUTRAL

Non-linear loads which contain harmonic currents

When a linear load is turned on, the voltage and current start and turn off together. When a non-linear load is turned on, the voltage starts but the current is purposely delayed.

Harmonic simply indicates that the current waveform is distorted. The closer the waveform is to a fundamental sine wave, the lower the harmonic content. With a fundamental sine wave, there are no high order harmonics.

A 3rd harmonic makes 3 alternations in one alternation of the fundamental wave form. A 5th harmonic makes 5 alternations in one alternation of the fundamental wave. The 7th harmonic makes 7 alternations, and so on.

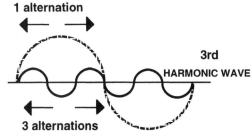

1 alternation

3rd
HARMONIC WAVE

3 alternations

The highest peak of the wave is determined by **adding** all of the odd harmonics together. The frequency is determined by the number of complete cycles per second, measured in Hertz. 60 cycles per second equals 60 Hertz, or 60 Hz.

On a 60 Hz AC system the 3rd harmonic is 180 Hz, the 5th harmonic is 300 Hz, the 7th harmonic is 420 Hz, etc.

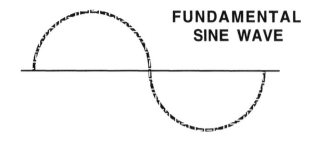

FUNDAMENTAL SINE WAVE

3rd HARMONIC WAVE FORM

A **harmonic wave** is a **distorted wave** pattern consisting of the fundamental wave and other **higher frequency waves** that are superimposed on the fundamental wave.

HARMONICS ARE ADDITIVE

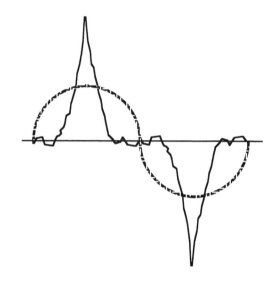

The harmonic currents are delayed then **added** together and then burst into action causing a high peak wave form and a higher frequency.

Heat is increased by an increase in current frequency. The heating effect on transformers, circuit breakers and conductors supplying **non-linear** loads is a function of **I^2R**.

The higher I^2R heating where harmonic currents are supplied is caused by what is known as **skin effect**. Skin effect is an increase in resistance due to the fact that **higher-frequency** currents flow on the **skin** of the conductor, rather than throughout the entire conductor.

AC tends to flow along the surface of a conductor. DC acts through the entire cross-sectional area of the conductor in a uniform manner. The name skin effect is given to the action whereby AC is forced toward the surface of the conductor. Because of skin effect, there is less useful copper conductive area with AC. As a result, there is an increase in resistance.

CROSS-SECTIONAL AREA DENSITY

DC   **AC**

For the 3rd harmonic, instead of 60 Hz it's now 180 Hz, there is a 42% change in the skin effect concentration point. For the 5th harmonic there is a 55% difference and a 62% difference for the 7th harmonic. The result is a proportionate increase of resistance.

As you can see, the harmonic currents raised the frequency, thus raising the resistance and the I²R heating effect.

In multiwire branch circuits, the odd numbered harmonics do not cancel out on the neutral, but are additive, resulting in a high neutral load. Because the heating effect on the conductor is proportional to I²R and because the conductor resistance will be greater at 180 Hz than at 60 Hz, the heating effect in the neutral conductor will be greater than that of the phase conductors.

This is the reason in section 310.15(B4c) of the Code it requires counting the neutral conductor in a 3ø, 4-wire circuit supplying **nonlinear loads.** The neutral conductor is actually **hotter** in temperature than the phase conductors.

An electrician is familar with the fluorescent light fixture containing a ballast. This fixture is referred to as discharge lighting since it contains a ballast (winding).

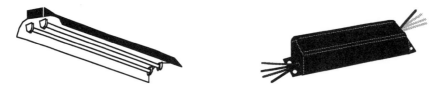

Harmonics cause problems to transformers and neutral conductors in multiwire feeders and branch circuits. The largest contributor to harmonic distortion is the static power converter used in adjustable speed drives.

310.15(B5) is a very interesting section which states you do **not** have to count the green or bare conductor (grounding or bonding). This conductor only carries current during a fault condition and if the circuit is designed properly will trip the circuit breaker in .008 of a second which is not a heat factor. But one must remember that this conductor carries **extremely high current** during this short time. The Code requires an effective grounding path. It's just important to make sure the conduits and grounding conductors are properly tightened as it is to check the hot wires.

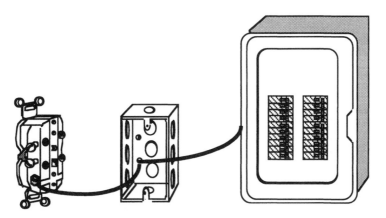

**310.15(B5) Grounding or bonding conductor
DO NOT COUNT**

AMBIENT TEMPERATURE

Ambient temperature is the temperature of the medium, such as air, water or earth into which the heat of the conductor is dissipated. It's the temperature surrounding the conductor.

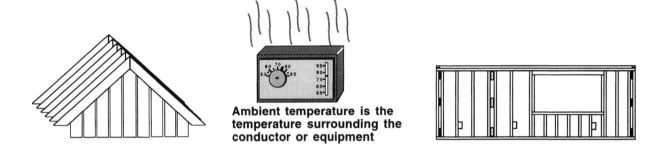

Ambient temperature is the temperature surrounding the conductor or equipment

A conductor in free air as shown below can carry more amperage than one that is installed in a conduit, cable, wall, attic, etc. where the higher ambient requires lowering the current flow on the conductor. This explains one reason why the power company can use smaller conductors.

DIFFERENT AMBIENT CONDITIONS

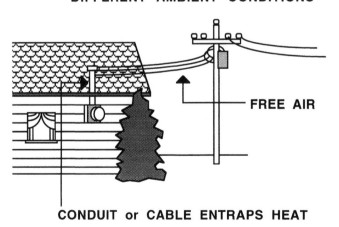

FREE AIR

CONDUIT or CABLE ENTRAPS HEAT

The Table 310-20c is from the **1971 Code**. This Table reflects the temperatures and insulations that were required for the heat. On the electrical exam the ambient temperature will be stated in the calculation.

Table 310-20(c) / Typical Ambient Temperatures

LOCATION	TEMPERATURE	Minimum Rating of Required Conductor Insulation
WELL VENTILATED, NORMALLY HEATED BUILDINGS	30° C (86° F)	* (See note below)
BUILDINGS WITH SUCH MAJOR HEAT SOURCES AS POWER STATIONS OR INDUSTRIAL PROCESSES	40° C (104° F)	75° C (167° F)
POORLY VENTILATED SPACES SUCH AS ATTICS	45° C (113° F)	75° C (167° F)
FURNACES AND BOILER ROOMS (min.)	40° C (104° F)	75° C (167° F)
(max.)	60° C (140° F)	90° C (194° F)
OUTDOORS IN SHADE IN AIR	40° C (104° F)	75° C (167° F)
IN THERMAL INSULATION	45° C (113° F)	75° C (167° F)
DIRECT SOLAR EXPOSURE	45° C (113° F)	75° C (167° F)
PLACES ABOVE 60° C (140° F)		110° C (230° F)

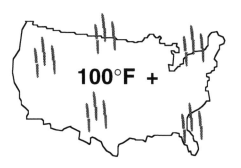

100°F +

Remember in the proper sizing of conductors you must consider the **worst** heat condition the conductor would ever encounter. I recently read an article in the newspaper where all 50 states in the U.S.A. have reached a temperature over 100 degrees F at some time. The ampacity Table 310.16 is based on an ambient temperature of 86 degrees F. If the conductor is subject to a temperature higher than 86 degrees F, the **correction factor** must be applied.

Table 310.16. Ampacities of Insulated Conductors Rated 0 -2000 Volts,
60° to 90°C (140° to 194°F) Not more Than Three Conductors in Raceway or Cable or Earth (Directly Buried),
Based on Ambient Air Temperature of 30°C (86°F).

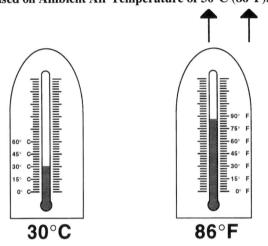

30°C   **86°F**

⌐— **When a conductor is installed in an
 ↓   ambient above or below 30°C or 86°F
     a correction factor must be applied**

CORRECTION FACTORS							
Ambient Temp. °C	For ambient temperatures other than 30°C (86°F), multiply the ampacities shown above by the appropritate factor shown below.						Ambient Temp. °F
21-25	1.08	1.05	1.04	1.08	1.05	1.04	70-77
26-30	1.00	1.00	1.00	1.00	1.00	1.00	78-86
31-35	.91	.94	.96	.91	.94	.96	87-95
36-40	.82	.88	.91	.82	.88	.91	96-104
41-45	.71	.82	.87	.71	.82	.87	105-113
46-50	.58	.75	.82	.58	.75	.82	114-122
51-55	.41	.67	.76	.41	.67	.76	123-131
56-60	....	.58	.71	....	.58	.71	132-140
61-70	....	.33	.58	....	.33	.58	141-158
71-80	....	....	.41	....	....	.41	159-176

For ambient temperatures above 30 degrees C or 86 degrees F **multiply** the **ampacities** shown above by the appropriate correction factor shown below. Remember, correction factors change with different temperatures and different **types of insulations**.

A #10 TW copper conductor in an ambient temperature of 106 degrees F has a correction factor of .71, whereas a #10 **THW** copper conductor in the same ambient temperature has a correction factor of .82. A #10 **THHN** copper conductor in the same ambient temperature has a correction factor of .87.

A #10 TW copper conductor has an ampacity of 30. In an ambient temperature of 106 degrees F the ampacity shall be reduced: 30 ampacity x .71 correction factor = 21.3 amps. This is the reduced ampacity and the maximum load that can be applied to this conductor at 106 degrees F without exceeding the temperature rating of 140 degrees F for TW insulation.

An error I have seen made by students trying to select the correct multiplier from the correction factor table is called a **line of sight** error. As you can see when selecting the 106 degrees F from the far right column, that you now have to go back to the second column from the left (TW insulation copper) to select the correction factor of .71. I suggest when using tables from the Code to use a **straight edge** such as a **ruler** so that you can follow the same line across the table and avoid selecting wrong numbers. Columns, numbers and lines have a tendency to "jump around". Your eyes can become weary after several exam hours of working calculations. **Use a straight edge**.

The left half of Table 310.16 is for **copper** and the right half of this table is for **aluminum or copper-clad aluminum** conductors. A #10 TW **aluminum** conductor has an ampacity of 25. In an ambient temperature of 106 degrees F, the correction factor is .71. The ampacity shall be reduced 25 ampacity x .71 correction factor = 17.75 amps. This is the reduced ampacity and maximum load on this conductor at 106 degrees F.

A #10 **THHN** copper conductor has an ampacity of 40. In an ambient temperature of 106 degrees F the correction factor **changes** to .87. 40 ampacity x .87 = 34.8 reduced ampacity, **but** the **maximum load** is limited to 30 amps by **overcurrent protection** device per the **asterisk (*)** at the bottom of Table 310.16:

" * 240.4(D)   Unless otherwise specifically permitted in (e) through (g), the **overcurrent protection** shall not exceed 15 amperes for #14 AWG, 20 amperes for #12 AWG, and 30 amperes for #10 AWG **copper**; or 15 amperes for #12 AWG and 25 amperes for #10 AWG **aluminum and copper-clad aluminum** after any **correction factors for ambient temperature and number of conductors have been applied**."

Example: A #14 TW copper conductor has an ampacity of 20. The **overcurrent protection** (fuse or circuit breaker) shall not exceed 15 amps.

When answering exam calculations, watch the **wording**. Ask yourself: "Is the question asking for **conductor ampacity** or asking for **overcurrent protection?**"

I've had students ask, "What good is it to have a conductor with an ampacity of 20, if you can only fuse it at 15 amps?"

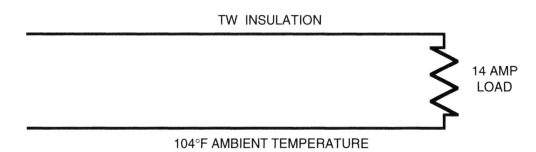

TW INSULATION

14 AMP LOAD

104°F AMBIENT TEMPERATURE

Even though a #14 conductor can only be **fused** at a maximum of 15 amps, the conductor is **derated** from the **20 ampacity** rather than 15.

In an ambient temperature of 104°F #14 TW copper has an ampacity of 20 x .82 correction factor = 16.4 reduced ampacity. A #14 TW copper conductor will carry a 14 amp load in an ambient temperature of 104°F.

In the 1978 Code a #14 TW copper conductor had an ampacity of **15**. From the 1978 Code 15 ampacity x .82 correction factor = 12.3 ampacity. A #14 TW copper conductor would not be permitted under the 1978 Code. A #12 TW copper conductor would have been the minimum size permitted. In the 1981 Code the ampacities were increased for some conductors due to better products of thermoplastics, etc.

A #14 TW copper conductor can carry 20 amperes continuously @ 86°F, but the devices you connect the conductor to are not rated for these higher currents. The asterisk (*) limit of 15 amps on the overcurrent protection is because the protective device will not protect the conductor from short-circuit currents, it will protect the conductor from overcurrent but not short circuit.

Conductors and devices must be used as listed in Section 110.3(B). An example of a daily **misuse** of Table 310.16 would be using the ampacities of a 90°C conductor such as the popular **THHN** insulation. Table 310.16 shows a #6 THHN copper conductor with an ampacity of 75, **but** this ampacity applies when the 90°C conductor is connected to devices with a rating of 90°C.

From the UL Electrical Construction Materials Directory and Code section 110.14(C): "The termination provisions on equipment are based on the use of 60°C conductors in circuits rated 100 amperes or less and the use of 75°C conductors in higher rated circuits.

If the termination provisions on the equipment are based on the use of other conductors, the equipment is either marked with both the size and temperature rating of the conductors to be used. If the equipment is marked only with the temperature rating of the conductors to be used, that temperature rating is required for the ambient temperature in the equipment and the 60°C ampacity (100 ampere or less circuits) or 75°C ampacity (over 100 ampere circuits) should be used to determine the size of conductors.

Higher temperature rated conductors may be used, though not required, if the size of the conductors is determined on the basis of the 60°C ampacity (100 ampere or less circuits) or 75°C ampacity (over 100 ampere circuits)."

Example: A #6 TW has a normal ampacity of 55 amps. Which means when the conductor is loaded to 55 amps in an ambient of 86°F or 30°C it will reach an **operating temperature** of 140°F or 60°C.

When the conductor insulation is exposed to a temperature **above** 86°F or 30°C it is subject to insulation damage when loaded to its ampacity value. This is why a **correction factor** is applied when the ambient temperature exceeds 86°F or 30°C.

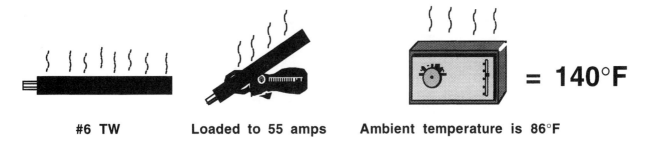

| #6 TW | Loaded to 55 amps | Ambient temperature is 86°F |

= 140°F

If you lay your ruler on 140°F and read the column for TW insulation (60°C-140°F) you'll see there is **no** correction factor. This simply means you are not permitted to use this insulation in this high of an ambient temperature.

133-140

The Extra Inch Puts You Miles Ahead With
Tom Henry's **CODE ELECTRICAL CLASSES, INC.**   407-671-0020

When the ambient temperature is **below** 86°F or 30°C the ampacity can be adjusted to a **higher** value than shown.

Example: The #6 TW has a normal ampacity of 55 amps. If the ambient temperature is 70°F the correction factor is now **1.08**. 55 ampacity x 1.08 = **59.4 ampacity**.

Cooler ambient allows a higher ampacity

TWO TYPES OF AMPACITY QUESTIONS

The first type of question will state the conductor, insulation type, and an ambient temperature either in Celsius (Centigrade) or Fahrenheit, and the question will ask the **ampacity** of the conductor.

   Example: What is the ampacity of a #6 TW conductor in an ambient temperature of 122°F?

   #6 TW = 55 ampacity x .58 correction factor = 31.9 reduced ampacity.

The second type of question will state a load, type of insulation, and an ambient temperature, and the question will ask the **size** of conductor required.

   Example: What is the minimum size copper conductor required for the circuit shown below?

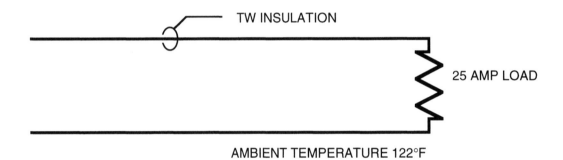

TW INSULATION

25 AMP LOAD

AMBIENT TEMPERATURE 122°F

$$\text{Use the formula: Required Table Ampacity} = \frac{\text{Load}}{\text{Correction Factor}}$$

You can select the minimum size conductor very easily by using this formula.

$$\frac{25 \text{ amp load}}{.58 \text{ correction factor}} = 43.1 \text{ required ampacity}$$

   Turn to Table 310.16 for copper TW insulation and select a conductor from this column that would carry at least 43.1 amps. This would require a #6 TW with an ampacity of 55.

   Note: Section 110.5: Conductors normally used to carry current shall be of **copper** unless otherwise provided in this Code. Where the conductor material is **not** specified, the sizes given in this Code shall apply to **copper** conductors.

To correctly apply Table 310.16 to reality and check the misuse of the table by using a #10 romex for a 25 amp load. Let's calculate the **minimum** size conductor required for a 3 ton A/C unit in a dwelling using nonmetallic sheathed NMB cable (romex) through the attic to the load center. The ambient temperature in the attic has reached 122°F.

3 ton A/C unit load 25 amps

10-2 G TYPE NMB

NMB has a 90°C insulation -BUT section 336.26 states it has an AMPACITY of 60°C (140°F)

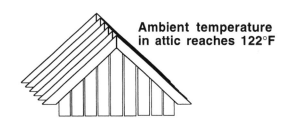

Ambient temperature in attic reaches 122°F

$$\text{Minimum wire size} = \frac{\text{LOAD}}{\text{CORRECTION FACTOR}}$$

$$\text{Minimum wire size} = \frac{25\ \text{amps}}{.58\ \text{correction factor}} = 43.1\ \text{required ampacity}$$

Table 310.16 required a #6 copper, 60°C (140°F) **minimum** size conductor. Now you can see how **heat** affects ampacity and the sizing of conductors.

Table 310.16 is a very **misused** table in reality.

Shown below is an example applying **both** factors, an ambient correction and adjustment factor from T. 310.15(B2a).

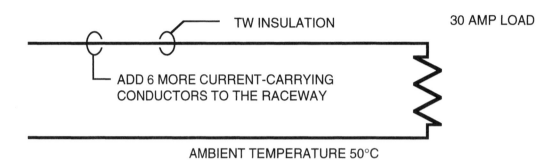

TW INSULATION   30 AMP LOAD

ADD 6 MORE CURRENT-CARRYING
CONDUCTORS TO THE RACEWAY

AMBIENT TEMPERATURE 50°C

Use the formula: Required Table Ampacity = $\dfrac{\text{Load}}{\text{Correction Factor x Adjustment Factor}}$

$$\frac{30 \text{ amp load}}{.58 \ \text{x} \ .70} = 73.89 \text{ required ampacity}$$

Turn to Table 310.16 for copper TW insulation and select a conductor from this column that would carry at least 73.89 amps. This would require a #3 TW with an ampacity of 85.

> **Ambient temperature is the temperature surrounding the conductor or equipment**

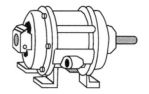

A motor circuit would be a different calculation.

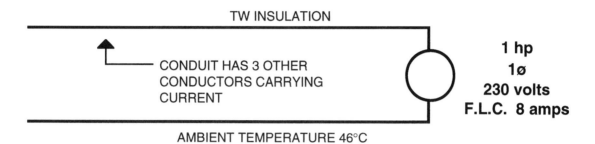

TW INSULATION

CONDUIT HAS 3 OTHER
CONDUCTORS CARRYING
CURRENT

1 hp
1ø
230 volts
F.L.C. 8 amps

AMBIENT TEMPERATURE 46°C

The load for a single-phase motor is found in Table 430.248 F.L.C. (full load current)

$$\frac{8 \text{ amp load}}{.58 \text{ x } .80} = 17.24$$

Section 430.22(A) requires an **increase** in ampacity of 125% for motor branch circuits.

17.24 x 125% = 21.5 required ampacity

Turn to Table 310.16 for copper TW insulation and select a conductor from this column that would carry at least 21.5 amps. This would require a #12 TW with an ampacity of 25.

The asterisk (*) that states a #12 copper conductor has a maximum overcurrent protection of 20 amps. The asterisk (*) rules for overcurrent protection do **not** apply to **motor circuits** per section 240.4(G) which states motor overcurrent protection is calculated from Part IV of 430.

The reason that motors have different overcurrent protection rules from lighting and appliance circuits, motors have an extra element called an **overload device**. You may refer to this overload device as **heaters** or **thermal running overload protective devices**.

The next chapter, which is "Motors", will explain how a motor circuit is better protected than a lighting and receptacle circuit.

**Overload
(heater)**

CONDUCTOR TERMINATIONS

The frequent misapplication of conductor temperature ratings occurs when the rating of the equipment is ignored when connecting the conductor. One must follow the rules of section 110.14(C).

Shown below are the ampacities and temperature ratings for a #10 conductor.

#10 TW 30 ampacity
60°C - 140°F temperature rating

#10 THW 35 ampacity
75°C - 167°F temperature rating

#10 THHN 40 ampacity
90°C - 194°F temperature rating

Conductors carry a specific temperature rating based on the *type* of insulation on the conductor.

Conductor sizing must be determined to where the conductors will terminate and the rating of the termination.

If a termination is rated for 60°C, this means that the temperature at that termination may rise up to 60°C when the equipment is loaded to its *ampacity*. Any additional heat at the connection above the 60°C conductor insulation rating could cause damage to the conductor insulation.

When a conductor is chosen to carry a specific load, the electrician must know the termination ratings of the equipment in the entire circuit.

When connecting the 90°C THHN insulation to 60°C rated equipment, the THHN cannot be loaded over the 60°C ampacity.

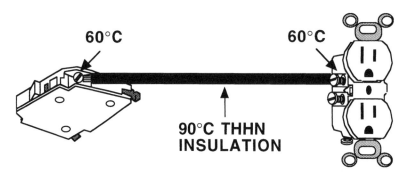

60°C   60°C

90°C THHN
INSULATION

If the temperature rating of the equipment is not considered and the THHN is loaded to the 90°C ampacity it will lead to overheating at the termination and *premature opening* of the breaker.

The breaker has a heat sink which determines when it will open, the added extra heat is a determining factor in the premature opening.

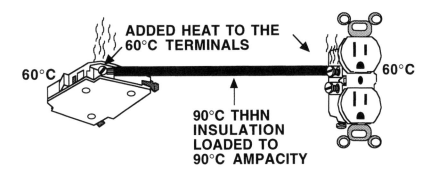

Electrical equipment such as circuit breakers, panelboards, receptacles, switches, terminal blocks, wire nuts, lugs, etc. have *temperature ratings* that must be observed.

The termination provisions are based on the use of 60°C ampacities for wire sizes #14 - #1 and 75°C ampacities for wire sizes #1/0 and larger. If using wire sizes #14-#1 in equipment marked "75°C only" or "60/75°C", it is intended that 75°C wire may be used at its full ampacity.

If the equipment is not marked, it is 60°C rated for 100 amps and less. Over 100 amps is 75°C rated. If the equipment is rated higher, it would have to be marked to indicate the higher temperature.

100 amps or less	Over 100 amps
Wire size #14 - #1	Wire size #1/0 and larger
60°C ampacity	75°C ampacity

The Code states in section 110.14(C) the temperature rating associated with the ampacity of the conductor shall be so selected not to exceed the lowest temperature rating of any conductor, device or connected termination.

This Code section is often violated, even ignored. A THHN 90°C conductor *cannot* be connected to a 60°C terminal and the conductor loaded to the 90°C ampacity.

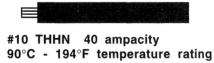

#10 THHN   40 ampacity
90°C - 194°F temperature rating

The THHN conductor is the most popular insulation used in circuits. Because of its thinner insulation more conductors can be installed in a conduit compared to conductors with a thicker insulation.

Where the violation occurs is when the installer loads the THHN to the 90°C ampacity!

The only way a THHN could be loaded to a 90°C ampacity would be if every piece of electrical equipment (lugs, receptacle, switch, panelboard, overcurrent device, etc.) in the *entire* circuit is rated at 90°C.

The first thing the installer must be made aware of is that electrical equipment terminations are rated at 60°C, 75°C, or 60/75°C. If there is no marking on the equipment it is 60°C for 100 amps or less. Over 100 amps is 75°C rated.

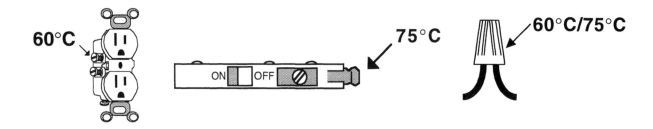

60°C   **75°C**   **60°C/75°C**

Circuit breakers are listed as suitable for 60°C only, 75°C only, or 60/75°C wire. Very little electrical equipment is tested for use with conductors operating over 75°C, although some large bolted pressure contact switches are suitable for conductors operating at 90°C.

When a conductor is chosen for the circuit, the electrician must know the termination ratings for the equipment in the *entire* circuit.

90°C RATED

The lug may be rated for 90°C but this does not give permission to the installer to use a 90°C conductor at 90°C ampacity. Every electrical component in the entire circuit must be 90°C rated.

When terminals are tested at 60°C or 75°C, the use of 90°C conductors loaded to their higher ampacity ratings can damage the terminals on circuit breakers, switches, etc. Electrical equipment has experienced termination failures even when the load current did not exceed the current rating of the circuit breaker or switch, etc.

When a 60°C rated circuit breaker terminal is fed by a conductor operating at 90°C, there will be substantial heat conducted from the 90°C metal to the 60°C terminal that can damage the terminal over a period of time, even though the load current does not exceed the 60°C terminal rating and does not exceed the 90°C ampacity.

The definition of ampacity is the current in amperes a conductor can carry *continuously* under the conditions without exceeding its (insulation) temperature rating. The greater the ampacity of a higher-temperature rated conductor establishes the ability of the conductor insulation to withstand the higher heat being produced by the higher current through the wire. But, it is *wrong* to assume that the equipment the conductor is being connected to is also capable of withstanding this higher heat.

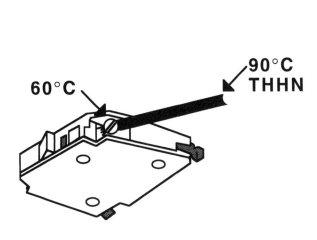
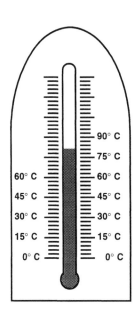

When two metallic parts are tightly connected having different operating temperatures (60°C - 90°C) the higher-temperature part (90°C) will give heat to the lower temperature part (60°C) and raise its temperature to above 60°C.

A 75°C temperature marking on a circuit breaker normally intended for wire sizes #14-#1 does not in itself allow the 75°C wire to be used at a 75°C ampacity unless the enclosure in which the circuit breaker is installed is also marked 75°C.

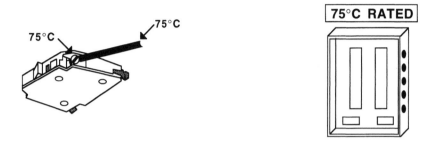

A conductor has *two* ends. Conductors must be sized by giving consideration to where each end will terminate and the temperature rating of the termination equipment.

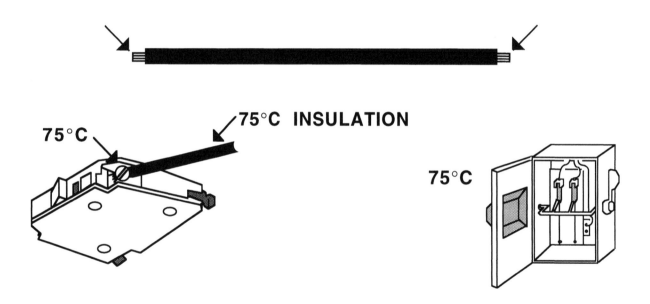

If a termination is rated for 75°C, this means that the temperature at that termination may rise up to 75°C when the equipment is loaded to its full ampacity. If 60°C conductors were used, the additional heat at the termination above 60°C conductor insulation rating could result in insulation damage.

Often, manufacturers are asked when electrical equipment will be available with terminations that will allow THHN 90°C conductors to be loaded to the 90°C ampacity. The answer is complex and requires not only significant equipment redesign to handle the extra heat, but also significant changes in the product testing/listing standards would also have to occur.

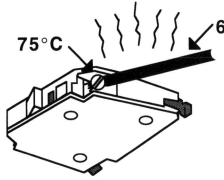

60°C INSULATION

The circuit breaker lug fully loaded will reach a temperature of 75°C which is 167°F. The 60°C conductor maximum operating temperature is 60°C which is 140°F. This is an increase of 27°F above the *maximum* operating temperature of the conductor. Over a period of time the conductor will show signs of insulation damage such as the insulation becoming hard and brittle close to the termination.

The panelboard has a 150 amp circuit breaker with a temperature of 75°C. It requires a conductor with an ampacity of at least 150 amperes. Table 310-16 shown below lists the ampacities of different conductors. We must select a conductor with an ampacity of at least 150 from the *75°C column* which is a #1/0. A #1 THHN 90°C conductor also has an ampacity of 150. But, a #1 THHN *cannot* be loaded to the 150 ampacity because the equipment is only rated at 75°C. Using a #1 THHN conductor in this application would lead to possible overheating at the termination or premature opening of the circuit breaker. A 60°C insulated conductor is not acceptable regardless of the size since the temperature at the termination (75°C) could rise to a value greater than the insulation rating of 60°C.

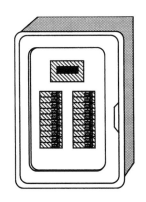

Table 310.16. Allowable Ampacities of Insulated Conductors

Size	Temperature Rating of Conductor. See Table 310.13.						Size
	60°C (140°F)	75°C (167°F)	90°C (194°F)	60°C (140°F)	75°C (167°F)	90°C (194°F)	
AWG kcmil	TYPES TW, UF	TYPES RHW, THHW, THW, THWN, XHHW, USE, ZW	TYPES TBS,SA, SIS, FEP, FEPB, MI, RHH, RHW-2, THHN, THHW, THW-2, THWN-2 USE-2, XHH XHHW, XHHW-2 ZW-2	TYPES TW, UF	TYPES RHW, THHW, THW, THWN, XHHW, USE	TYPES TBS, SA, SIS, THHN, THHW, THW-2, THWN-2, RHH, RHW-2, USE-2, XHH, XHHW, XHHW-2, ZW-2	AWG kcmil
	COPPER			ALUMINUM OR COPPER-CLAD ALUMINUM			
18	....	....	14	....	....	....	....
16	....	....	18	....	....	....	....
14*	20	20	25	....	....	....	....
12*	25	25	30	20	20	25	12*
10*	30	35	40	25	30	35	10*
8	40	50	55	30	40	45	8
6	55	65	75	40	50	60	6
4	70	85	95	55	65	75	4
3	85	100	110	65	75	85	3
2	95	115	130	75	90	100	2
1	110	130	150	85	100	115	1
1/0	125	150	170	100	120	135	1/0
2/0	145	175	195	115	135	150	2/0
3/0	165	200	225	130	155	175	3/0
4/0	195	230	260	150	180	205	4/0

A circuit breaker is rated 75°C and the receptacle to which the branch circuit conductor is connected is rated 60°C. The conductor must have an insulation rating of at least 75°C (due to the rating of the breaker), and the conductor must be sized based on the ampacity of a 60°C conductor (due to the rating of the receptacle).

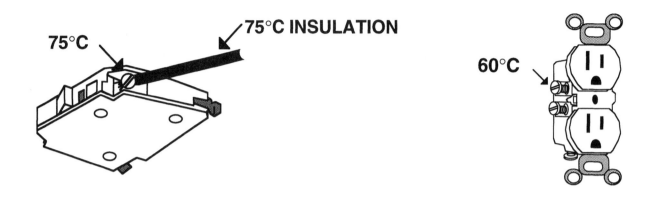

The general rule is 100 amps or less is wire sizes #14 - #1 with 60°C ampacity and for over 100 amps the wire sizes are #1/0 and larger with 75°C ampacity. But, there are two exceptions: (1) Conductors with higher temperature ratings such as 75°C can be used but at the ampacity of the equipment temperature rating as shown above. (2) Equipment termination provisions can be used with higher rated conductors at the ampacity of the higher rated conductors, provided the equipment is listed at the higher rating. This means a 20 amp receptacle can be rated 75°C even though it is 100 amps or less.

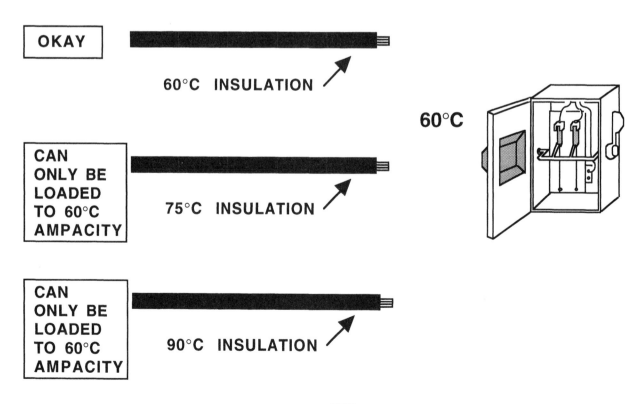

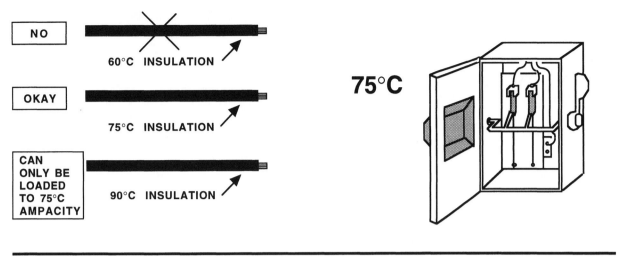

NO
60°C INSULATION

OKAY
75°C INSULATION

CAN ONLY BE LOADED TO 75°C AMPACITY
90°C INSULATION

75°C

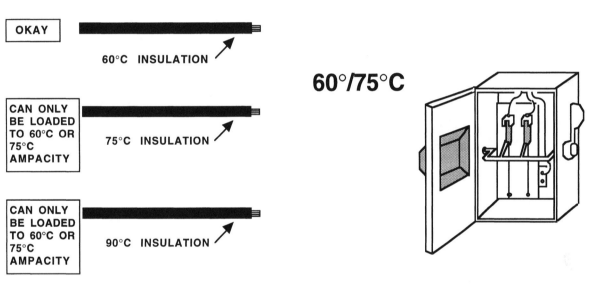

OKAY
60°C INSULATION

CAN ONLY BE LOADED TO 60°C OR 75°C AMPACITY
75°C INSULATION

CAN ONLY BE LOADED TO 60°C OR 75°C AMPACITY
90°C INSULATION

60°/75°C

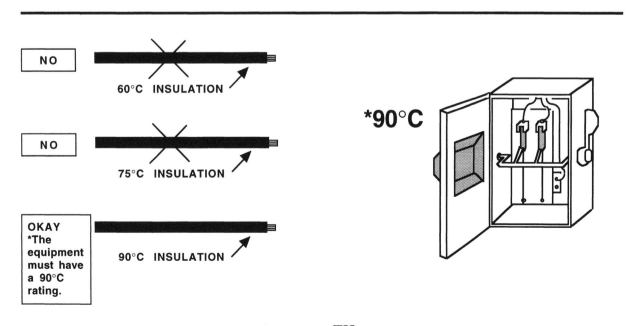

NO
60°C INSULATION

NO
75°C INSULATION

OKAY *The equipment must have a 90°C rating.
90°C INSULATION

*90°C

ADVANTAGES OF 90° C CONDUCTORS

As you have seen different types of insulations have different ampacities and temperature ratings. Insulation also changes the size of the conductor and this is important when considering conduit fill.

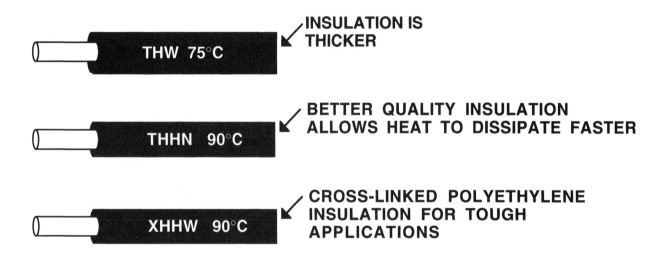

A #12 THW has a thicker insulation .026 sq.in. compared to the thinner insulation of a #12 THHN at .0133 sq.in.

You could install 8 - #12 THW's in a 3/4" EMT conduit or 16 - #12 THHN's.

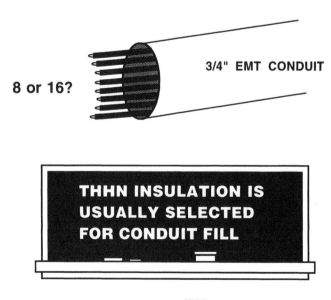

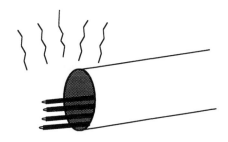

Code Table 310.15(B2a) states that where the number of current-carrying conductors in a raceway or cable exceeds *three,* the allowable ampacity must be reduced to compensate for the increased heating effect due to reduced ventilation of an enclosed group of closely spaced conductors.

Adjustment Factors.
(a) **More than Three Conductors in a Raceway or Cable.** Where the number of conductors in a raceway or cable exceeds three, the ampacities shall be reduced as shown in the following table:

Number of Conductors	Percent of Values in Tables as Adjusted for Ambient Temperature if Necessary
4 through 6	80
7 through 9	70
10 through 20	50
21 through 30	45
31 through 40	40
41 and above	35

Selecting THHN 90°C insulation is an advantage in designing when applying the derating factors (correction factor and/or adjustment factor) to the normal ampacity of the conductor.

Example: The circuit is installed in a conduit that has a total of seven current carrying conductors. The equipment in the circuit has a rating of 60°C.

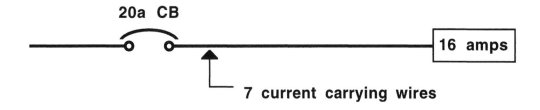

20a CB

16 amps

7 current carrying wires

The Code requires the normal ampacity to be reduced for the seven current carrying conductors.

A #12 TW ampacity is 25 x 70% =17.5 amps the maximum current permitted.

A #12 THW ampacity is 25 x 70% = 17.5 amps is the maximum current permitted.

A #12 THHN has a normal ampacity of 30 x 70% = 21 amps is the maximum current permitted on the conductor. A #12 TW or #12 THW with a derated ampacity of 17.5 is considered protected by the next higher size breaker which is a 20. The advantage of a #12 THHN is it has a derated ampacity of 21 which is above the breaker rating of 20 amps. The THHN insulation eliminates any chance of overload damage to the insulation.

DERATED AMPACITY = 17.5

#12 TW   25 ampacity
60°C - 140°F temperature rating

DERATED AMPACITY = 17.5

#12 THW   25 ampacity
75°C - 167°F temperature rating

DERATED AMPACITY = 21

#12 THHN   30 ampacity
90°C - 194°F temperature rating

Example: A branch circuit has a noncontinuous load of 29 amps. The circuit is installed in a conduit that has a total of four current carrying conductors. The equipment in the circuit has a rating of 60°C.

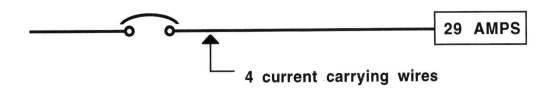

29 AMPS

4 current carrying wires

A #10 TW ampacity is 30 x 80% = 24 amps the maximum current permitted. A #10 TW would violate the Code in this example as the load is 29 amps.

A #10 THW ampacity is 35 x 80% = 28 amps is the maximum current permitted. A #10 THW would also be a violation as the load is 29 amps.

A #10 THHN has a normal ampacity of 40 x 80% = 32 amps is the maximum current permitted on the conductor. Next go to the 60°C column and select a conductor that will carry the 29 amp load. A #10 THHN can be used in this condition. The THHN conductor can safely carry 32 amps without damage to the *conductor insulation*. But, the 60°C column shows a #10 conductor cannot be loaded to more than 30 amps without possible damage to the *termination*.

Otherwise you would have to use a #8 TW (40a x 80% = 32a) or a #8 THW (50a x 80% = 40a). By selecting THHN insulation you can use a smaller #10 conductor.

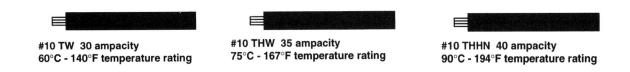

#10 TW 30 ampacity
60°C - 140°F temperature rating

#10 THW 35 ampacity
75°C - 167°F temperature rating

#10 THHN 40 ampacity
90°C - 194°F temperature rating

**THHN HAS A HIGHER
AMPACITY WHICH IS
USED IN DERATING**

Table 310.16 gives ampacities under two conditions: There are not more than three current-carrying conductors in a raceway or cable and the raceway or cable containing the conductors is operating in an ambient temperature not exceeding 30°C of 86°F.

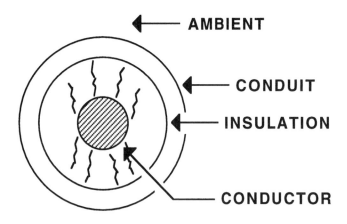

Definition of **ambient**: "That which encompasses on all sides". Ambient temperature is the temperature of the medium, such as earth, air or water, into which the heat of the conductor is dissipated.

The current flowing through the conductor produces heat (I²R). This heat must dissipate through the insulation into the raceway or cable. From the raceway or cable the heat must dissipate into the ambient.

You can see from the illustration how the conductor material, size, insulation type, and ambient temperature decide the allowable ampacity of a conductor.

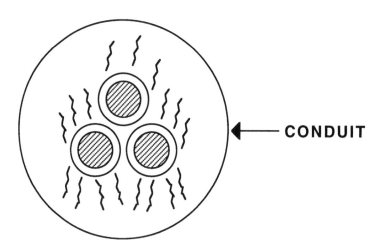

The above diagram shows three current-carrying conductors with the heat being released from the circumference of the conductors to the conduit.

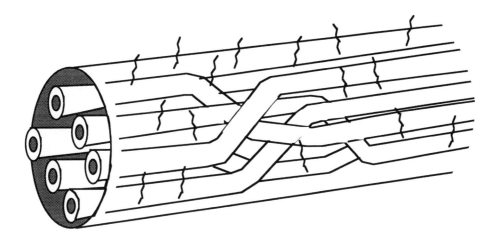

The above illustration shows a conduit with six current-carrying conductors. **All** of the conductors are not close to the conduit wall to dissipate the heat. This condition requires the ampacity of each conductor to be reduced per Table 310.15(B2a). Conductors installed in **parallel** require reducing the ampacity per T. 310.15(B2a). Section 310.4 states: Conductors installed in parallel shall comply with the provisions of T. 310.15(B2a).

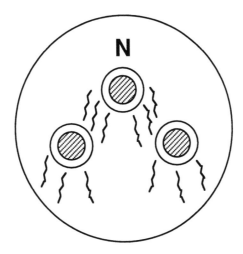

310.15(B4a): A **neutral** conductor which carries only the unbalanced current from the other conductors, as in the case of normally balanced circuits of three or more conductors, **shall not be counted** when applying the provisions of T. 310.15(B2a).

Example: If the load is balanced, the current in the neutral is zero, and the two ungrounded conductors will run cooler because the neutral conductor is in intimate contact with them throughout the circuit and will serve to carry off part of the heat.

Using #4 THW copper conductors, 100 feet in length each. From Table 8, Chapter 9 the resistance of a #4 uncoated copper conductor is 0.308 ohms per thousand feet. 0.308 x .100 feet = 0.0308 ohm per conductor.

Let's say the circuit is balanced with each ungrounded conductor carrying a load of 60 amps. Heat = I²R 60a x 60a x 0.0308 x 2 conductors = 221.76 watts.

Now assume the load is **not** balanced, the ungrounded conductor Line 1 carries 80 amps, Line 2 carries 40 amps, and the neutral carries the **unbalanced** of 40 amps.

The heat loss would be:

Line 1 =   80a x 80a x 0.0308 ohm = 197.12 watts

Line 2 =   40a x 40a x 0.0308 ohm =   49.28 watts

Neutral =   40a x 40a x 0.0308 ohm =   49.28 watts

                                                                  295.68 watts

The total of 295.68 watts is **more** than the loss of 221.76 watts in the case of the balanced load. Therefore the balanced load is the best condition for heat. Any amount of load **imbalance** will only make heat conditions worse.

Any conductor in a raceway or cable has one of six possible values of ampacity, depending on the conditions of application.

The six conditions of ampacity using a #4 THW copper conductor as an example:

Condition 1. Ambient temperature is 30°C. Not more than three current-carrying conductors in raceway or cable. Under these conditions, #4 THW copper conductor has an ampacity of 85, as shown in Table 310.16.

Condition 2. Ambient temperature is 25°C which is **below** 30°C. Not more than three current-carrying conductors in raceway or cable. Under these conditions the value of 85 amps from Table 310-16 must be multiplied by the factor from "Ampacity Correction Factors". For THW insulation at 25°C the correction factor is 1.05. 85 ampacity x 1.05 = 89.25 **increased** ampacity.

Condition 3. Ambient temperature is 45°C which is **above** 30°C. Not more than three current-carrying conductors in raceway or cable. Under these conditions the value of 85 amps must be multiplied by the correction factor of .82. 85 ampacity x .82 = 69.7 reduced ampacity.

Condition 4. Ambient temperature is 30°C. **Four** current-carrying conductors in raceway or cable. As required by T.310.15(B2a), the value of 85 amps must be multiplied by 80% to determine the conductor ampacity. 85 ampacity x 80% = 68 reduced ampacity.

Condition 5. Ambient temperature is 45°C. **Four** current-carrying conductors in raceway or cable. The ambient temperature of 45°C requires a correction factor of .82. 85 ampacity x .82 = 69.7 reduced ampacity. This value must be reduced again by 80% for **four** current-carrying conductors per T.310.15(B2a). 69.7 ampacity x 80% = 55.76 reduced ampacity.

Condition 6. Ambient temperature is 25°C. **Four** current-carrying conductors in raceway or cable. The ambient temperature of 25°C requires a correction factor of 1.05. 85 ampacity x 1.05 = 89.25 **increased** ampacity. This value must be reduced by 80% for **four** current-carrying conductors per T.310.15(B2. 89.25 ampacity x 80% = 71.4 reduced ampacity.

•Terminations shall be as listed per 110.14(C).

**AMPACITY IS THE CURRENT
A CONDUCTOR CAN CARRY
CONTINUOUSLY**

1. Determine the allowable ampacity of 13 - #12 THHN conductors in a raceway, when passing through an area where the ambient temperature is 40° C.

(a) 13.65 amps   (b) 15.0 amps   (c) 26.4 amps   (d) 30.0 amps

2. A raceway contains nine #12 THHN conductors from a 120/240v, single-phase panelboard. The conductors supply three 120/240v, three-wire circuits made up of L1, L2 and a grounded conductor (neutral). What is the allowable ampacity for each of the #12 conductors?

(a) 20   (b) 21   (c) 24   (d) 25

3. What is the ampacity of four #4/0 THWN copper current carrying conductors in a raceway installed through an ambient temperature of 45° C?

(a) 150.9 amps   (b) 160.1 amps   (c) 163.5 amps   (d) 213.2 amps

4. A 20" length of conduit that separates two cabinets contains 30 current-carrying conductors, the ambient temperature is 27°C. These conductors are to be derated ____.

(a) twice   (b) 45%   (c) 1.08   (d) not required at all

5. What is the ampacity of a #3/0 THWN conductor installed in an ambient temperature of 104°F?

(a) 100 amps   (b) 200 amps   (c) 160 amps   (d) 176 amps

6. Where two different ampacities apply to adjacent portions of a circuit, the higher ampacity shall be permitted to be used beyond the point of transition, a distance equal to 10 feet or ____ percent of the circuit length figured at the higher ampacity, whichever is less.

(a) 10%   (b) 15%   (c) 20%   (d) 25%

1. Determine the size of conductors required to supply a 75 amp non-motor load. The device terminations are rated at 75°C. Use copper conductors, conductor insulation type is THHN.

(a) #6   (b) #3   (c) #4   (d) none of these

2. The source is 3ø 208/120v. The load is three banks of fluorescent lights connected line to neutral. The three current carrying conductors and neutral are all in the same conduit. If the line current is 50 amps, what size THWN conductors would be required.

(a) 8   (b) 6   (c) 4   (d) 3

3. The ampacity of a copper #10 THWN-2 is ___ when there are three conductors in the conduit and the ambient temperature is 70°F.

(a) 30   (b) 32.4   (c) 35   (d) 41.6

4. How many conductors would be counted in a branch circuit raceway for the purpose of derating conductor ampacity given the following:

3 bare conductors - 3 black insulated conductors - 3 white insulated conductors - 3 red insulated conductors

The service is single-phase, the load is balanced on each circuit and there are no harmonic currents on the neutrals.

(a) 3   (b) 6   (c) 9   (d) 12

5. What is the ampacity of a #18 SVE cord with three conductors carrying current in an ambient temperature of 30°C?

(a) 5 amps   (b) 7 amps   (c) 8 amps   (d) 10 amps

6. What is the allowable ampacity of a #4 THW in free air in an ambient temperature of 104°F?

(a) 74.8 amps   (b) 69.7 amps   (c) 110 amps   (d) 125 amps

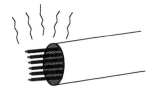

1. The overcurrent protection of a #10 THW conductor, when there are not more than three conductors in a raceway, and the ambient temperature is 28°C, would be ____ amps.

(a) 30   (b) 35   (c) 25   (d) 20

2. The ampacity of a #14 THW conductor, when there are six conductors in a conduit and the temperature is 30°C, would be ____ amps.

(a) 25   (b) 22   (c) 20   (d) 16

3. The ampacity of a #12 TW conductor when there are not more than three conductors in a raceway and the ambient temperature is 36°C would be ____ amps.

(a) 25   (b) 22   (c) 20.5   (d) 16

4. What is the allowable ampacity of a #12 TW copper conductor in a raceway with an ambient temperature of 75°F?

(a) 20 amps   (b) 25 amps   (c) 27 amps   (d) 30 amps

5. What is the maximum current allowed on a #12 THHN copper conductor in an ambient temperature of 122°F with a total of six current-carrying conductors in the conduit?

(a) 19.68 amps   (b) 24.6 amps   (c) 32.8 amps   (d) 20 amps

6. What is the maximum current allowed on a #10 THW when in a conduit with 5 other current-carrying #10 THW's and two bare #10 grounding conductors? (all are copper conductors) (this is a total of 8 conductors in the conduit).

(a) 30 amps   (b) 21 amps   (c) 28 amps   (d) 20 amps

1. A raceway contains two #12 THW conductors. The raceway is installed in an ambient temperature of 115°F. What is the ampacity of this conductor?

(a) 25 amps   (b) 20 amps   (c) 18.75 amps   (d) 14.50 amps

2. A cable contains seven current-carrying #10 TW conductors in an ambient temperature of 30°C. What is the ampacity of this conductor?

(a) 21 amps   (b) 17.22 amps   (c) 24.6 amps   (d) 24 amps

3. What is the allowable ampacity of a #2/0 THW aluminum conductor with an ambient temperature of 23°C?

(a) 175 amps   (b) 183.75 amps   (c) 141.75 amps   (d) 135 amps

4. Three #8 XHHW conductors are installed in a wet location with an ambient temperature of 45°C. What is the ampacity of this conductor?

(a) 32.8 amps   (b) 41 amps   (c) 45.1 amps   (d) 29 amps

5. What is the ampacity of each conductor of a group of twenty-five #14 copper RHH conductors all in one conduit with an ambient temperature of 45°C?

(a) 25 amps   (b) 15.23 amps   (c) 17.4 amps   (d) 9.7875 amps

6. The maximum overcurrent protection of a copper #10 RHW conductor is _____ when there are three conductors in a conduit and the ambient temperature is 104°F.

(a) 30   (b) 30.8   (c) 35   (d) 40

1. 24 - #12 THW current-carrying conductors are installed in a conduit 18" in length. What is the total derating percent of value?

(a) 70%   (b) 80%   (c) 60%   (d) no derating required

2. What is the allowable ampacity of a #10 TW copper conductor in an ambient temperature of 70°F?

(a) 30   (b) 35   (c) 32.4   (d) 31.5

3. A single-phase 240/120 volt service has six #3/0 THW copper conductors in parallel installed in a single raceway. What is the ampacity of each conductor?

(a) 200 amps   (b) 400 amps   (c) 160 amps   (d) 140 amps

4. What is the ampacity of 4 #6 THW copper current-carrying conductors enclosed in schedule 80 PVC conduit 8 feet in length entering a trench?

(a) 65 amps   (b) 52 amps   (c) 44 amps   (d) 40 amps

5. What is the ampacity of each of four #8 XHHW copper conductors in a conduit above the dropped-ceiling on a 4-wire, three-phase wye circuit where the load is all flourescent lighting?

(a) 40 amps   (b) 50 amps   (c) 44 amps   (d) 55 amps

6. What is the minimum size 60°C copper conductor permitted for a 3 ton air-conditioning unit with a load of 25 amps in an ambient temperature of 122°F?

(a) #12 TW   (b) #10 TW   (c) #8 TW   (d) #6 TW

CHAPTER 3

MOTORS

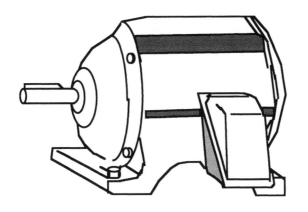

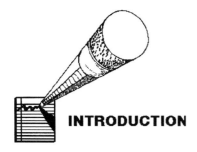

INTRODUCTION

This chapter will cover the proper sizing of separate overload protective devices, branch circuit conductors, branch circuit overcurrent protection, feeder conductors, and feeder overcurrent protection for motors.

A motor is not very smart, it will actually work itself to death if we don't protect it.

Section 430.6(A) General Motor Applications. **Table Values**. Other than for motors built for low speeds or high torques, and for multispeed motors, the values given in Table 430.247, Table 430.248, Table 430.249, and Table 430.250 **SHALL BE** used to determine the ampacity of conductors or ampere ratings of switches, branch-circuit short-circuit and ground-fault protection, **INSTEAD** of the actual current rating marked on the motor nameplate. Where a motor is marked in amperes, but not horsepower, the horsepower rating shall be assumed to be that corresponding to the values given in the Tables, **interpolated** if necessary.

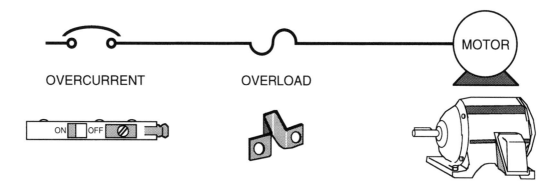

OVERCURRENT   OVERLOAD   MOTOR

ON   OFF

In motor circuits the over**current** device is the fuse or circuit breaker to protect against short-circuit and ground-fault. The separate over**load** protective device is the thermal protection for excessive heat. The overload protective device is often referred to as the **heaters**.

Section 430.6(A2) states the heaters shall be based on the motor nameplate current rating, but when sizing the conductors, fuses, or circuit breakers you shall use the Tables to select the current rating.

Table 430.247 Full-load current in amperes, **D.C. motors**

Table 430.248 Full-load current in amperes, **Single-phase A.C. motors**

Table 430.249 Full-load current in amperes, **Two-phase A.C. motors**

Table 430.250 Full-load current, **Three-phase A.C. motors**

For the exam Tables 430.248 and 430.250 would be referred to the most. Be careful when using these Tables to select the proper Table for single-phase or three-phase. The mistake I see students make is selecting currents from the wrong Table.

Table 430.248 SINGLE-PHASE

Table 430.248. Full Load Currents in Amperes
Single-Phase Alternating-Current Motors
The following values of full-load currents are for motors running at usual speeds and motors with normal torque characteristics. The rated voltages listed are rated motor voltages. The currents listed shall be permitted for system voltage ranges of 110 to 120 and 220 to 240.

HP	115V	208V	230V
1/6	4.4	2.4	2.2
1/4	5.8	3.2	2.9
1/3	7.2	4.0	3.6
1/2	9.8	5.4	4.9
3/4	13.8	7.6	6.9
1	16	8.8	8
1-1/2	20	11	10
2	24	13.2	12
3	34	18.7	17
5	56	30.8	28
7-1/2	80	44	40
10	100	55	50

The Table shows the amperes for 115, 208 and 230 volt single-phase motors.

The currents shown shall be permitted for system voltage ranges of 110 to 120 volts and 220 to 240 volts.

Example: A 1 hp **240 volt** motor would have a F.L.C. of 8 amps. A 1 hp **110 volt** motor would have a F.L.C. of 16 amps.

Section 430.6(A1) states: **interpolated** if necessary.

Example: What is the full-load current for a **4 hp** 230 volt single-phase motor?

Interpolated: 5 hp = 28 amps   3 hp = 17 amps   28 - 17 = 11 amp difference. The difference in hp is 5 hp - 3 hp = 2 hp difference. Interpolated = 11 amps divided by 2 hp = 5.5 amps difference per hp.   3 hp = 17 amps + 5.5 amps = **22.5 amps F.L.C. for a 4 hp motor.**

Motor va input = E x I   Motor output = 746 watts per hp

Example: What is the efficiency of a 1 hp 115 volt single-phase motor?

EFFICIENCY = OUTPUT/INPUT   746w output   115v x 16a = 1840 input   746/1840 = **40.5%**

Table 430.250 THREE-PHASE

Table 430.250. Full-Load Current **Three-Phase** Alternating -Current Motors

	Induction type Squirrel-Cage and Wound-Rotor Amperes							Synchronous Type Unity Power Factor* Amperes			
HP	115 Volts	200 Volts	208 Volts	230 Volts	460 Volts	575 Volts	2300 Volts	230 Volts	460 Volts	575 Volts	2300 Volts
1/2	4.4	2.5	2.4	2.2	1.1	0.9					
3/4	6.4	3.7	3.5	3.2	1.6	1.3					
1	8.4	4.8	4.6	4.2	2.1	1.7					
1 1/2	12.0	6.9	6.6	6.0	3.0	2.4					
2	13.6	7.8	7.5	6.8	3.4	2.7					
3		11.0	10.6	9.6	4.8	3.9					
5		17.5	16.7	15.2	7.6	6.1					
7 1/2		25.3	24.2	22	11	9					
10		32.2	30.8	28	14	11					
15		48.3	46.2	42	21	17					
20		62.1	59.4	54	27	22					
25		78.2	74.8	68	34	27		53	26	21	
30		92	88	80	40	32		63	32	26	
40		120	114	104	52	41		83	41	33	
50		150	143	130	65	52		104	52	42	
60		177	169	154	77	62	16	123	61	49	12
75		221	211	192	96	77	20	155	78	62	15
100		285	273	248	124	99	26	202	101	81	20
125		359	343	312	156	125	31	253	126	101	25
150		414	396	360	180	144	37	302	151	121	30
200		552	528	480	240	192	49	400	201	161	40
250					302	242	60				
300					361	289	72				
350					414	336	83				
400					477	382	95				
450					515	412	103				
500					590	472	118				

*For 90 and 80 percent power factor, the above figures shall be multiplied by 1.1 and 1.25 respectively.

The currents listed shall be permitted for system voltage ranges of 110 to 120, 220 to 240, 440 to 480, and 550 to 600 volts.

THREE-PHASE VOLT-AMPS = E x I x **1.732**

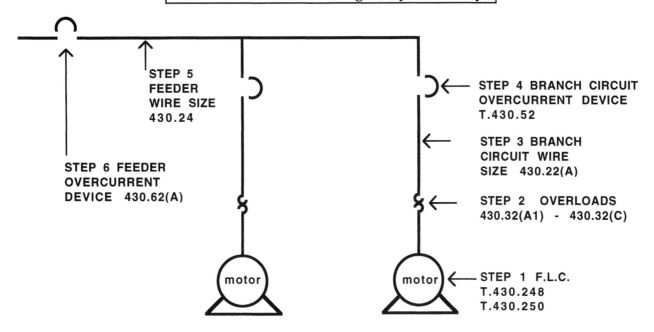

| MOTOR FORMAT   Designed by *Tom Henry* |

STEP 5
FEEDER
WIRE SIZE
430.24

STEP 4 BRANCH CIRCUIT
OVERCURRENT DEVICE
T.430.52

STEP 3 BRANCH
CIRCUIT WIRE
SIZE 430.22(A)

STEP 6 FEEDER
OVERCURRENT
DEVICE 430.62(A)

STEP 2   OVERLOADS
430.32(A1) - 430.32(C)

motor

motor

STEP 1 F.L.C.
T.430.248
T.430.250

STEP 1   FLC (full load current)   Table 430.248   1 ø current   Table 430.250 3 ø current

STEP 2   Motor running over**load** protection. Thermal protector called a "heater".
• 430.32(A1) Minimum size   • 430.32(C) Maximum size
• If motor **nameplate** is given, use it, if not use FLC from Tables

STEP 3   Branch circuit conductor sizing   430.22   FLC x 125% = Required ampacity
• Turn to Table 310.16 and select the conductor with the required ampacity

STEP 4   Branch circuit over**current** device shall be selected from Table 430.52. First select the
type of motor (1 ø, 3 ø, AC, DC, wound rotor, etc.) next select the **type** of
protective device (non-time delay fuse, dual element fuse, inverse time breaker) now
select the **percentage** from the proper column and multiply it times the FLC of the motor.
Use 240.6 to select the **standard size** overcurrent device. • When the value found does
not match a standard size the Code permits the **next higher STANDARD size** for a
branch circuit overcurrent device (430.52 ex.1).

STEP 5   Feeder conductor size 430.24. Multiply the **largest** rated motor in FLC by 125% and add
the FLC of all other motors connected to the **SAME** feeder conductor for the total amps.

STEP 6   Feeder overcurrent protection 430.62(A). Select the **largest** branch circuit **overcurrent
device** and add all the other motor FLC connected on the **same** feeder conductor to find
the amperage required to select the feeder fuse or CB. • The Code does **NOT** permit going
to a higher size if the value does not match a standard size from 240.6. Drop **DOWN** to
the next smaller standard size. Code permits going up only on a branch circuit.

> **STEP 1**   F.L.C. Tables 430.248 1 ø   430.250 3 ø

> **STEP 2**   Section 430.32(A1) More than 1 horsepower separate overload device.

Motor Service Factor.

Motor ratings are based on a **service factor** stamped on the nameplate of the motor, ranging from 1.00 to 1.35. If for a specific motor the service factor is 1.00, it means that if the motor is installed in a location where the ambient temperature is not over 40° C or 104° F, it can deliver its rated horsepower continuously without harm. But if the service factor is, for example 1.15, it means that the motor can be used up to 1.15 times its rated horsepower under the same conditions. For example, a 10 hp motor has a service factor of 1.15, the motor can be allowed to develop 11.5 hp without causing undue deterioration to the insulation. The **higher** service factor provides temporary extra power if needed.

Temperature Rise.

Current passing through the windings of a motor results in an increase in the motor temperature. The difference between the winding temperature of the motor when running and the ambient temperature is called the **temperature rise**.

The temperature rise produced at full load is not harmful provided the motor ambient temperature does not exceed 40° C (104°F).

Higher temperature caused by increased current or higher ambient temperatures produces a deteriorating effect on the motor insulation and lubrication.

All Other Motors.

Motors with a service factor **less** than 1.15 or a temperature rise **more** than 40° C would be classified **all other motors**.

Example: What is the **minimum** size running overload protection for a 1 1/2 hp 230v single-phase squirrel cage motor?
Solution: Table 430.248 F.L.C. = 10 amps. Section 430.32(A1) **all other motors** 115%. 10 amps x 115% = **11.5** overload protection.

Example: What is the minimum size running overload protection for this same motor with a **service factor of 1.2**?
Solution: F.L.C. 10 amps x **125%** = **12.5** overload protection.

Now the motor can develop 12.5 amps before the thermal overload would trip. A motor with a marked service factor 1.15 or higher or a marked temperature rise 40° C or less is a better built motor.

Example: What is the **maximum** size running overload protection for a 10 hp 460v three-phase motor with a 40° C temperature rise?
Solution: F.L.C. = 14 amps. Section 430.32(C) **maximum** 140%. 14 amps x 140% = **19.6**

430.32(A1) is the **recommended** minimum size. If the overload selected from 430.32(A1) is not sufficient to start the motor or to carry the load, the next higher size selected from 430.32(C) shall be permitted.

STEP 3	Section 430.22(A): Branch circuit conductors supplying a single motor shall have an ampacity not less than **125%** of the motor full-load current rating.

The 125% increase in conductor ampacity is for the overloading of the motor, with "all other motors" the F.L.C. can be exceeded 115%. With a marked service factor or temperature rise the motor can be loaded even higher. This is the reason for the 125% increase in conductor ampacity.

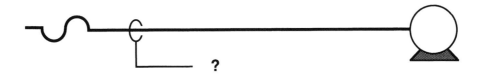

?

Example: What size TW insulation copper conductor is required for a 1 hp single-phase 115 v motor?

Solution: Table 430.248 F.L.C. = 16 amps x 125% = 20 **required ampacity**. Table 310.16 TW insulation a **#14 TW** copper has an **ampacity of 20.**

The Table 310.16 * asterisk states a #14 conductor maximum **overcurrent protection (fuse or circuit breaker)** is 15 amps. In this example we are selecting a **conductor size,** not overcurrent protection. Besides, 240.4(G) states the asterisk does **not** apply to motor circuits. Overcurrent devices for motors are sized from Article 430 Part IV.

CALCULATING THE WIRE SIZE IS THE *MINIMUM* WIRE SIZE PERMITTED

STEP 4

Section 430.52: The motor branch circuit short-circuit and ground-fault protective device shall be capable of carrying the starting current of a motor. A protective device having a rating or setting not exceeding the maximum value calculated according to the values given in Table **430.52** shall be used.

430.52. Maximum Rating or Setting of Motor Branch-Circuit and Groundfault Protective Devices

Type of Motor	Percent of Full-Load Current			
	Nontime Delay Fuse**	Dual Element (Time Delay) Fuse**	Instantaneous Trip Breaker	Inverse Time Breaker*
Single-phase Motors AC **polyphase** motors other than wound rotor	300	175	800	250
Squirrel Cage - Other than Design B evergy-efficient	300	175	800	250
Design B energy-efficient	300	175	1100	250
Synchronous	300	175	800	250
Wound rotor	150	150	800	150
Direct-Current (constant voltage)	150	150	250	150

The first column of Table 430.52 lists the types of motors. The word **polyphase** is the **three-phase** motor. Wound-rotor is a type sometimes asked on an exam. Wound-rotor is an AC motor with slip rings used in speed control applications.

The next four columns list the percentages for the different types of overcurrent protection.

The non-time delay fuse will hold five times its rated current for about one-fourth of a second. Dual element (time delay) fuses hold five times their rating for ten seconds.

Fuses will not open **all** ungrounded conductors at the same time (simultaneously).

TABLE 430.52 IS FOR THE SIZING OF *BRANCH CIRCUIT* FUSES OR BREAKERS

Circuit breakers will hold approximately three times the breaker rating for different periods of time based on the breaker frame size.

SIZING OVERCURRENT PROTECTION EXAMPLES

Example: A motor with a F.L.C. of 10 amps would require what size **inverse time** breaker?

Solution: F.L.C. 10 amps x 250% = 25 amp circuit breaker.

Always check section 240.6 for standard sizes before selecting a multiple choice answer on the exam. 240.6 lists a 25 amp as a **standard** size.

Example: What size dual element fuse is required for a 1 1/2 hp single-phase 230v motor?

Solution: Table 430.248: 1 1/2 hp 230v F.L.C. = 10 amps x **175%** = 17.5 amps. 17.5 amps is **not** a **standard** size fuse. Section 430.52 ex.1 permits the **next higher** standard size fuse to be used. 240.6: The **next higher** standard fuse size is 20 amp.

Example: What is the maximum size nontime delay fuse for a 7 1/2 hp, three-phase 208v motor?

Solution: Table 430.250: 7 1/2 hp, 208v F.L.C. = 24.2 amps x **300%** Table 430.52 = 72.6 amps. The next higher size per section 240.6 is 80 amps.

Example: What is the maximum size inverse time breaker for a 2 hp, single-phase, 115v motor.

Solution: Table 430.248: 2hp, 115v F.L.C. = 24 amps x **250%** Table 430.52 = 60 amps.

Example: What is the maximum size inverse time breaker for a 25 hp, three-phase, 480v motor?

Solution: Table 430.250: 25 hp, 480v F.L.C. = 34 amps x **250%** = 85 amps. 240.6 next standard size is a 90 amp circuit breaker.

Example: What is the maximum size dual element fuse for a 5 hp, **D.C.,** 120v motor?

Solution: Table 430.**247:** 5 hp, 120v F.L.C. = 40 amps x **150%** = 60 amps. 240.6, 60 amp is standard.

Example: What is the maximum size nontime delay fuse for a 10 hp, single-phase, 230v **wound-rotor** type motor?

Solution: Table 430.248: 10 hp, 230v F.L.C. = 50 amps x **150%** = 75 amps. 240.6, 75 amp is **not** a standard size, the next higher standard size is 80 amps. • Always check 240.6 before selecting an exam answer, as you can see 75 amp sounds standard, but it's not!

Example: Which is a standard size fuse, a 75 amp or a 601 amp?

Solution: 240.6 **exception**: Additional standard ratings for fuses shall be considered 1, 3, 6, 10 and **601**.

 STEP 5   Feeder conductor size. Section 430.24: Conductors supplying **two** or more motors shall have an ampacity equal to the sum of the full-load current rating of all the motors **plus** 25% of the **highest rated** motor in the group.

Section 430.17: Highest rated **(largest in current)** motor. In determining compliance with Sections 430.24, 430.53(B), and 430.53(C), the highest rated **(largest in current)** motor shall be considered to be that motor having the **highest** rated **full-load current.** The full-load current used to determine the highest rated motor shall be equivalent value corresponding to the motor horsepower rating selected from Tables 430.247, 430.248, 430.249, and 430.250.

The **largest** motor is **not** always the motor with the largest horsepower. The largest motor is the motor with the highest full-load current. •Remember, we size wire to amperes **not** horsepower.

CALCULATING THE FUSE OR BREAKER IS THE MAXIMUM SIZE PERMITTED

Example: Which of the following motors is the largest motor, a 5 hp, single-phase, 115v or a 10 hp, single-phase 208v?

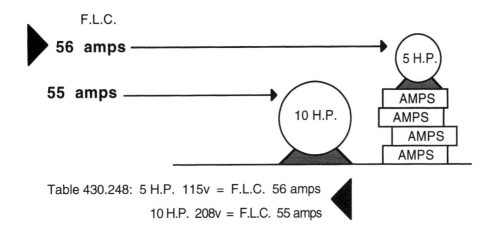

F.L.C.

56 amps ———————————————————→ 5 H.P.

55 amps —————————————————→ 10 H.P.

AMPS
AMPS
AMPS
AMPS

Table 430.248: 5 H.P. 115v = F.L.C. 56 amps

10 H.P. 208v = F.L.C. 55 amps

SIZING FEEDER CONDUCTOR EXAMPLES

Example: What is the feeder conductor ampacity required for two 2 hp single-phase 115v motors?

Solution: Table 430.248: 2 hp, 115v F.L.C. = 24 amps x 125% = 30 amps + 24 amps = 54 required ampacity. Table 310.16 would require a #6 TW copper conductor minimum.

Example: Two-25 hp, three-phase, 208v motors are fed by the same feeder, the feeder conductor would be required to carry a minimum of how many amps?

Solution: Table 430.250: 25 hp, 208v F.L.C. = 74.8 amps x 125% = 93.5 amps + 74.8 amps = 168.3 required ampacity. Table 310.16 would require a #2/0 THW copper conductor.

LARGEST MOTOR IN F.L.C.
NOT HORSEPOWER

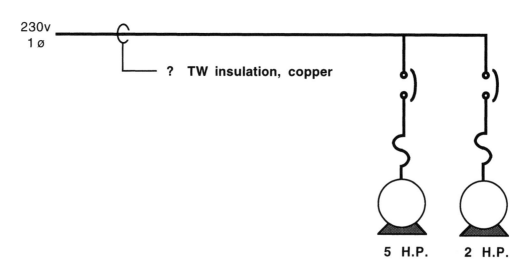

Example: What is the minimum size copper feeder conductor permitted using TW insulation for a 5 hp, single-phase, 230v motor and a 2 hp, single-phase, 230v motor?

Solution: Table 430.248: 5 hp, 230v F.L.C. = 28 amps x 125% = 35 amps + 12 amps = 47 required ampacity. Table 310.16 would require a #6 TW copper conductor minimum.

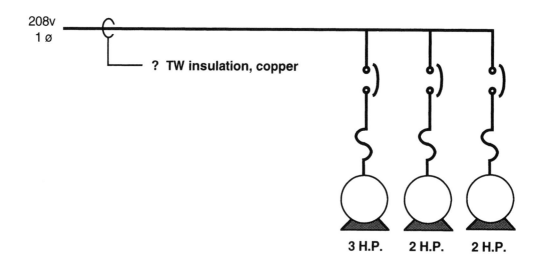

Example: What is the minimum size copper feeder conductor using TW insulation for a 3 hp, single-phase, 208v motor and two - 2 hp, single-phase, 208v motors?

Solution: Table 430.248: 3 hp, 208v F.L.C. = 18.7 amps x 125% = 23.375 amps + 13.2 amps + 13.2 amps = 49.775 required ampacity. Table 310.16 would require a #6 TW copper conductor minimum.

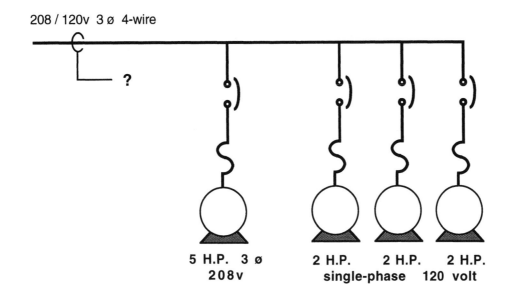

Example three-phase 4-wire feeder: The smallest feeder conductor permitted to one 5 hp, three-phase and three - 2 hp, **single-phase, 120v** motors would require a minimum ampacity of how many amps?

Solution: Table 430.250: 5 hp, 208v F.L.C. = 16.7 amps. Table 430.248: 2 hp, 120v F.L.C. = 24 amps. 430.17 largest motor in **current** would be the 2 hp at 24 amps. Feeder conductor = 24 amps x 125% = 30 amps + 16.7 amps = **46.7 required ampacity**. Table 310.16 would require a #6 TW copper conductor minimum.

The example above is the motor calculation most students answer incorrectly. Turn to page 72 and read **STEP 5**: Multiply the largest rated motor (24 amps) by 125% and add the current of **all** other motors on the **same** feeder conductor (16.7). There are only **two** motors per conductor, **not four**.

Draw a sketch of the three-phase 4-wire system and **connect** the motors (remember as an electrician you are required to **balance** loads per 210.11(B). Now you can see there are **two** motors connected on each feeder conductor not four. Each feeder conductor requires an ampacity of 24 amps x 125% = 30 amps + 16.7 amps = 46.7 ampacity.

•Sketch is shown on the next page.

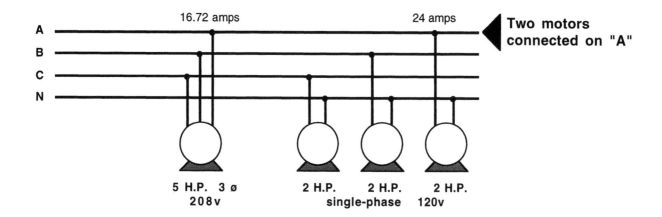

When the exam question mentions a three-phase motor with **single-phase 120 volt motors**, draw a sketch and make the motor connections for the proper voltages (208v is line to line and 120v is line to neutral). Now count how many motors you have on the **SAME** conductor. This is the **key** in answering this type of question. The error generally made is counting four motors instead of **two**.

Example: What is the minimum size copper feeder conductor using TW insulation for a 7 1/2 hp, three-phase, 208v motor and three - 3 hp, single-phase, 120v motors?

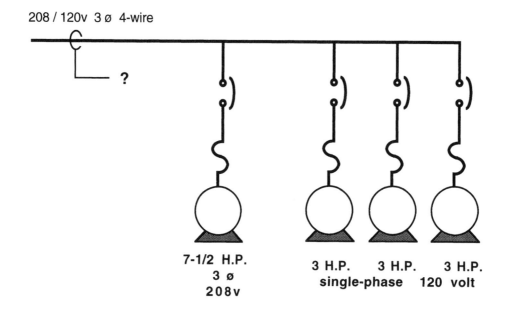

Solution: Table 430.250: 7 1/2 hp, 208v F.L.C. = 24.2 amps. Table 430.248: 3 hp, 120v F.L.C. = 34 amps. The largest motor is the 3 hp at 34 amps. 34 amps x 125% = 42.5 amps + 24.2 amps = 66.7 required ampacity. Table 310.16 would require a #4 TW copper conductor minimum.

Example: What is the minimum size copper feeder conductor using TW insulation for a 5 hp, single-phase, 240v motor and three - 3 hp, single-phase, 240v motors?

Draw a sketch:

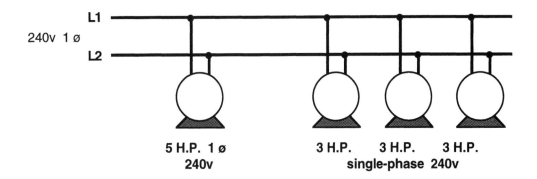

Solution: Table 430.248: 5 hp, 240v F.L.C. = 28 amps. 3 hp, 240v F.L.C. = 17 amps. The largest motor is the 5 hp at 28 amps x 125% = 35 amps + 17 amps + 17 amps + 17 amps = 86 required ampacity. Table 310.16 would require a #2 TW copper conductor minimum.

Always draw a sketch and connect the motors, then you can determine how many motors you have on the **SAME** feeder conductor. As you can see in this example you have four motors connected on each feeder conductor.

ALWAYS DRAW A SKETCH
AND CONNECT THE
MOTORS TO THE PHASE
CONDUCTORS

STEP 6 Feeder overcurrent protection.

Section 430.62(A): A feeder supplying a specific fixed motor load(s) and consisting of conductor sizes based on Section 430.24, shall be provided with a protective device having a rating or setting **not** greater than the **largest** rating or setting of the branch circuit short-circuit and ground-fault protective device **(fuse or breaker)** for any motor of the group (based on Table 430.52, or Section 440.22(A) for hermetic refrigerant motor-compressors), **plus** the sum of the **full-load currents** of the other motors of the group.

Where the **same** rating or setting of the branch circuit short-circuit and ground-fault protective device is used on two or more of the branch circuits of the group, **one** of the protective devices shall be considered the **largest** for the above calculations.

Example: What size inverse time breaker is required for the feeder overcurrent device?

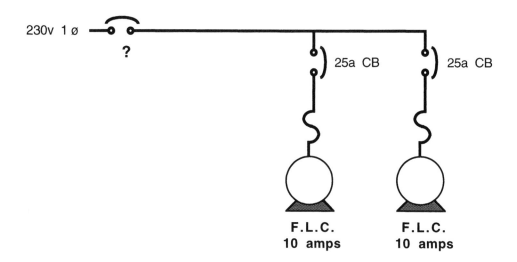

Solution: Feeder overcurrent protection = The largest branch circuit breaker **25 amps** + the other F.L.C. **10 amps** = 35 amps maximum permitted.

Section 240.6: **35 amps** is a standard size.

Example: What size dual element fuse is required for the feeder overcurrent protection?

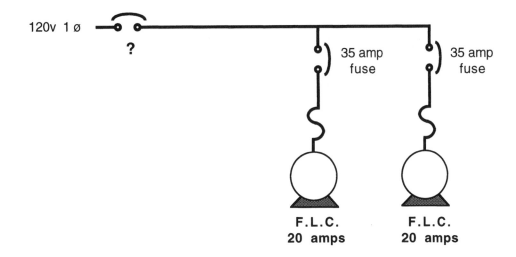

120v 1 ø

?

35 amp
fuse

35 amp
fuse

F.L.C.
20 amps

F.L.C.
20 amps

Solution: Feeder overcurrent protection = The largest branch circuit fuse **35 amps** + the other F.L.C. **20 amps** = 55 amps maximum.

Section 240.6: 55 amp fuse is not a standard size, you can **NOT** go up to the next higher standard size on **FEEDER** protection, you must drop **DOWN** to the next standard size of **50 amps**.

The maximum dual element fuse permitted is 50 amps.

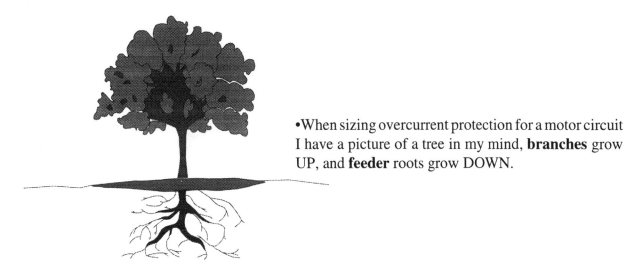

•When sizing overcurrent protection for a motor circuit I have a picture of a tree in my mind, **branches** grow UP, and **feeder** roots grow DOWN.

THERE IS *NO* EXCEPTION TO 430.62 PERMITTING THE NEXT HIGHER SIZE

Example: What size nontime delay fuse is required for the feeder overcurrent protection?

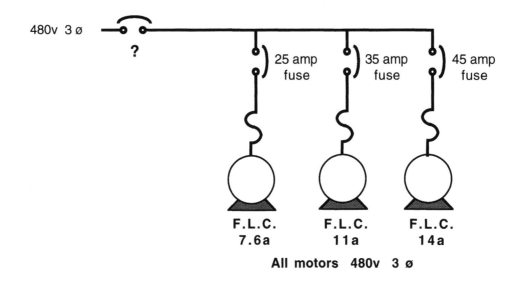

Solution: Feeder overcurrent protection = The largest branch circuit fuse 45 amps + the other F.L.C. 11 amps + 7.6 amps = 63.6 amps maximum permitted.

Section 240.6: Use 60 amp fuse.

GO *DOWN* ON A FEEDER FUSE OR CIRCUIT BREAKER SIZE

Example: What size dual element fuse is required for the feeder overcurrent protection?

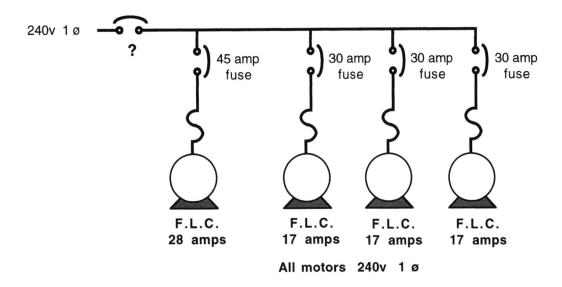

240v 1 ø

?

45 amp
fuse

30 amp
fuse

30 amp
fuse

30 amp
fuse

**F.L.C.
28 amps**

**F.L.C.
17 amps**

**F.L.C.
17 amps**

**F.L.C.
17 amps**

All motors   240v 1 ø

Solution: Feeder overcurrent protection = The largest branch circuit fuse 45 amps + the other F.L.C. 17 amps + 17 amps + 17 amps = 96 amps maximum permitted.

Section 240.6: 96 amps is not a standard size fuse, drop down to the next standard size 90 amp fuse.

Feeder fuse = 90 amps.

ALWAYS CHECK SECTION
240.6 FOR STANDARD SIZE

Example: What size inverse time circuit breaker is required for the feeder overcurrent protection?

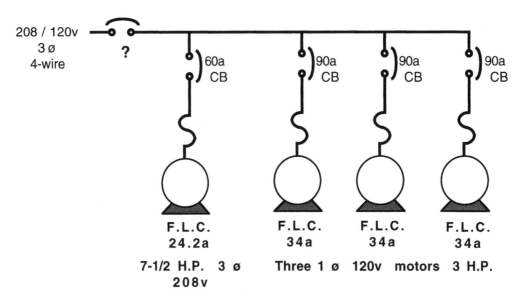

208 / 120v
3 ø
4-wire

?

60a
CB

90a
CB

90a
CB

90a
CB

F.L.C.
24.2a

F.L.C.
34a

F.L.C.
34a

F.L.C.
34a

7-1/2 H.P. 3 ø
208v

Three 1 ø 120v motors 3 H.P.

•Draw a sketch:

24.2 amps F.L.C.   90a CB

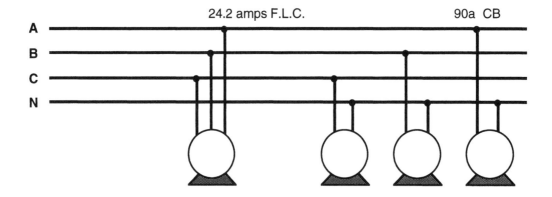

A
B
C
N

Solution: Feeder overcurrent protection = The largest branch circuit breaker 90 amps + the other F.L.C. on the **SAME CONDUCTOR** 24.2 amps = 114.2 amps maximum permitted.

Section 240.6: Drop down to standard size fuse of 110 amps.

•When solving motor calculations for a feeder conductor, and feeder overcurrent protection for three-phase motors and **single-phase 120 volt** motors, draw a sketch and connect the motors. This is very helpful in determining the number of motors on the **SAME CONDUCTOR**.

Summary

The most confusing thing for the electrician to understand is with a motor circuit the overcurrent device (fuse or breaker) is permitted to be larger in size than the ampacity of the wire. A #14 conductor with an ampacity of 20 can be fused to 25 amps in a motor circuit.

Section 240.4 requires for conductors to be protected against overcurrent in accordance with their ampacities, **unless otherwise permitted**. 240.4(G) states that motor circuit conductors shall be permitted to be protected against overcurrent in accordance with the rules of Article 430 which was covered in this chapter.

It makes sense to have **special** rules for motor sizing and the protection of the motor is **not** sacrificed at all. Actually the motor circuit, even with a larger fuse size than the ampacity of the wire, is still a better protected circuit than a lighting or receptacle circuit. How can it be? Very simple, a motor circuit has an **overload** (heater) protective device which a receptacle circuit does not have.

OVERLOAD

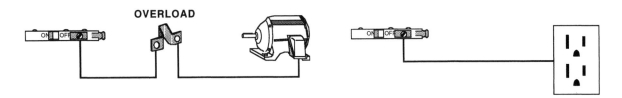

To further illustrate this point, use an example such as a table lamp in the living room of your home. Using a 100 watt light bulb the current flow in a 120 volt branch circuit would be less than one amp. If this was the only item turned on in the branch circuit the 20 amp breaker is protecting the lamp and the #18 gauge wire which has an ampacity of 10 amps per Table 400.5(A). This is permitted in Code section 240.5(A1).

20a CB

#12 wire

#18 cord

100 watt lamp

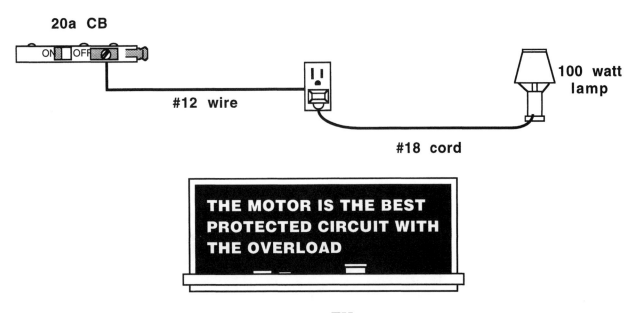

THE MOTOR IS THE BEST PROTECTED CIRCUIT WITH THE OVERLOAD

We have learned in Chapter 3 that a 10 amp motor would have the overload sized at 115% which equals 11.5 amps. The #14 wire has an ampacity of 20 and the current flowing through the circuit would shut off when the overload trips at 11.5 amps thus protecting not only the motor but also the wire from thermal overloads. The 20 amp breaker provides ground-fault and short-circuit protection for the motor circuit. Whereas with the branch circuit in your living room the breaker has to provide both functions, thermal currents and ground-fault and short-circuit protection, as the circuit contains no overload.

20a CB   **11.5a**   **10a F.L.C.**

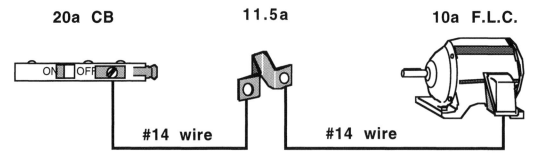

The asterisk * in the Table of Ampacity applies to lighting and appliance circuits but **not** motor circuits. The overcurrent device for a motor is sized in accordance with Table 430.52 as we learned in Step 4 of our motor format. And if you're an electrician wiring motor circuits it's easy to understand why the asterisk * **can't** apply to motor circuits.

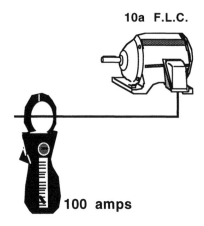

At the moment an AC motor is energized, the starting current rises rapidly to as many as 10 times or more the normal current. Thus, for a period of time, the overcurrent protective devices in the motor circuit must be able to tolerate the rather substantial temporary overload. After the first half-cycle, the starting current subsides to around 6 times the normal current for several seconds. This is called the *locked rotor current*. Special requirements for protection of motors requires that the motor overload protective device withstand the temporary overload caused by motor starting currents, and at the same time, protects the motor from continuous or damaging overloads.

If you applied the 240.4(D) to the #14 wire which only allows a 15 amp breaker, the breaker could trip on starting. This is the reason the asterisk * does **not** apply to motor circuits per 240.4(G).

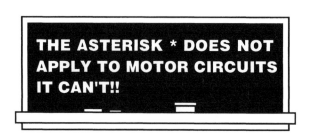

```
CHAPTER 3  TEST 1  MOTORS
```

1. The branch circuit conductor for a 3/4 hp, single-phase, 115v motor would require a minimum ampacity of _____ amps.

(a) 17.25   (b) 13.8   (c) 8.6   (d) 6.9

2. The full-load current of a three-phase, 20 hp induction motor on 208v is _____ amps.

(a) 27   (b) 29.7   (c) 54   (d) 59.4

3. The motor running overload protection for a single-phase, 3 hp motor would be _____ amps on 115 volts.

(a) 39.1 - 42.5   (b) 44.2 - 47.6   (c) 19.55 - 22.1   (d) 21.25 - 23.8

4. The branch circuit overcurrent protection is _____% of the full-load current for a DC motor using dual element fuses.

(a) 150   (b) 175   (c) 250   (d) 300

5. Size the feeder conductor for a 3 hp, single-phase, 208v motor and two - 2 hp, single-phase, 208v motors. Use 60°C insulation.

(a) #10   (b) #8   (c) #6   (d) #4

6. Size the feeder protection using an inverse time breaker for three - 5 hp, single-phase, 230v motors. Each motor has a 70 amp CB for branch circuit protection.

(a) 90 amp CB   (b) 110 amp CB   (c) 125 amp CB   (d) 150 amp CB

CHAPTER 3   TEST 2   MOTORS

1. What is the minimum size heater to protect a 5 hp, three-phase, 208v motor? The motor has a marked service factor of 1.15.

(a) 19.23a   (b) 20.875a   (c) 35a   (d) 38.5a

2. What minimum size branch circuit conductor is necessary for a 10 hp, three-phase, 230v induction motor using 60°C insulation?

(a) #10   (b) #8   (c) #6   (d) #4

3. What is the feeder conductor ampacity required for two - 2 hp, single-phase, 115v motors?

(a) 48a   (b) 54a   (c) 60a   (d) 72a

4. The maximum branch circuit protection for a 2 hp, single-phase, 208v motor would be _____ amps. Use inverse time breaker.

(a) 20   (b) 25   (c) 35   (d) 50

5. The smallest feeder conductor to one 5 hp, three-phase, 208v motor and three - 2 hp, single-phase, 120v motors should have an ampacity of _____ amps.

(a) 50   (b) 100   (c) 150   (d) 175

6. What size dual element fuse is required for the branch circuit protection for a three-phase, 50 hp, 480v motor?

(a) 100a   (b) 125a   (c) 150a   (d) 175a

CHAPTER 3 TEST 3 MOTORS

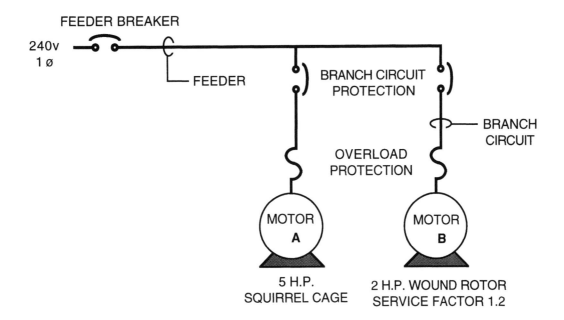

FEEDER BREAKER

240v
1 ø

FEEDER

BRANCH CIRCUIT
PROTECTION

BRANCH
CIRCUIT

OVERLOAD
PROTECTION

MOTOR
A

MOTOR
B

5 H.P.
SQUIRREL CAGE

2 H.P. WOUND ROTOR
SERVICE FACTOR 1.2

FIND:	MOTOR A	MOTOR B
Full load current	_____	_____
Overload protection, minimum size	_____	_____
Branch circuit conductor size (TW)	_____	_____
Branch circuit protection, inverse time	_____	_____
Feeder size (TW)	_____	
Feeder protection, inverse time	_____	

CHAPTER 3   TEST 4   MOTORS

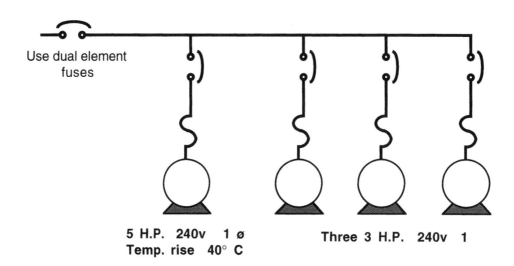

Use dual element
fuses

5 H.P. 240v   1 ø
Temp. rise   40° C

Three 3 H.P.   240v   1

1. What size heaters are required for the 3 hp motor?

(a) 17.0 (b) 19.55 (c) 21.25 (d) none of these

2. If the nameplate of one of the 3 hp motors was 15 amps, what size heater would be required?

(a) 17.0 (b) 17.25 (c) 21.25 (d) 19.55

3. What is the branch circuit conductor size, 60°C insulation, for the 5 hp motor?

(a) #14 (b) #12 (c) #8 (d) #10

4. What is the required feeder conductor size? Use TW insulation.

(a) #3 (b) #4 (c) #6 (d) #2

5. What is the maximum branch circuit overcurrent protection for the 3 hp motor?

(a) 30 (b) 35 (c) 45 (d) 50

6. What is the maximum branch circuit overcurrent protection for the 5 hp motor?

(a) 45 (b) 50 (c) 60 (d) 70

7. What is the feeder overcurrent protection size?

(a) 100 (b) 95 (c) 90 (d) 110

CHAPTER 3 TEST 5 MOTORS

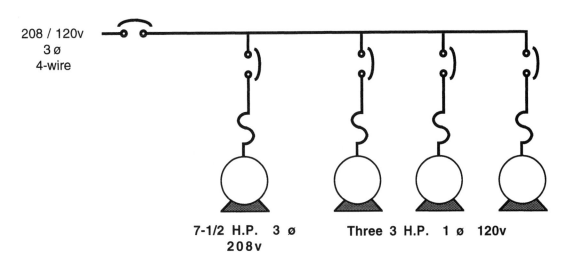

208 / 120v
3 ø
4-wire

7-1/2 H.P. 3 ø   Three 3 H.P. 1 ø 120v
208v

All motors are squirrel-cage 40 degree C rise

1. What is the overload protection size for a 3 hp motor?

(a) 22a   (b) 39.1a   (c) 34a   (d) 42.5a

2. What is the minimum size branch circuit conductor size for the 7 1/2 hp motor using TW insulation?

(a) #14   (b) #12   (c) #10   (d) #8

3. What is the branch circuit overcurrent protection size for the 3 hp motor, using an inverse time breaker?

(a) 85a   (b) 65a   (c) 70a   (d) 90a

4. What is the va input to the fully loaded 7 1/2 hp motor?

(a) 5034   (b) 5060   (c) 5612   (d) 8718

5. What is the required feeder conductor size using TW insulation?

(a) #2/0   (b) #1/0   (c) #2   (d) #4

6. What size feeder overcurrent protection using an inverse time breaker?

(a) 110a   (b) 125a   (c) 175a   (d) 200a

CHAPTER 3   TEST 6   MOTORS

1. What size dual element time-delay fuse is required for a 15hp, 230 volt, three-phase motor?

(a) 75 amp   (b) 80 amp   (c) 85 amp   (d) 90 amp

2. What size inverse time circuit breaker should be selected for a branch circuit to a 3ø, 3hp, 208v motor?

(a) 15 amps   (b) 20 amps   (c) 25 amps   (d) 35 amps

3. What size dual-element fuse does the Code require for a 2hp, 208 volt, single-phase motor?

(a) 20 amps   (b) 30 amps   (c) 35 amps   (d) 40 amps

4. If the full load current of a 2hp, 115 volt, 1ø motor is 24 amps, the branch circuit protection to this motor should not be set at more than ____ amps using dual-element time-delay fuses.

(a) 30   (b) 40   (c) 50   (d) 60

5. What is the maximum size overload relay permitted for a single-phase 2hp, 208v motor?

(a) 15.18   (b) 16.5   (c) 17.16   (d) none of these

6. The ampacity of the feeder to one 3hp, 3ø, 208v motor and one 2hp, 3ø, 208v motor would be at least ____ amps.

(a) 22.55   (b) 21   (c) 19   (d) 18

7. What size THW feeder is required for a single-phase 3/4 hp, 120 volt and a three-phase 2hp, 208 volt motor?

(a) #12 THW   (b) #10 THW   (c) #8 THW   (d) none of these

8. What size inverse-time circuit breaker is required for a feeder supplying a 1ø, 3hp, 208v motor, and a 3ø, 5hp, 208v motor?

(a) 40 amp   (b) 50 amp   (c) 60 amp   (d) none of these

CHAPTER 3-A

MOTOR CONTROLS

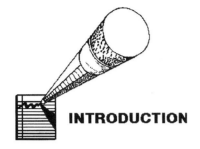

INTRODUCTION

MOTOR CONTROLS

The intent of Chapter 3-A is to familiarize you with the type of exam questions on motor controls.

Some electrical exams ask for the sequence from stop to full run position, requiring a detailed **show your work** type answer. Whereas other exams ask a **multiple choice** type question from a **part** of the sequence, or a question from general motor control wiring knowledge.

Motor control type questions generally are asked on a Master examination and not Journeyman.

The following examples will cover both types of questioning.

The intent of this Chapter is not to teach you motor controls, but to familiarize you with exam questioning on motor controls. If motor controls and reading schematics is a problem for you, I strongly recommend a class on motor controls.

Example: In your own words, using the following diagram, list the sequence from **stop** position to **full run** position.

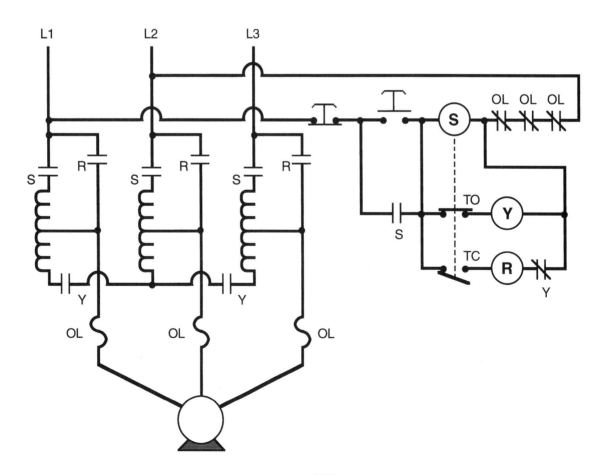

STEP BY STEP SEQUENCE

First step, close the line switch energizing L1, L2, and L3.

L1 becomes energized and follows a path to one side of the start button through the normally closed interlocks on the stop button.

L2 (which also becomes energized when the line switch is closed) follows a path through the three normally closed overload protection interlocks (OL) to make one side of "S" coil hot, also "Y" coil, and follows a path through "Y" normally closed interlock to make one side of "R" coil hot.

When pushing the start button you complete L1 circuit to "S" coil energizing "S" coil, which has a holding circuit. When "S" coil is energized, "S" normally open interlock closes holding voltage to "S" coil after the start button is released. "Y" coil is also energized at the same moment as "S" coil through the "TO" normally closed interlock. Also "Y" normally closed interlock will open to "R" coil.

At this point with "S" coil and "Y" coil energized the normally open "S" contacts on L1-L2-L3 motor circuit and the two normally open "Y" contacts in the motor circuit will close allowing voltage from L1-L2-L3 to flow through the "S" contacts through the autotransformer winding coils and through the overloads (heaters) to the motor windings causing the motor to start.

When the motor circuit reaches the pre-set time, the timer times out, "TO" interlock will open causing "Y" coil to de-energize, thus closing normally closed "Y" interlock to "R" coil circuit. At this same moment "TC" interlock will close energizing "R" coil, closing the normally open "R" contacts on L1-L2-L3 in the motor circuit. When "R" contacts close they will bypass the autotransformer windings and follow a path through the overloads (heaters) to the motor windings putting the motor in a **full running** position.

Automatic autotransformer reduced-voltage starters:

"Y" normally open power contacts: Autotransformer motor starters have a period between the start and run positions when the motor is temporarily disconnected from the power lines. The open period starts when the start contactor is de-energized, and ends when the run starter is energized. This de-energized period, called the "open circuit transition", can be objectionable. A sharp spike of current may be drawn when the motor is reconnected across the line in the run position. To overcome this inrush of current caused by the "open circuit transition" from reduced voltage to across-the-line running, a closed circuit transition is very often used.

If the run contactor is closed before the start contactor is opened, high currents that might damage the windings and contacts will flow in the transformer. Since this method cannot be satisfactorily used, some answer to the problem must be found by using some additional equipment.

The most well known solution is called the **"Korndorfer Method"** . This approach uses a third contactor to open the common connection to the autotransformer before the run contactor is energized. The third contactor may "short out" a reactor without damage to it. Thus, the run contactor is energized without having to de-energize the start contactor, resulting in a closed circuit transition.

Example: Answer the following multiple choice questions, answers and detail are on next page.

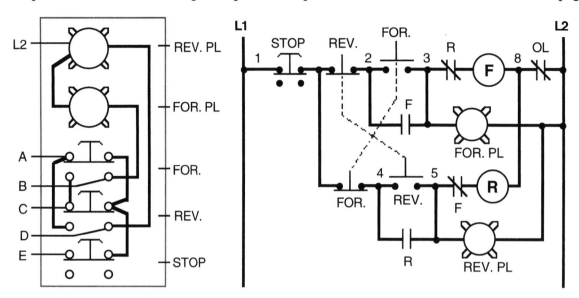

1. Conductor "A" on the push button station is conductor number _____ shown in the control circuit schematic.

(a) 1   (b) 2   (c) 3   (d) 4   (e) 5

2. Conductor "B" on the push button station is conductor number _____ shown in the control circuit schematic.

(a) 1   (b) 2   (c) 3   (d) 4   (e) 5

3. Conductor "C" on the push button station is conductor number _____ shown in the control circuit schematic.

(a) 1   (b) 2   (c) 3   (d) 4   (e) 5

4. Conductor "D" on the push button station is conductor number _____ shown in the control circuit schematic.

(a) 1   (b) 2   (c) 3   (d) 4   (e) 5

5. Conductor "E" on the push button station is conductor number _____ shown in the control circuit schematic.

(a) 1   (b) 2   (c) 3   (d) 4   (e) 5

1. Conductor "A" is connected to a terminal on the normally closed forward button, with a jumper connected to the normally open reverse button. On the wiring diagram locate the forward normally closed button. Note the jumper connected to the normally open reverse button. Conductor "A" is number **4**.

2. Conductor "B" is connected to a terminal on the normally open forward button, with a jumper connected to a light. On the wiring diagram locate the forward normally open button. Note the jumper connected to the light. Conductor "B" is number **3**.

3. Conductor "C" is connected to a terminal on the normally closed reverse button, with a jumper connected to the normally open forward button. On the wiring diagram locate the normally closed reverse button. Note the jumper connected to the normally open forward button. Conductor "C" is number **2**.

4. Conductor "D" is connected to a terminal on the normally open reverse button, with a jumper connected to a light. On the wiring diagram locate the normally open reverse button. Note the jumper connected to the light. Conductor "D" is number **5**.

5. Conductor "E" is connected to a terminal on the normally closed stop button, with no other connections on the terminal. Locate the stop button on the wiring diagram. Note conductor "E" is connected from L1 to the stop button. Conductor "E" is number **1**.

CHAPTER 3-A TEST 1 MOTOR CONTROLS

1. In motor controls, a maintaining contact is a ____ contact.

(a) delay-on   (b) delay-off   (c) normally closed   (d) normally open

2. When a motor is to be controlled from two different locations, the start buttons are connected in ____ while the stop buttons are connected in ____.

(a) series, parallel   (b) series, series   (c) parallel, parallel   (d) parallel, series

3. A ____ is a device actuated by the operation of some devices with which it is directly associated, to govern succeeding operations of some or allied devices.

(a) interlock   (b) relay   (c) starter   (b) coil

4. An operation in which the motor runs when the pushbutton is pressed and will stop when the pushbutton is released is called ____.

(a) plugging   (b) clipping   (c) reversing   (d) inching

5. A ____ is the simplest form of a motor controller.

(a) relay   (b) drum switch   (c) toggle switch   (d) magnetic contactor

6. A diagram showing the physical location of coils, contacts, motors and the like in their actual positions would be a ____ diagram.

(a) schematic   (b) power flow   (c) ladder   (d) wiring

7. If a motor runs but fails to stop even if the stop button is pressed, the cause is probably ____.

(a) the overload contact did not operate   (b) the fuse has blown
(c) the holding circuit interlock was welded   (d) all of these

8. A method for stopping a three-phase motor quickly by momentarily connecting the motor for reverse rotation is called ____.

(a) plugging   (b) inching   (c) jogging   (d) latching

CHAPTER 3-A   TEST 2   MOTOR CONTROLS

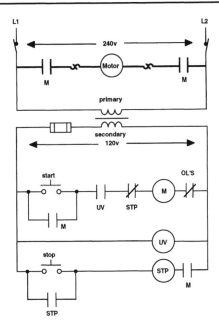

1. Which of the following statements is true?

(a) The stop button is normally closed
(b) The stop button is normally open
(c) The UV relay is on 240 volts
(d) The start button is sealed by the STP auxiliary contact

2. If the fused disconnect were open the motor would stop because _____.

(a) of undervoltage   **(b) the "M" contacts open**
(c) "M" coil de-energizes   **(d) all of these would happen**

3. Which of the following must occur first before the motor can start?

(a) ⊣├─ **UV closes**   **(b)** ⊣╱├─ **STP opens**   **(c)** ⊣├─ **M closes**   **(d)** ⊣╱├─ **OL opens**

4. When STP coil is energized and sealed in by the auxiliary STP contact, what de-energizes the STP circuit?

(a) ⊣├─ **UV closes**   **(b)** ⊣╱├─ **STP opens**   **(c)** ⊣├─ **M opens**   **(d)** ⊣╱├─ **STP closes**

5. Which of the following is true with the motor running?

(a) ⊣├─ **UV is open**   **(b)** ⊣├─ **STP is closed**

(c) The UV coil is energized   **(d) The** ⊣╱├─ **OL overload is open**

CHAPTER 3-A   TEST 3   MOTOR CONTROLS

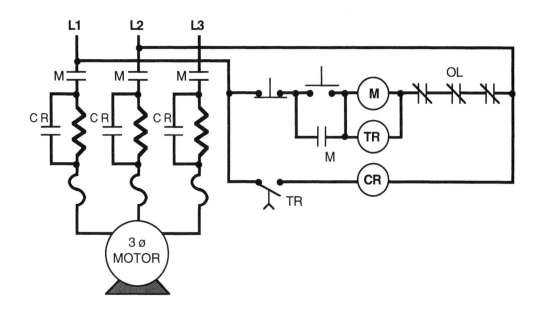

1. This is a _____ type starter.
(a) **full voltage**   (b) **autotransformer**   (c) **reactor**   (d) **resistor**

2. The resistors are:
(a) **in series with the heaters**   (b) **in parallel with the M contacts**
(c) **in series with the M contacts**   (d) **in parallel with the CR contacts**

3. When the motor is at full speed:
(a) **all normally open CR contacts are closed**
(b) **all normally open M contacts are open**
(c) **OL contacts are open**
(d) **all normally open CR contacts are open**

4. Which is true?
(a) **CR contacts close before M contacts close**
(b) **⊣⊢ M opens when Ⓣ𝐑 is energized**
(c) **when Ⓒ𝐑 is energized the motor will go to full run position**
(d) **when ⊣⊢ M closes Ⓒ𝐑 is energized**

5. To add another "START" button, you would connect it in:
(a) **series**   (b) **series-parallel**   (c) **parallel**   (d) **L3**

CHAPTER 3-A   TEST 4   MOTOR CONTROLS

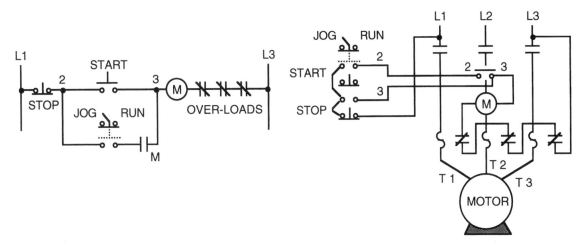

1. This is a _____ type starter.
(a) reactor   (b) autotransformer   (c) resistor   (d) full voltage

2. Which of the following is a true statement?
(a) the Stop station is in parallel with the control circuit
(b) the over-loads are in series with (M)
(c) the heaters are in series with (M)
(d) ⊣⊢M is in parallel with (M)

3. Which of the following is a <u>false</u> statement?
(a) the over-loads are in series with L3
(b) the Stop station is in series with (M)
(c) the heaters are in parallel with the motor
(d) in the jog mode, ⊣⊢M has been bypassed

4. With the control circuit in the jog mode, which is the proper sequence of operation?
(a) Start is pushed, energizing ⊣⊢M and (M); Stop is pushed, (M) releases, jog cycle is complete
(b) Start is pushed, energizing (M), Stop is pushed before ⊣⊢M can lock in
(c) Start is pushed, and (M) is energized, ⊣⊢M is bypassed in the jog mode, (M) remains energized only when Start is in the closed position
(d) Start is pushed, ⊣⊢M closes and energizes (M), ⊣⊢M then times out and opens the circuit to (M)

5. With the control circuit in the run mode, which is the proper sequence of operation?
(a) Start is pushed, ⊣⊢M is bypassed, (M) is energized
(b) Start is pushed, energizing (M), ⊣⊢M locks in
(c) Start is pushed, ⊣⊢M locks in, (M) is de-energized
(d) Start is pushed, ⊣⊢M locks in, energizing (M)

CHAPTER 3-A   TEST 5   MOTOR CONTROLS

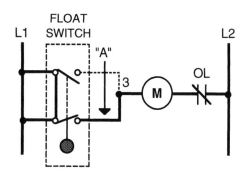

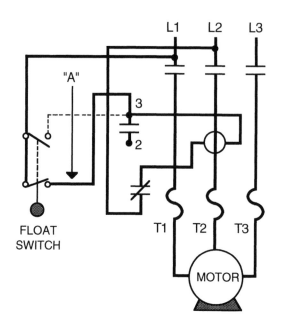

FLOAT SWITCH CONTROLS STARTER

The diagram shows a float switch intended for tank operation. When the water reaches "low" level the float switch closes. Pumping action will continue until the water reaches the "high" level. For sump pumping remove wire "A" and connect as per the dotted line. At "low" level the float switch operates and stops the pumping action. Sump pumping action will not commence until the water reaches the "high" level.

FLOAT SWITCH SHOWN IN FUEL TANK

1. This is a _____ type starter.
(a) full voltage   (b) resistor   (c) reversible   (d) reactor

2. When used for sump pump, if conductor identified as "A" were not installed as per instructions, this control circuit would not function properly because:
(a) the H.C. (pts 2 & 3) have been bypassed
(b) the motor would reverse rotation
(c) pump would only function when container is empty
(d) overloads are bypassed

3. A remote momentary stop station should be added to _____.
   I. L1   II. L2   III. L3
(a) I only   (b) I and II only   (c) I and III only   (d) none

CHAPTER 3-B

TAPS

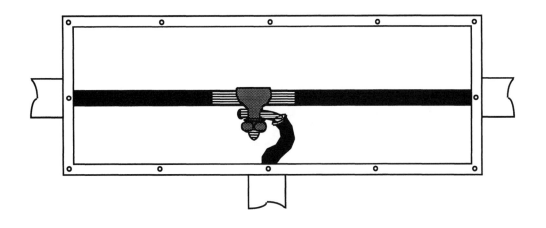

```
BRANCH CIRCUIT TAPS
```

The general Code rules 210.19 and 240.4 require the use of an overcurrent device at the point of which a conductor receives its supply, exceptions to this rule are made in the case of taps.

GENERAL RULE

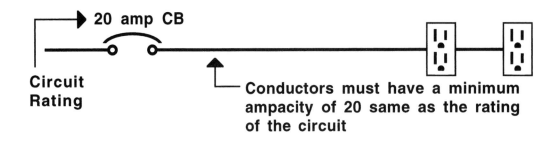

20 amp CB

Circuit Rating

Conductors must have a minimum ampacity of 20 same as the rating of the circuit

The general rule is when two different sizes of wire are connected together the rating of the overcurrent device cannot be greater than what is required for the smallest wire as shown below.

GENERAL RULE

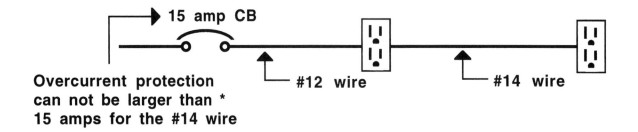

15 amp CB

Overcurrent protection can not be larger than * 15 amps for the #14 wire

#12 wire

#14 wire

There are a number of exceptions to this general rule. Often it is necessary to connect a wire to another continuous wire. This is called a tap connection.

In some cases it's not necessary to run wires of the same size as the branch circuit wires to individual loads on the circuit. A good example of this exception to the general rule is the table lamp in the living room. The cord to the lamp may be a #18 wire plugged into a 20 amp branch circuit of #12 wires.

210.19(A3) ex.1 permits branch circuit tap conductors supplying electric ranges, wall-mounted ovens, and counter-mounted electric cooking units supplied from a 50 amp branch circuit to have an ampacity of not less than 20.

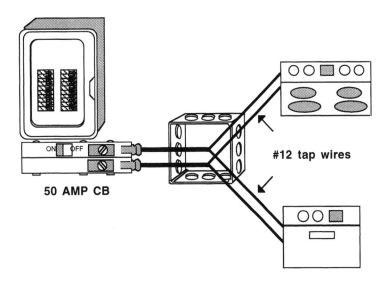

#12 tap wires

50 AMP CB

Section 210.19(A4) ex.1 states tap conductors for branch circuits serving other than cooking appliances shall have an ampacity not less than 15 for circuits rated less than 40 amperes and not less than 20 for circuits rated 40 or 50 amperes and only where these tap conductors supply any of the following loads:

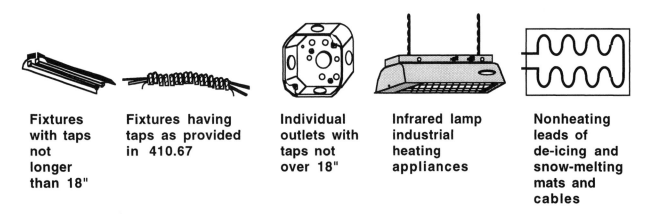

Fixtures with taps not longer than 18"

Fixtures having taps as provided in 410.67

Individual outlets with taps not over 18"

Infrared lamp industrial heating appliances

Nonheating leads of de-icing and snow-melting mats and cables

FEEDER TAPS

To meet the practical demands of field application feeder taps are permitted by the Code.

Feeder conductors shall be permitted to be tapped, without overcurrent protection at the tap where all of the following conditions are met:

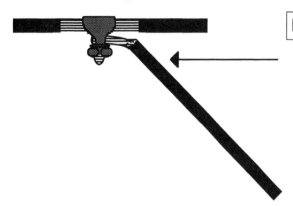

FEEDER TAPS NOT OVER 10' LONG

(a) The ampacity of the tap conductor is

(1) Not less than the combined computed loads on the circuits supplied by the tap conductors, and

(2) Not less than the rating of the device supplied by the tap conductors or not less than the rating of the overcurrent-protective device at the termination of the taps conductors.

(b) The tap conductors do not extend beyond the switchboard, panelboard, disconnecting means, or control devices they supply.

(c) Except at the point of connection to the feeder, the tap conductors are enclosed in a raceway, which shall extend from the tap to the enclosure of an enclosed switchboard, panelboard, or control devices, or back of an open switchboard.

(d) For field installations where the tap conductors leave the enclosure or vault in which the tap is made, the rating of the overcurrent device on the line side of the tap conductors shall not exceed 10 times the ampacity of the tap conductor.

Short circuit protection for feeder taps is obtained by limiting the maximum length of each tap conductor (not raceway) to 10 feet. This assures a minimum circuit impedance corresponding to the practical circuit conditions to be encountered. Any short circuit in this short length of tap conductor would open the feeder overcurrent device.

LENGTH OF TAP CONDUCTOR IS A MAXIMUM OF 10 FEET, NOT THE RACEWAY

Feeder taps **not over 25'** long, conductors shall be permitted to be tapped, without overcurrent protection at the tap, to a feeder where all of the following conditions are met:

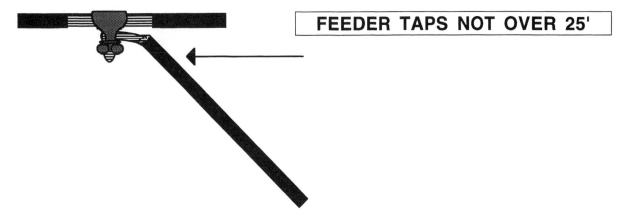

FEEDER TAPS NOT OVER 25'

(a) The ampacity of the tap conductors cannot be less than 1/3 of the rating of the overcurrent device protecting the feeder conductors.

(b) The tap conductors terminate in a single CB or single set of fuses that will limit the load to the ampacity of the tap conductors. This device shall be permitted to supply any number of additional overcurrent devices on its load side.

(c) The tap conductors shall be suitably protected from physical damage or are enclosed in a raceway.

ALL 3 CONDITIONS MUST BE MET FOR A TAP NOT OVER 25 FEET

Transformer feeder taps with primary plus secondary **not over 25'** long, conductors shall be permitted to be tapped, without overcurrent protection at the tap, to a feeder where all of the following conditions are met:

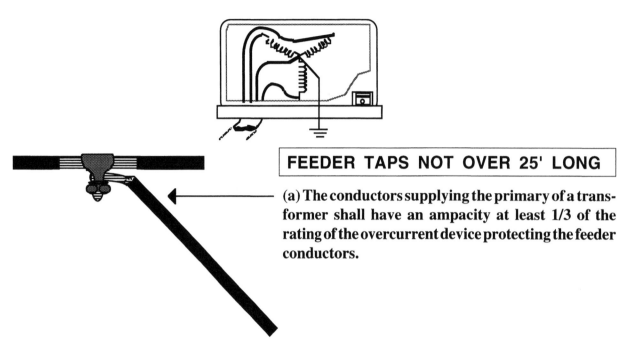

FEEDER TAPS NOT OVER 25' LONG

(a) The conductors supplying the primary of a transformer shall have an ampacity at least 1/3 of the rating of the overcurrent device protecting the feeder conductors.

(b) The conductors supplied by the secondary of the transformer shall have an ampacity that, when multiplied by the ratio of the secondary-to-primary voltage, is at least 1/3 of the rating of the overcurrent device protecting the feeder conductors.

(c) The total length of one primary plus one secondary conductor, excluding any portion of the primary conductor that is protected at its ampacity, is not over 25'.

(d) The primary and secondary conductors are suitably protected from physical damage.

(e) The secondary conductors terminate in a single CB or set of fuses that will limit the load to that allowed in section 310.15.

ALL 5 CONDITIONS MUST BE MET FOR A TAP NOT OVER 25' FOR TRANSFORMERS

Feeder taps **over 25'** long, conductors over 25 feet shall be permitted to be tapped from feeders in **high bay manufacturing buildings** over 35 feet high at walls, and the installation complies with all of the following conditions.

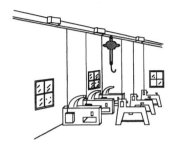

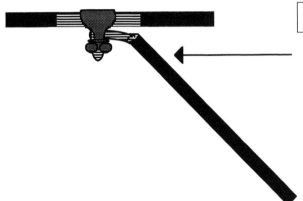

FEEDER TAPS OVER 25' LONG

(a) Conditions of maintenance and supervision ensure that only qualified persons will service the systems

(b) The tap conductors are not over 25' long horizontally and not over 100' total length.

(c) The ampacity of the tap conductors is not less than 1/3 of the rating of the overcurrent device protecting the feeder conductors.

(d) The tap conductors terminate at a single CB or a single set of fuses that will limit the load to the ampacity of the tap conductors. This single overcurrent device shall be permitted to supply any number of additional overcurrent devices on its load side.

(e) The tap conductors are suitably protected from physical damage or are enclosed in a raceway.

(f) The tap conductors are continuous from end-to-end and contain no splices.

(g) The tap conductors are sized #6 copper or #4 aluminum or larger.

(h) The tap conductors do not penetrate walls, floors, or ceilings.

(i) The tap is made no less than 30' from the floor.

MOTOR FEEDER TAPS

Feeder tap conductors shall have an ampacity not less than required by Part II (430.22 & 430.24), shall terminate in a branch circuit protective device and, in addition, shall meet **one** of the following requirements:

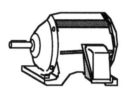

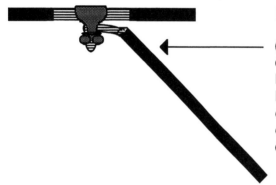

MOTOR FEEDER TAPS

(1) The tap conductors shall be enclosed by either an enclosed controller or by a raceway. Be not more than 10 feet in length.
For field installation be protected by an overcurrent device on the line side of the tap conductor, the rating or setting of which shall not exceed 1000% of the tap conductor ampacity.

OR

(2) Have an ampacity of at least 1/3 that of the feeder conductors, be protected from physical damage and be not more than 25' in length.

OR

(3) Have the same ampacity as the feeder conductors.

• There is an exception for feeder taps OVER 25' in high-bay manufacturing buildings.

Without the 1000% limitation of the overcurrent device (10:1 ratio) it would allow a tap of any size. A #10 wire could be tapped from a bus having overcurrent protection set at 1200 amps. This is a 40:1 ratio. Under a fault condition, the #10 wire would burn off, creating other shock and fire hazards. The 1000% limitation is a much safer design.

(1) The 10' or less tap conductors shall be enclosed by either an enclosed controller or by a raceway. When installed in a raceway or enclosed controller the taps can be the same size as the branch circuit conductors.

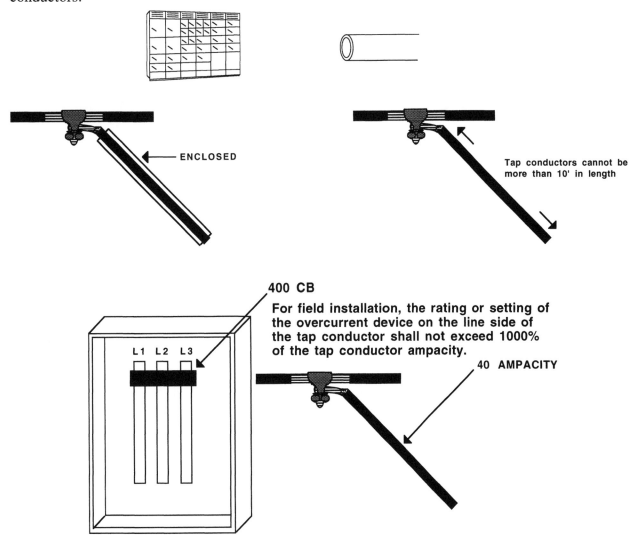

400 CB

For field installation, the rating or setting of the overcurrent device on the line side of the tap conductor shall not exceed 1000% of the tap conductor ampacity.

40 AMPACITY

OR (2) have an ampacity at least 1/3 that of the feeder conductors, be protected from physical damage and be not more than 25' in length. **Or** (3) have the same ampacity as the feeder conductors.

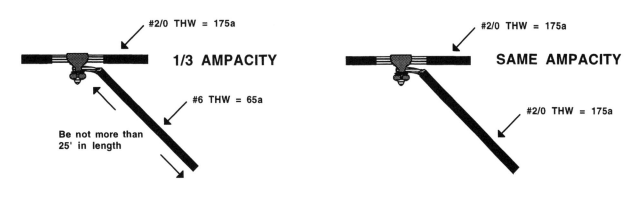

Shown below is an exam calculation tap question. The next page will show the answers.

208/120v three-phase 4-wire
Dual-element time delay fuses
THW insulation
Discharge lighting load

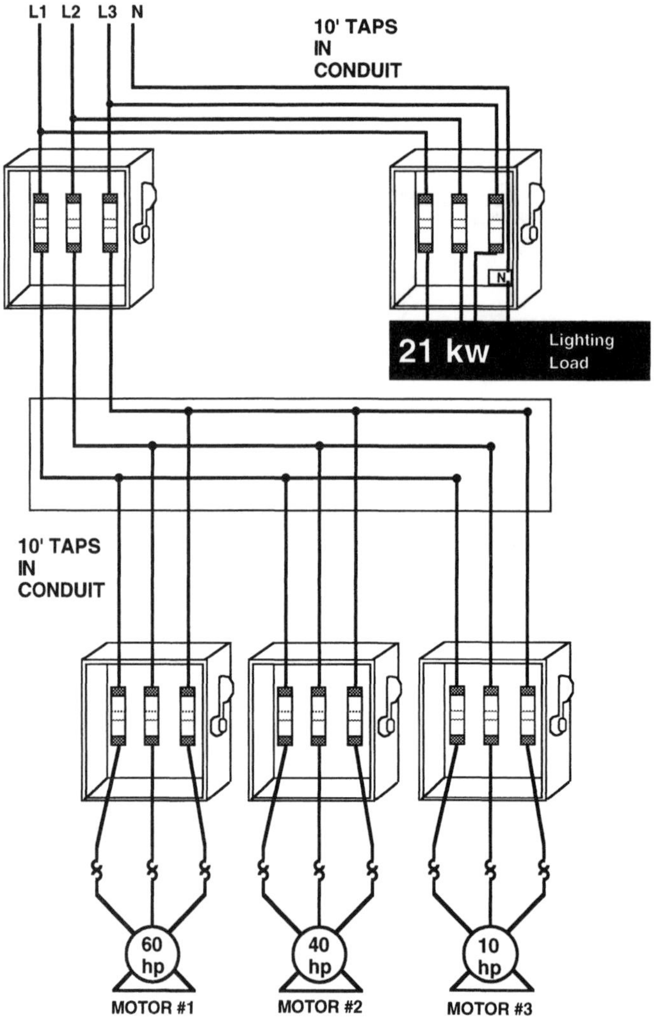

L1 L2 L3 N

10' TAPS
IN
CONDUIT

21 kw   Lighting Load

10' TAPS
IN
CONDUIT

60 hp   40 hp   10 hp
MOTOR #1   MOTOR #2   MOTOR #3

1. **Full load current**:
Motor #1 _____

Motor #2 _____

Motor #3 _____

2. **Size overloads**:
Motor #1 _____

Motor #2 _____

Motor #3 _____

3. **Branch circuit wire size**:
Motor #1 _____

Motor #2 _____

Motor #3 _____

4. **Branch fuse size**:
Motor #1 _____

Motor #2 _____

Motor #3 _____

5. **Disconnect size**:
Motor #1 _____

Motor #2 _____

Motor #3 _____

6. **Tap conductor size**:
Motor #1 _____

Motor #2 _____

Motor #3 _____

7. **Feeder conductor size**: _____

8. **Feeder fuse size**: _____

9. **Feeder disconnect size**: _____

10. **Tap conductors size (to lighting load)**: _____

Solution:

1.   Motor #1 = Table 430.250 F.L.C. **169 amps**
        Motor #2 = Table 430.250 F.L.C. **114 amps**
        Motor #3 = Table 430.250 F.L.C. **30.8 amps**

2.   Motor #1 =   169 x 115% (430.32A1) = **194.35 amps**
        Motor #2 =   114 x 115% (430.32A1) = **131.1   amps**
        Motor #3 =   30.8 x 115% (430.32A1) = **35.42 amps**

3.   Motor #1 = 169   x 125% (430.22) = 211.25 required ampacity T.310-16 = **#4/0 THW**
        Motor #2 = 114   x 125% (430.22) = 142.5 required ampacity T.310-16 = **#1/0 THW**
        Motor #3 = 30.8 x 125% (430.22) =   38.5 required ampacity T. 310-16 = **#8 THW**

4.   Motor #1 = 169   x 175% (T.430.52 dual-element) = 295.75   240.6 = **300 amps**
        Motor #2 = 114   x 175% (T.430.52 dual-element) = 199.5 240.6 = **200 amps**
        Motor #3 = 30.8 x 175% (T.430.52 dual-element) = 53.9 240.6 = **60 amps**

5.   Motor #1 = 169 x 115% (430.110A) = 194.35 amps minimum = 200 amp **non-fusible** or
        a **400 amp fusible disconnect** for a 300 amp branch circuit fuse
        Motor #2 = 114 x 115% (430.110A) = 131.1   amps minimum = 150 amp **non-fusible** or
        a **200 amp fusible disconnect** for a 200 amp branch circuit fuse
        Motor #3 = 30.8 x 115% (430.110A) = 35.42 amps minimum = 60 amp **non-fusible** or
        a **60 amp fusible disconnect** for a 60 amp branch circuit fuse

6.   10 foot taps in conduit cannot be smaller than the branch circuit conductor size required by
        section 430.22:
        Motor #1 = **#4/0 THW tap conductor**
        Motor #2 = **#1/0 THW tap conductor**
        Motor #3 = **#8 THW tap conductor**

7.   169 x 125% (430.24) = 211.25 + 114 + 30.8 = 356.05 required ampacity = **#500 kcmil**

8.   300 amp fuse + 114 + 30.8 = 444.8 amps   240.6 = **400 feeder fuse**

9.   169 + 114 + 30.8 = 313.8 x 115% (430.110A) = 360.87 amps minimum = **400 amp fuses**

10.   21,000w/208v x 1.732 = 58.29 amps actual lighting load. The overcurrent protection for this
        continuous load would be 58.29 x 125% (215.2A1) = 72.86 amps   240.6 = 80 amp O.C.P.
        The ampacity of the taps cannot be smaller than the rating of the O.C.P. device at the
        termination of the taps which is 80 amps. T.310.16 = **#4 THW tap conductor.** • The
        overcurrent device on the line side (which is not given in this question) could not exceed the
        1000% (10:1 ratio) or 800 amps.

Section 240.6 of the Code lists standard sizes for fuses and circuit breakers but not disconnects.

The standard sizes for disconnects are found in a manufacturer's catalog which would list the following: 30, 60, 100, 200, 400, 600, 800 and 1200.

Fuses are in sizes with different configurations such as plug fuses, cartridge and knife-blade fuses.

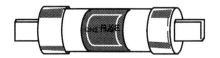

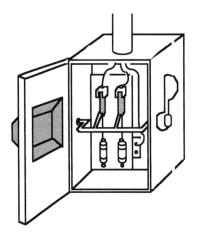

DISCONNECT SIZE	FUSE SIZE
30 amps	15 - 30 amps
60 amps	35 - 60 amps
100 amps	70 - 100 amps
200 amps	110 - 200 amps
400 amps	225 - 400 amps
600 amps	450 - 600 amps
800 amps	700 - 800 amps
1200 amps	1000 - 1200 amps

CHAPTER 3-B   TEST 1   MOTOR TAPS

208/120v three-phase 4-wire
Dual-element time delay fuses
THW insulation
Discharge lighting load

L1 L2 L3   N

15' TAPS
IN
CONDUIT

21' TAPS
IN
CONDUIT

19 kw
Lighting
Load

50 hp   20 hp   10 hp
MOTOR #1   MOTOR #2   MOTOR #3

1. **Full load current**:
Motor #1 _____

Motor #2 _____

Motor #3 _____

2. **Size overloads**:
Motor #1 _____

Motor #2 _____

Motor #3 _____

3. **Branch circuit wire size**:
Motor #1 _____

Motor #2 _____

Motor #3 _____

4. **Branch fuse size**:
Motor #1 _____

Motor #2 _____

Motor #3 _____

5. **Disconnect size**:
Motor #1 _____

Motor #2 _____

Motor #3 _____

6. **Tap conductor size**:
Motor #1 _____

Motor #2 _____

Motor #3 _____

7. **Feeder conductor size**: _____

8. **Feeder fuse size**: _____

9. **Feeder disconnect size**: _____

10. **Tap conductors size (to lighting load)** : _____

113TH

CHAPTER 4

BOX and CONDUIT SIZING

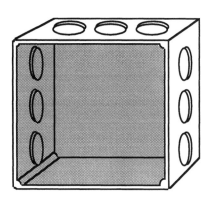

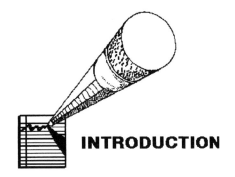

INTRODUCTION

The Code contains provisions considered necessary for safety. Compliance therewith and proper maintenance will result in an installation essentially free from hazard but **not** necessarily efficient, convenient, or adequate for good service or **future expansion** of electrical use.

This Chapter will show how to calculate the **maximum** number of wires the Code allows in a box or conduit.

Hazards often occur because of overloading of wiring systems by methods or usage NOT in conformity with the Code. This occurs because initial wiring did not provide for increases in the use of electricity. An initial adequate installation and reasonable provisions for system changes will provide for future increases in the use of electricity.

Limiting the number of wires and circuits in a single enclosure will minimize the effects from a short-circuit or ground fault in one circuit.

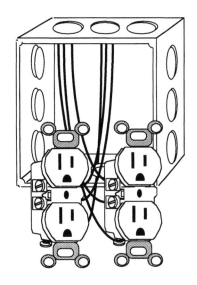

Installing more than the Code maximum permitted conductors in a box has caused accidents and fires. Forcing the receptacles into a crowded box tends to loosen the connections thus resulting in a high resistance fault (heat).

Boxes shall be of sufficient size to provide free space for all enclosed conductors. In no case shall the volume of the box be less than the fill calculation.

BOX FILL CALCULATIONS - CUBIC INCHES

Based on AWG sizes not insulation sizes.

Proper calculations in box fill will result in conductors not being jammed into the box causing nicks or damage to the conductor insulation resulting in possible grounds or short circuits.

•Note: Box fill requirements don't apply to terminal housings supplied with motors.

When determining the maximum number of conductors permitted in a box, Table 314.16(A) would apply for conductor sizes #18 through #6. Table 314.16(A) shows the number of conductors **all the same size** permitted in a box. But, the number of conductors permitted as shown in Table 314.16(A) represents an **empty** box. If the box contains internal clamps, fixture studs, hickeys, switches or receptacles, the number of conductors shown in Table 314.16(A) would have to be **reduced**.

Table 314.16(A). Metal Boxes

Box Dimension, Inches Trade Size or Type	Min. Cu. In. Cap.	Maximum Number of Conductors*						
		No. 18	No. 16	No. 14	No. 12	No. 10	No. 8	No. 6
4 x 1-1/4 Round or Octagonal	12.5	8	7	6	5	5	4	0
4 x 1-1/2 Round or Octagonal	15.5	10	8	7	6	6	5	0
4 x 2-1/8 Round or Octagonal	21.5	14	12	10	9	8	7	0
4 x 1-1/4 Square	18.0	12	10	9	8	7	6	0
4 x 1-1/2 Square	21.0	14	12	10	9	8	7	0
4 x 2-1/8 Square	30.3	20	17	15	13	12	10	6
4-11/16 x 1-1/4 Square	25.5	17	14	12	11	10	8	0
4-11/16 x 1-1/2 Square	29.5	19	16	14	13	11	9	0
4-11/16 x 2-1/8 Square	42.0	28	24	21	18	16	14	6
3 x 2 x 1-1/2 Device	7.5	5	4	3	3	3	2	0
3 x 2 x 2 Device	10.0	6	5	5	4	4	3	0
3 x 2 x 2-1/4 Device	10.5	7	6	5	4	4	3	0
3 x 2 x 2-1/2 Device	12.5	8	7	6	5	5	4	0
3 x 2 x 2-3/4 Device	14.0	9	8	7	6	5	4	0
3 x 2 x 3-1/2 Device	18.0	12	10	9	8	7	6	0
4 x 2-1/8 x 1-1/2 Device	10.3	6	5	5	4	4	3	0
4 x 2-1/8 x 1-7/8 Device	13.0	8	7	6	5	5	4	0
4 x 2-1/8 x 2-1/8 Device	14.5	9	8	7	6	5	4	0
3-3/4 x 2 x 2-1/2 Masonry Box / Gang	14.0	9	8	7	6	5	4	0
3-3/4 x 2 x 3-1/2 Masonry Box / Gang	21.0	14	12	10	9	8	7	0
FS — Minimum Internal Depth 1-3/4 Single Cover/Gang	13.5	9	7	6	6	5	4	0
FD — Minimum Internal Depth 2-3/8 Single Cover/Gang	18.0	12	10	9	8	7	6	3
FS — Minimum Internal Depth 1-3/4 Multiple Cover/Gang	18.0	12	10	9	8	7	6	0
FD — Minimum Internal Depth 2-3/8 Multiple Cover/Gang	24.0	16	13	12	10	9	8	4

* Where no volume allowances are required by Sections 314.16(B2) through 314.16(B5).

Table 314.16(A) shall apply where no fittings or devices, such as fixture studs, cable clamps, hickeys, switches or receptacles, are contained in the box and where no grounding conductors are part of the wiring within the box. Where one or more of these types of fittings, such as fixture studs, cable clamps, or hickeys are contained in the box, the number of conductors shown in the table shall be reduced by one for each type of fitting; an additional deduction of two conductors shall be made for each mounting yoke or strap containing one or more devices or equipment; and a further deduction of one conductor shall be made for one or more grounding conductors entering the box. Where a second set of equipment grounding conductors, as permitted by Section 250.146(D), is present in the box, then an additional deduction of one conductor shall be made. A conductor running through the box shall be counted as one conductor, and each conductor originating outside of the box and terminating inside the box is counted as one conductor. Conductors, no part of which leaves the box, shall not be counted.

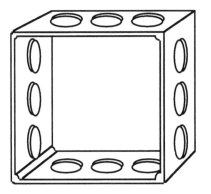

The number of conductors shown in Table 314.16(A), are for an **empty*** box.

* Where no volume allowances are required by Sections 314.16(B2) through 314.16(B5).

FIXTURE STUD   CABLE CLAMP   HICKEY   SWITCH   RECEPTACLE

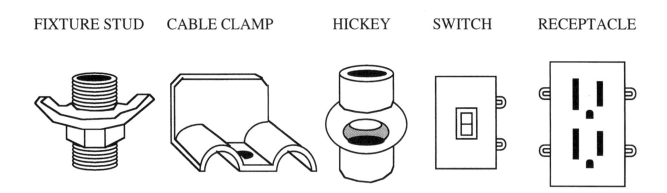

The number of conductors shown in Table 314.16(A) shall be reduced by **one** for each type of fitting; an additional deduction of **two** conductors shall be made for each **mounting yoke or strap** containing **one or more** devices or equipment per 314.16(B2,3,4).

•Note: Each **strap** holding a device (switch or receptacle) counts as **two** conductors, if the strap holds a duplex or triplex receptacle, it still counts as **two** conductors.

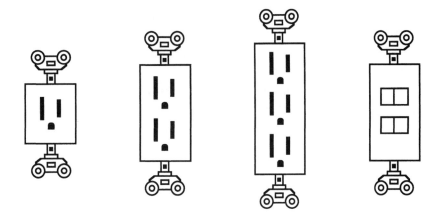

•Note: Do **not** count box connectors, no reduction is required as they are not **internal** cable clamps.

314.16(B1 through 5) Counting conductors

A deduction of **one** conductor shall be made for one **or more** grounding conductors (green or bare wire) entering a box per 314.16(B5).

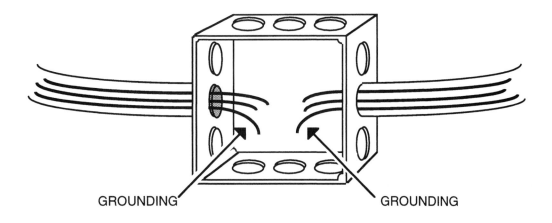

GROUNDING   GROUNDING

Where a second set of equipment grounding conductors, as permitted by Section 250.146(D), is present in the box, then an **additional** deduction of **one** conductor is made.

Section 250.146(D): Where required for the reduction of electrical noise (electromagnetic interference) on the grounding circuit, a receptacle in which the grounding terminal is purposely insulated from the receptacle mounting means shall be permitted. The receptacle grounding terminal shall be grounded by an insulated equipment grounding conductor run with the circuit conductors. This grounding conductor shall be permitted to pass through one or more panelboards without connection to the panelboard grounding terminal as permitted in Section 408.40ex., so as to terminate directly at an equipment grounding conductor terminal of the applicable derived system or service.

(FPN): Use of an isolated equipment grounding conductor does not relieve the requirement for grounding the raceway system and outlet box.

In the box shown below with two equipment grounding conductors (count one) and one isolated grounding conductor (count one) you would count a total of **two**.

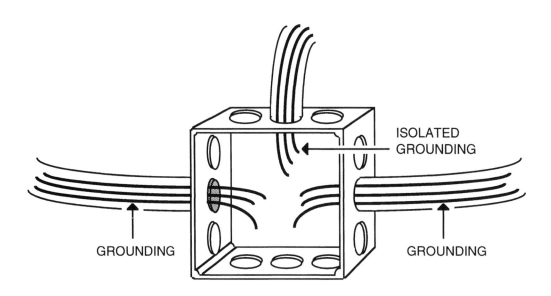

A conductor running through the box shall be counted as **one** conductor per 314.16(B1).

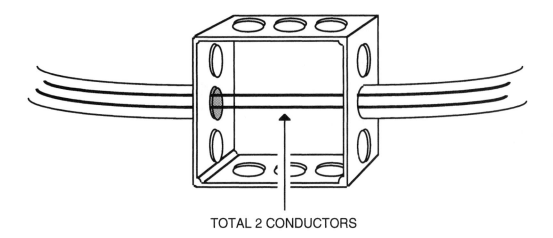

TOTAL 2 CONDUCTORS

Each conductor originating outside of the box and terminating inside the box is counted as **one** conductor.

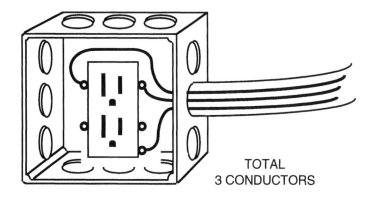

TOTAL
3 CONDUCTORS

Conductors, no part of which leaves the box, shall **not** be counted per 314.16(B1.

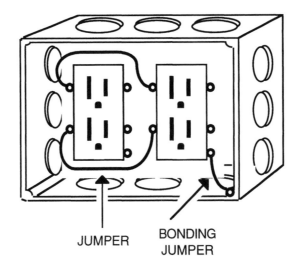

JUMPER   BONDING
              JUMPER

Example: Using Table 314.16(A): A 3" x 2" x 2 3/4" device box will hold 6 - #12 conductors. This box will accommodate a maximum of:

A 12-2 with ground romex cable = 3 conductors
cable clamps   = 1 conductor
one duplex receptacle   = 2 conductors
                                  6 conductors

   Now let's reverse the calculation, we know the number of conductors, but need to determine the correct cubic inch box size. Go to Table **314.16(B)**.

Table 314.16(B).   Volume Required per Conductor

Size of Conductor	Free Space Within Box for Each Conductor
No. 18	1.50 cubic inches
No. 16	1.75 cubic inches
No. 14	2.00 cubic inches
No. 12	2.25 cubic inches
No. 10	2.50 cubic inches
No. 8	3.00 cubic inches
No. 6	5.00 cubic inches

Table 314.16(B) is a very useful table for everyday box sizing. The electrician should memorize, #14 conductor = 2 cubic inches, and a #12 conductor = 2.25 cubic inches. These two conductors are the most often used in calculating the correct box size using devices. Example, if the electrician is installing #14 conductors, count the conductors, clamps, devices, and multiply the total conductors times 2 cubic inches and this will determine the minimum cubic inch capacity required. Boxes not shown in Table 314.16(A) are required to have the cubic inch capacity marked (314.16(A2).

Example: Table 314.16(A) shows a 4 11/16" x 1 1/4" square box will hold 11 - #12 conductors. If this box contained three #12-2 with ground nonmetallic sheathed cables, cable clamps, and two duplex receptacles (two straps).

3 - #12 black conductors = 3 conductors
3 - #12 white conductors = 3 conductors
3 - #12 bare conductors = 1 conductor
3 - cable clamps   = 1 conductor
2 - duplex receptacles   = 4 conductors
                            ‾‾‾‾‾‾‾‾‾‾‾‾‾
                            12 conductors

12 - #12 conductors x 2.25 cubic inches = 27 cubic inch box required, a 4 11/16" x 1 1/4" square box at 25.5 cubic inches would be a **violation**.

Example: Using mixed size conductors. The box shown below contains two #12-2 with ground nonmetallic sheathed cables to a duplex receptacle, and one #14-2 with ground nonmetallic sheathed cable to a switch. The box contains cable clamps. What is the cubic inch capacity required?

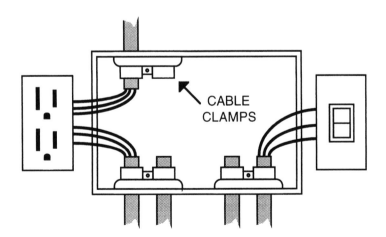

CABLE
CLAMPS

Solution:

2 - #12 black conductors = 2 conductors
2 - #12 white conductors = 2 conductors
2 - #12 bare conductors = 1 conductor
1 - receptacle strap   = 2 conductors
2 - cable clamps   = 1 conductor
                    8 - #12 conductors = 8 x 2.25 cubic inches = 18 cubic inches

1 - #14 black conductor = 1 conductor
1 - #14 white conductor = 1 conductor
1 - switch strap   = 2 conductors
1 - #14 bare conductor = 0 counted as a #12 (370.16b5)
1 - cable clamp   = 0 counted as a #12 (370.16b2)
                    4 - #14 conductors = 4 x 2 cubic inches = 8 cubic inches

18 cubic inches + 8 cubic inches = **26 cubic inch box required minimum.**

    Table 314.16(A) and Table 314.16(B) show conductor sizes **through #6**. For conductor sizes **#4 and larger** 314.28 is used for calculations.

CONDUCTORS #4 and LARGER

    314.28(A). Minimum size. For raceways 3/4 inch trade size or larger, containing conductors of #4 or larger, and for cables containing conductors #4 or larger, the minimum dimensions of pull or junction boxes installed in a raceway or cable run shall comply with the following:

(1) **Straight Pulls**. In straight pulls the length of the box shall not be less than eight times the trade diameter of the largest raceway.

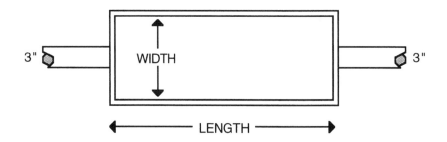

LENGTH = 3" conduit x 8 = 24" minimum.

WIDTH - The box must be wide enough to provide proper installation of the conduit locknuts and
            bushings within the box.

Example: Straight pull, what is the minimum length of this pull box?

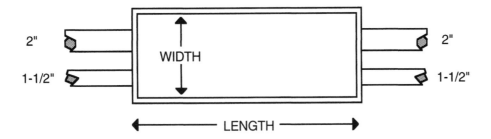

LENGTH = Largest raceway 2" x 8 = 16" minimum length.

WIDTH = Width necessary for locknuts and bushings.

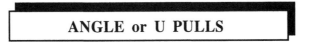

ANGLE or U PULLS

   Article 314.28(A2)¡ **Angle or U pulls**. Where angle or U pulls are made, the distance between each raceway entry inside the box and the opposite wall of the box shall not be less than six times the trade diameter of the largest raceway. This distance shall be increased for additional entries by the amount of the maximum sum of the diameters of all other raceway entries in the same row on the same wall of the box. Each row shall be calculated individually, and the single row that provides the maximum distance shall be used.
   The distance between raceway entries enclosing the same conductor shall not be less than six times the trade diameter of the larger raceway.

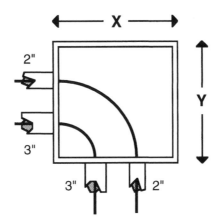

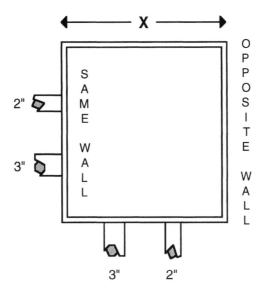

Sizing the angle pull box:

Starting with dimension **"X"**, we are calculating the distance from the **same wall** (the wall with the conduit enclosing the conductors in an angle pull) to the **opposite wall** (of the angle pull).

This distance shall not be less than **six** times the trade diameter of the **largest** raceway (6 x 3" conduit = 18") **plus** the diameters of all other raceway entries in any one row on the **same wall** of the box. 6 x 3" = 18" **plus** 2" conduit = 20".   Dimension **"X" = 20" minimum**.

Next calculate dimension **"Y"**:

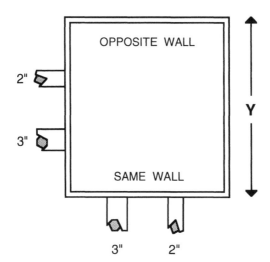

Largest raceway on **same wall** (3" x 6 = 18") **plus** all other raceways on the **same wall** (2"). 3" x 6 = 18" + 2" = 20".   Dimension **"Y" = 20" minimum**.

Example: Calculate dimension **"Z"**.

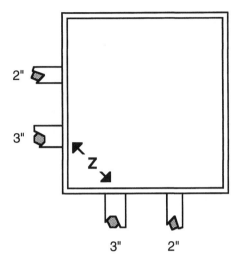

The distance between raceway entries enclosing the same conductor shall not be less than **six times** the trade diameter of the larger raceway.

Solution: 3" conduit x 6 = 18". Dimension **"Z" = 18" minimum**.

Example: Calculate dimension **"X"** in a **U Pull**.

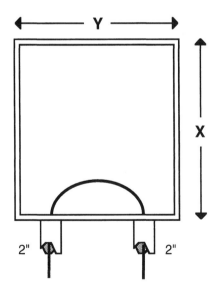

Solution: 2" conduit x 6 = 12" + 2" = 14". Dimension **"X" = 14" minimum**.
Dimension **"Y"** = width necessary for locknuts and bushings.

Example: Calculate the distance between raceways in a **U Pull**.

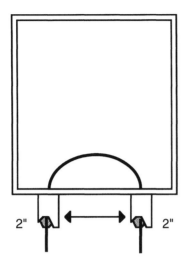

Solution: 2" conduit x 6 = **12" minimum distance between raceways**.

Example: Combination of a straight pull and an angle pull in the same box. Calculate dimension **"Y"**.

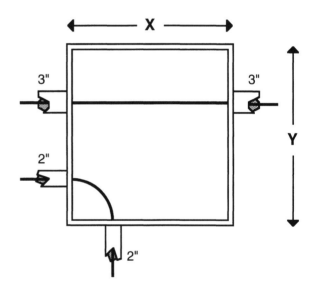

Solution: Same wall = 2" conduit x 6 = 12" plus all other entries on the **same wall**, there are none.   Dimension **"Y" = 12" minimum**.

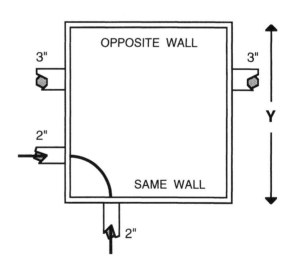

Example: Calculate dimension **"X"**.

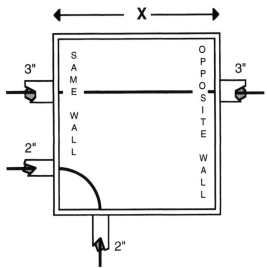

Solution: Same wall = 2" conduit x 6 = 12" plus 3" = 15". But, we also have a straight pull in dimension "X", straight pull = 3" conduit x 8 = 24".   Dimension **"X" = 24" minimum**.

CONDUIT FILL - AREA SQUARE INCHES

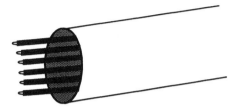

The number and size of conductors in any raceway shall not be more than will permit dissipation of the heat and ready installation and withdrawal of the conductors without damage to the conductors or to their insulation.

Raceways shall be installed complete between outlet, junction, or splicing points **prior** to the installation of conductors.

Table 1 is based on common conditions of proper cabling and alignment of conductors where the length of the pull and the number of bends are within reasonable limits. It should be recognized that for certain conditions, a larger size conduit or a lesser conduit fill should be considered,

Table 1.   Percent of Cross Section of Conduit and Tubing for Conductors

Number of Conductors	All conductor types
1	53
2	31
Over 2	40

TABLE 1 NOTES

1. See Annex C for maximum number of conductors and fixture wires, **all of the same size**, permitted in a conduit or tubing.

2. Table 1 applies only to **complete** conduit or tubing systems and is **not** intended to apply to sections of conduit or tubing used to protect exposed wiring from physical damage.

3. Equipment grounding or bonding conductors, where installed, shall be **included** when calculating conduit or tubing fill. The actual dimensions of the equipment grounding or bonding conductor (insulated or bare) shall be used in the calculation.

4. Where conduit or tubing nipples having a maximum length not to exceed **24 inches** are installed between boxes, cabinets, and similar enclosures, the nipple shall be permitted to be **filled 60%** of its total cross-sectional area, and section 310.15(B2a) adjustment factors need **not** apply to this condition.

7. Where the calculated number of conductors, **all of the same size**, includes a decimal fraction, the next higher whole number shall be used where this decimal is **0.8** or larger.

8. When **bare** conductors are permitted by other sections of this Code, the dimensions for **bare** conductors in **Table 8** of Chapter 9 shall be permitted.

A NIPPLE CAN BE FILLED
60% OF THE
CROSS-SECTIONAL AREA

Table 4. Dimensions and Percent Area of Conduit and Tubing

Trade Size Inches	Electrical Metallic Tubing					Electrical Nonmetallic Tubing				
	Internal Diameter Inches	Total Area 100% Sq. In.	2 Wires 31% Sq. In.	Over 2 Wires 40% Sq. In.	1 Wire 53% Sq. In.	Internal Diameter Inches	Total Area 100% Sq. In.	2 Wires 31% Sq. In.	Over 2 Wires 40% Sq. In.	1 Wire 53% Sq. In.
1/2	0.622	0.304	0.094	**0.122**	0.161	0.560	0.246	0.076	**0.099**	0.131
3/4	0.824	0.533	0.165	**0.213**	0.283	0.760	0.454	0.141	**0.181**	0.240
1	1.049	0.864	0.268	**0.346**	0.458	1.000	0.785	0.243	**0.314**	0.416
1 1/4	1.380	1.496	0.464	**0.598**	0.793	1.340	1.410	0.437	**0.564**	0.747
1 1/2	1.610	2.036	0.631	**0.814**	1.079	1.570	1.936	0.600	**0.774**	1.026
2	2.067	3.356	1.040	**1.342**	1.778	2.020	3.205	0.994	**1.282**	1.699
2 1/2	2.731	5.858	1.816	**2.343**	3.105	-	-	-	-	-
3	3.356	8.846	2.742	**3.538**	4.688	-	-	-	-	-
3 1/2	3.824	11.545	3.579	**4.618**	6.119	-	-	-	-	-
4	4.334	14.753	4.573	**5.901**	7.819	-	-	-	-	-

Trade Size Inches	Flexible Metal Conduit					Intermediate Metal Conduit				
	Internal Diameter Inches	Total Area 100% Sq. In.	2 Wires 31% Sq. In.	Over 2 Wires 40% Sq. In.	1 Wire 53% Sq. In.	Internal Diameter Inches	Total Area 100% Sq. In.	2 Wires 31% In Sq. In.	Over 2 Wires 40% Sq. In.	1 Wire 53% Sq. In.
3/8	0.384	0.116	0.036	**0.046**	0.161	-	-	-	**-**	-
1/2	0.635	0.317	0.098	**0.127**	0.168	0.660	0.342	0.106	**0.137**	0.181
3/4	0.824	0.533	0.165	**0.213**	0.283	0.864	0.586	0.182	**0.235**	0.311
1	1.020	0.817	0.253	**0.327**	0.433	1.105	0.959	0.297	**0.384**	0.508
1 1/4	1.275	1.277	0.396	**0.511**	0.677	1.448	1.647	0.510	**0.659**	0.872
1 1/2	1.538	1.858	0.576	**0.743**	0.985	1.683	2.225	0.690	**0.890**	1.178
2	2.040	3.269	1.013	**1.307**	1.732	2.150	3.630	1.125	**1.452**	1.923
2 1/2	2.500	4.909	1.522	**1.963**	2.602	2.557	5.135	1.592	**2.054**	2.722
3	3.000	7.069	2.191	**2.827**	3.746	3.176	7.922	2.456	**3.169**	4.199
3 1/2	3.500	9.621	2.983	**3.848**	5.099	3.671	10.584	3.281	**4.234**	5.610
4	4.000	12.566	3.896	**5.027**	6.660	4.166	13.631	4.226	**5.452**	7.224

Table 4 shows area of **square inches**. The Table is divided different types of conduits and tubing.

The third column from the left, **"TOTAL 100%"** is the **cross-sectional area** of the conduit. The most often referred to column would be **"OVER 2 Wires 40%"**. Most conduit and raceway systems generally have **over** two conductors installed in them. •*Note: Hi-lite the 40% column.*

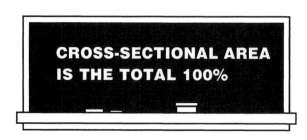

CROSS-SECTIONAL AREA
IS THE TOTAL 100%

Table 4 (Continued)

Trade Size Inches	Liquidtight Flexible Nonmetallic Conduit (Type LFNC-B*)					Liquidtight Flexible Nonmetallic Conduit (Type LFNC-A*)				
	Internal Diameter Inches	Total Area 100% Sq. In.	2 Wires 31% Sq. In.	Over 2 Wires 40% Sq. In.	1 Wire 53% Sq. In.	Internal Diameter Inches	Total Area 100% Sq. In.	2 Wires 31% Sq. In.	Over 2 Wires 40% Sq. In.	1 Wire 53% Sq. In.
3/8	0.494	0.192	0.059	**0.077**	0.102	0.495	0.192	0.060	**0.077**	0.102
1/2	0.632	0.314	0.097	**0.125**	0.166	0.630	0.312	0.097	**0.125**	0.165
3/4	0.830	0.541	0.168	**0.216**	0.287	0.825	0.535	0.166	**0.214**	0.283
1	1.054	0.873	0.270	**0.349**	0.462	1.043	0.854	0.265	**0.342**	0.453
1 1/4	1.395	1.528	0.474	**0.611**	0.810	1.383	1.502	0.466	**0.601**	0.796
1 1/2	1.588	1.981	0.614	**0.792**	1.050	1.603	2.018	0.626	**0.807**	1.070
2	2.033	3.246	1.006	**1.298**	1.720	2.603	3.343	1.036	**1.337**	1.772

*Corresponds to Section 351-22(2)   *Corresponds to Section 351-22(1)

Trade Size Inches	Liquidtight Flexible Metal Conduit					Rigid Metal Conduit				
	Internal Diameter Inches	Total Area 100% Sq. In.	2 Wires 31% Sq. In.	Over 2 Wires 40% Sq. In.	1 Wire 53% Sq. In.	Internal Diameter Inches	Total Area 100% Sq. In.	2 Wires 31% In Sq. In.	Over 2 Wires 40% Sq. In.	1 Wire 53% Sq. In.
3/8	0.494	0.192	0.059	**0.077**	0.102	-	-	-	-	-
1/2	0.632	0.314	0.097	**0.125**	0.166	0.632	0.314	0.097	**0.125**	0.166
3/4	0.830	0.541	0.168	**0.216**	0.287	0.836	0.549	0.170	**0.220**	0.291
1	1.054	0.873	0.270	**0.349**	0.462	1.063	0.887	0.275	**0.335**	0.470
1 1/4	1.395	1.528	0.474	**0.611**	0.810	1.394	1.526	0.473	**0.610**	0 809
1 1/2	1.588	1.981	0.614	**0.792**	1.050	1.624	2.071	0.642	**0.829**	1.098
2	2.033	3.246	1.006	**1.298**	1.720	2.083	3.408	1.056	**1.363**	1.806
2 1/2	2.493	4.881	1.513	**1.953**	2.587	2.489	4.866	1.508	**1.946**	2.579
3	3.085	7.475	2.317	**2.990**	3.962	3.090	7.499	2.325	**3.000**	3.974
3 1/2	3.520	9.731	3.017	**3.893**	5.158	3.570	10.010	3.103	**4.004**	5.305
4	4.020	12.692	3.935	**5.077**	6.727	4.050	12.882	3.994	**5.153**	6.828
5	-	-	-	-	-	5.073	20.212	6.266	**8.085**	10.713
6	-	-	-	-	-	6.093	29.158	9.039	**11.663**	15.454

This continuing page of Table 4 lists liquidtight flexible **NON**metallic conduits in types LFNC - B and LFNC-A and liquidtight flexible **METAL** conduit and **rigid metal conduit**.

Table 4. Dimensions and Percent Area of Conduit and Tubing (Areas Of Conduit or Tubing for the Combinations of Wires Permitted in Table 1, Chapter 9) (continued)

Trade Size Inches	Internal Diameter Inches	Total Area 100% Sq. In.	2 Wires 31% Sq. In.	Over 2 Wires 40% Sq. In.	1 Wire 53% Sq. In.	Internal Diameter Inches	Total Area 100% Sq. In.	2 Wires 31% Sq. In.	Over 2 Wires 40% Sq. In.	1 Wire 53% Sq. In.
	Rigid PVC Conduit, Schedule 80					Rigid PVC Conduit Schedule 40 and HDPE Conduit				
1/2	0.526	0.217	0.067	**0.087**	0.115	0.602	0.285	0.088	**0.114**	0.151
3/4	0.722	0.409	0.127	**0.164**	0.217	0.804	0.508	0.157	**0.203**	0.269
1	0.936	0.688	0.213	**0.275**	0.365	1.029	0.832	0.258	**0.333**	0.441
1 1/4	1.255	1.237	0.383	**0.495**	0.656	1.360	1.453	0.450	**0.581**	0.770
1 1/2	1.476	1.711	0.530	**0.684**	0.907	1.590	1.986	0.616	**0.794**	1.052
2	1.913	2.874	0.891	**1.150**	1.523	2.047	3.291	1.020	**1.316**	1.744
2 1/2	2.290	4.119	1.277	**1.647**	2.183	2.445	4.695	1.455	**1.878**	2.488
3	2.864	6.442	1.997	**2.577**	3.414	3.042	7.268	2.253	**2.907**	3.852
3 1/2	3.326	8.688	2.693	**3.475**	4.605	3.521	9.737	3.018	**3.895**	5.161
4	3.786	11.258	3.490	**4.503**	5.967	3.998	12.554	3.892	**5.022**	6.654
5	4.768	17.855	5.535	**7.142**	9.463	5.016	19.761	6.126	**7.904**	10.473
6	5.709	25.598	7.935	**10.239**	13.567	6.031	28.567	8.856	**11.427**	15.141
	Type Rigid A, Rigid PVC Conduit					Type EB, PVC Conduit				
1/2	0.700	0.385	0.119	**0.154**	0.024	-	-	-	-	-
3/4	0.910	0.650	0.202	**0.260**	0.345	-	-	-	-	-
1	1.175	1.084	0.336	**0.434**	0.575	-	-	-	-	-
1 1/4	1.500	1.767	0.548	**0.707**	0.937	-	-	-	-	-
1 1/2	1.720	2.324	0.720	**0.929**	1.231	-	-	-	-	-
2	2.155	3.647	1.131	**1.459**	1.933	2.221	3.874	1.201	**1.550**	2.053
2 1/2	2.635	5.453	1.690	**2.181**	2.890	-	-	-	-	-
3	3.230	8.194	2.540	**3.278**	4.343	3.330	8.709	2.700	**3.484**	4.616
3 1/2	3.690	10.694	3.315	**4.278**	5.668	3.804	11.365	3.523	**4.546**	6.023
4	4.180	13.723	4.254	**5.489**	7.273	4.289	14.448	4.479	**5.779**	7.657
5	-	-	-	-	-	5.316	22.195	6.881	**8.878**	11.763
6	-	-	-	-	-	6.336	31. 530	9.774	**12.612**	16.711

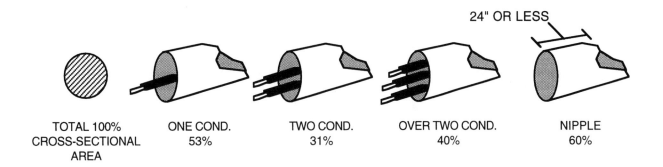

TOTAL 100%
CROSS-SECTIONAL
AREA

ONE COND.
53%

TWO COND.
31%

OVER TWO COND.
40%

24" OR LESS

NIPPLE
60%

Example: 1/2" Electrical Metallic Tubing (EMT) trade size conduit:

100% = .304
31% = .094
40% = .122
53% = .161
60% = .1824 (nipple fill **60%** of the 100% = 60% x .304 = .182)

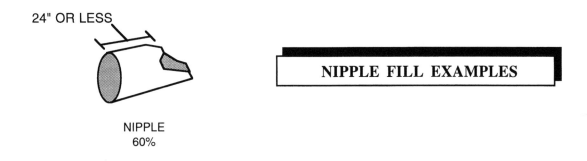

24" OR LESS

NIPPLE
60%

NIPPLE FILL EXAMPLES

1. A 2" rigid metal nipple can be filled to what area of square inch?

Table 4 - Rigid Metal Conduit - Trade Size 2" - Total Area 100% = 3.408 x 60% = **2.045**

2. A 1 1/2" rigid PVC conduit schedule 80 nipple can be filled to what area of square inch?

Table 4 - Rigid PVC Conduit Schedule 80 - Trade Size 1 1/2" - Total Area 100% = 1.711 x 60% = **1.027**

3. A 3" intermediate metal conduit (IMC) nipple can be filled to what area of square inch?

Table 4 - Intermediate Metal Conduit - Trade Size 3" - Total Area 100% = 7.922 x 60% = **4.753**

TABLE 5   AREA OF SQUARE INCH

Table 5 has four pages listing the dimensions of **insulated** and **covered** conductors, the area square inch for a **bare** conductor is found in Table 8.

The different types are listed under different pages in Table 5. When calculating conduit fill we will be using the column "Approx. Area Sq. In." in Table 5. Column 1 shows the insulation type, Column 2 lists the size of wire and Column 6 lists the area of square inch.

•Note: Hi-lite Column 6 in "Approx. Area Sq. In." your book.

EXAMPLES

Example: What is the area square inch for a #6 THW conductor?

Solution: THW insulation is shown on the second page of Table 5 - #6 THW = **.0726 square inch**.

Example: What is the area square inch for a #10 TW conductor?

Solution: TW insulation is shown on the first page of Table 5 - #10 TW = **.0243 square inch**.

Example: What is the area square inch for a #2/0 XHHW conductor?

Solution: XHHW insulation is shown on the fourth page of Table 5 - #2/0 = **.2190 square inch**.

Selecting the area of square inch for the previous three examples, was merely following the conductor size to the proper type insulation page and selecting the area of square inch. Exam questions often select conductor sizes #14, #12, and #10,

Example: What is the area square inch for a #14 THW conductor?

THW insulation is shown page one of Table 5. A #14 THW has an area of square inch of **.0139**.

Example: What is the area square inch for a #12 TW conductor?

TW insulation is shown on page one of Table 5. A #12 TW has an area square inch of **.0181.**

RHH, RHW, RHW-2 WITH OUTER COVERING

Example: What is the area square inch for a #14 RHH conductor **with** an outer cover?

Solution: RHH insulation is listed on page one of Table 5. The area of square inch for a #14 RHH conductor WITH and outer covering is **.0293.**

*RHH, RHW, RHW-2 WITHOUT OUTER COVERING

Example: What is the area square inch for a #14 RHH conductor **without** an outer cover?

Solution: The key word is **without** an outer cover. On page one of Table 5 at the very bottom of the page a note reads: ***Types RHH, RHW, and RHW-2 without outer covering.**

The insulation types RHH*, RHW*, RHW-2* all have an asterisk (*) this is the indicator for WITHOUT covering. A #14 RHH without outer covering has an area square inch of **.0209.**

This only applies to insulation types RHH, RHW, and RHW-2. If it is **with** an outer cover there is NO asterisk (*) beside it. If it is **without** outer cover it HAS an asterisk (*) beside it.

WITH OUTER COVER = RHH, RHW, RHW-2
WITHOUT OUTER COVER = RHH*, RHW*, RHW-2*

Page two of Table lists the other RHH, RHW, and RHW-2 conductors in sizes #12 through #2000.

Table 5. Dimensions of Insulated Conductors and Fixture Wires

Type: FFH-2, RFH-1, RFH-2, RH, RHH*, RHW*, RHW-2*, RHH, RHW, RHW-2, SF-1, SF-2, SFF-1, SFF-2, TF, TFF, THHW, THW, THW-2 , TW, XF, XFF

Type	Size	Approx. Diam In.	Approx. Area Sq. In.
RFH-2	18	0.136	0.0145
FFH-2	16	0.148	0.0172
RHW-2, RHH	14	0.193	0.0293
RHW	12	0.212	0.0353
	10	0.236	0.0437
RHH	8	0.326	0.0835
RHW	6	0.364	0.1041
RHW-2	4	0.412	0.1333
	3	0.44	0.1521
	2	0.472	0.1750
	1	0.582	0.2660
	1/0	0.622	0.3039
	2/0	0.688	0.3505
	3/0	0.72	0.4072
	4/0	0.778	0.4754
	250	0.895	0.6291
	300	0.95	0.7088
	350	1.001	0.7870
	400	1.048	0.8266
	500	1.133	1.0082
	600	1.243	1.2135
	700	1.314	1.3561
	750	1.348	1.4272
	800	1.38	1.4957
	900	1.444	1.6377
	1000	1.502	1.7719
	1250	1.729	2.3479
	1500	1.852	2.6938
	1750	1.966	3.0357
	2000	2.072	3.3719
SF-2, SFF-2	18	0.121	0.0115
	16	0.133	0.0139
	14	0.148	0.0172
SF-1, SFF-1	18	0.091	0.0065
RFH-1, AF, XF, XFF	18	0.106	0.0080
AF, TF, TFF, XF, XFF	16	0.118	0.0109
TW, XF, XFF, THHW, THW, THW-2	**14**	0.133	**0.0139**
TW	12	0.0152	0.0181
	10	0.0176	0.0243
	8	0.0236	0.0437
RHH*, RHW*, RHW-2*	**14**	0.163	**0.0209***
	12	0.182	0.0260

* Types RHH, RHW, and RHW-2 without outer covering

Table 5. Dimensions of Insulated Conductors and Fixture Wires (Continued)

Type: RHH*, RHW*, RHW-2*, THHN, THHW, THW, THW-2, TFN, TFFN, THWN, THWN-2, XF, XFF

Type	Size	Approx. Diam In.	Approx.Area Sq. In.
RHH*, RHW*, RHW-2*	12	0.182	**0.0260**
THHW, THW, XF, XFF	10	0.206	**0.0333**
RHH*, RHW*, RHW-2*	8	0.266	**0.0556**
THHW, THW, THW-2			
TW, THW	6	0.304	**0.0726**
THHW	4	0.352	**0.0973**
THW-2	3	0.38	**0.1134**
RHH*	2	0.412	**0.1333**
RHW*	1	0.492	**0.1901**
RHW-2*	1/0	0.532	**0.2223**
	2/0	0.578	**0.2624**
	3/0	0.63	**0.3117**
	4/0	0.688	**0.3718**
	250	0.765	**0.4596**
	300	0.82	**0.5281**
	350	0.871	**0.5958**
	400	0.918	**0.6619**
	500	1.003	**0.7901**
	600	1.113	**0.9729**
	700	1.184	**1.1010**
	750	1.218	**1.1652**
	800	1.25	**1.2272**
	900	1.314	**1.3561**
	1000	1.372	**1.4784**
	1250	1.539	**1.8602**
	1500	1.662	**2.1695**
	1750	1.776	**2.4773**
	2000	1.882	**2.7818**
TFN	18	0.084	0.0055
TFFN	16	0.096	0.0072
THHN	14	0.111	0.0097
THWN	12	0.13	0.0133
THWN-2	10	0.164	0.0211
	8	0.216	0.0366
	6	0.254	0.0507
	4	0.324	0.0824
	3	0.352	0.0973
	2	0.384	0.1158
	1	0.446	0.1562
	1/0	0.486	0.1855
	2/0	0.532	0.2223
	3/0	0.584	0.2679
	4/0	0.642	0.3237
	250	0.711	0.3970
	300	0.766	0.4608

* Types RHH, RHW, and RHW-2 without outer covering

TABLE 5. (CONTINUED)

TYPE: FEP, FEPB, PAF, PAFF, PF, PFA, PFAH, PFF, PGF, PGFF, PTF, PTFF, TFE, THHN, THWN, THWN-2, Z, ZF, ZFF

Type	Size	Approx. Diam In.	Approx.Area Sq. In.
THHN	350	0.817	0.5242
THWN	400	0.864	0.5863
THWN-2	500	0.949	0.7073
	600	1.051	0.8676
	700	1.122	0.9887
	750	1.156	1.0496
	800	1.188	1.1085
	900	1.252	1.2311
	1000	1.31	1.3478
PF, PGFF, PGF, PFF,	18	0.086	0.0058
PTF, PAF, PTFF, PAFF	16	0.098	0.0075
PF, PGFF, PGF, PFF PTF, PAF, PTFF, PAFF, TFE, FEP, PFA FEPB, PFAH	14	0.113	0.0100
TFE, FEP	12	0.132	0.0137
PFA, FEPB	10	0.156	0.0191
PFAH	8	0.206	0.0333
	6	0.244	0.0468
	4	0.292	0.0670
	3	0.32	0.0804
	2	0.352	0.0973
TFE, PFAH	1	0.422	0.1399
TFE	1/0	0.462	0.1676
PFA	2/0	0.508	0.2027
PFAH, Z	3/0	0.56	0.2463
	4/0	0.618	0.3000
ZF, ZFF	18	0.076	0.0045
	16	0.088	0.0061
Z, ZF, ZFF	14	0.103	0.0083
Z	12	0.122	0.0117
	10	0.156	0.0191
	8	0.196	0.0302
	6	0.234	0.0430
	4	0.282	0.0625
	3	0.33	0.0855
	2	0.362	0.1029
	1	0.402	0.1269

TABLE 5. Dimensions of Insulated Conductors and Fixture Wires (Continued)

TYPE: KF-1, KF-2, KFF-1, KFF-2, XHH, XHHW, XHHW-2, ZW

Type	Size	Approx. Diam In.	Approx.Area Sq. In.
XHHW, ZW XHHW-2 XHH	14	0.133	0.0139
	12	0.152	0.0181
	10	0.176	0.0243
	8	0.236	0.0437
	6	0.274	0.0590
	4	0.322	0.0814
	3	0.35	0.0962
	2	0.382	0.1146
XHHW XHHW-2 XHH	1	0.442	0.1534
	1/0	0.482	0.1825
	2/0	0.528	0.2190
	3/0	0.58	0.2642
	4/0	0.638	0.3197
	250	0.705	0.3904
	300	0.76	0.4536
	350	0.811	0.5166
	400	0.858	0.5782
	500	0.943	0.6984
	600	1.053	0.8709
	700	1.124	0.9923
	750	1.158	1.0532
	800	1.19	1.1122
	900	1.254	1.2351
	1000	1.312	1.3519
	1250	1.479	1.7180
	1500	1.602	2.0157
	1750	1.716	2.3127
	2000	1.822	2.6073
KF-2 KFF-2	18	0.063	0.0031
	16	0.075	0.0044
	14	0.09	0.0064
	12	0.109	0.0093
	10	0.133	0.0139
KF-1 KFF-1	18	0.057	0.0026
	16	0.069	0.0037
	14	0.084	0.0055
	12	0.103	0.0083
	10	0.127	0.0127

RHH, RHW, RHW-2   SUMMARY

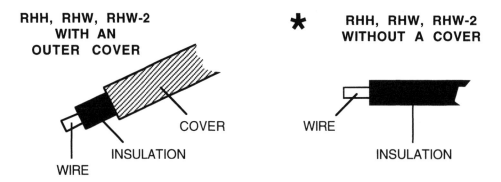

RHH, RHW, RHW-2
WITH AN
OUTER COVER

COVER

INSULATION

WIRE

★ RHH, RHW, RHW-2
WITHOUT A COVER

WIRE

INSULATION

Example: What is the area square inch for a #12 RHW conductor without an outer covering?

Solution: Table 5 lists a #12 RHW* conductor without an outer covering at **.0260 sq.in.**

Example: How many #4 RHH conductors with an outer covering can you install in a 1" EMT conduit?

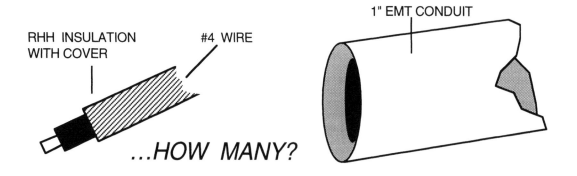

RHH INSULATION
WITH COVER

#4 WIRE

1" EMT CONDUIT

...HOW MANY?

Solution: Use Tables 4 & 5 for this calculation.

Table 4 - 1" EMT conduit 40% fill = .346 square inch
Table 5 - #4 RHH conductor = .1333 square inch

.346/.1333 = 2.59 or **2 conductors.**

BARE CONDUCTORS - AREA SQUARE INCHES

Example: What is area square inch for a #8 bare conductor in a raceway?

This is an excellent exam question because you have so many Code rules to consider.
#8 bare, copper or aluminum? Section 110.5 says when not specified, it's **copper**.

Table 8 must be used to find the area square inch for a **BARE** conductor.

Table 8. Conductor Properties

Size AWG / kcmil	Area Circ. Mils	Stranding Quan-tity	Stranding Diam. In.	Overall Diam. In.	Overall Area In.²	Copper Uncoated ohm / kFT	Copper Coated ohm / kFT	Aluminum ohm / kFT
18	1620	1	—	0.040	0.001	7.77	8.08	12.8
18	1620	7	0.015	0.046	0.002	7.95	8.45	13.1
16	2580	1	—	0.051	0.002	4.89	5.08	8.05
16	2580	7	0.019	0.058	0.003	4.99	5.29	8.21
14	4110	1	—	0.064	0.003	3.07	3.19	5.06
14	4110	7	0.024	0.073	0.004	3.14	3.26	5.17
12	6530	1	—	0.081	0.005	1.93	2.01	3.18
12	6530	7	0.030	0.092	0.006	1.98	2.05	3.25
10	10380	1	—	0.102	0.008	1.21	1.26	2.00
10	10380	7	0.038	0.116	0.011	1.24	1.29	2.04
8	16510	1	—	0.128	0.013	0.764	0.786	1.26
8	16510	7	0.049	0.146	0.017	0.778	0.809	1.28
6	26240	7	0.061	0.184	0.027	0.491	0.510	0.808
4	41740	7	0.077	0.232	0.042	0.308	0.321	0.508
3	52620	7	0.087	0.260	0.053	0.245	0.254	0.403
2	66360	7	0.097	0.292	0.067	0.194	0.201	0.319
1	83690	19	0.066	0.332	0.087	0.154	0.160	0.253
1/0	105600	19	0.074	0.372	0.109	0.122	0.127	0.201
2/0	133100	19	0.084	0.418	0.137	0.0967	0.101	0.159
3/0	167800	19	0.094	0.470	0.173	0.0766	0.0797	0.126
4/0	211600	19	0.106	0.528	0.219	0.0608	0.0626	0.100
250	—	37	0.082	0.575	0.260	0.0515	0.0535	0.0847
300	—	37	0.090	0.630	0.312	0.0429	0.0446	0.0707
350	—	37	0.097	0.681	0.364	0.0367	0.0382	0.0605
400	—	37	0.104	0.728	0.416	0.0321	0.0331	0.0529
500	—	37	0.116	0.813	0.519	0.0258	0.0265	0.0424
600	—	61	0.099	0.893	0.626	0.0214	0.0223	0.0353
700	—	61	0.107	0.964	0.730	0.0184	0.0189	0.0303
750	—	61	0.111	0.998	0.782	0.0171	0.0176	0.0282
800	—	61	0.114	1.030	0.834	0.0161	0.0166	0.0265
900	—	61	0.122	1.094	0.940	0.0143	0.0147	0.0235
1000	—	61	0.128	1.152	1.042	0.0129	0.0132	0.0212
1250	—	91	0.117	1.289	1.305	0.0103	0.0106	0.0169
1500	—	91	0.128	1.412	1.566	0.00858	0.00883	0.0141
1750	—	127	0.117	1.526	1.829	0.00735	0.00756	0.0121
2000	—	127	0.126	1.632	2.092	0.00643	0.00662	0.0106

These resistance values are valid ONLY for the parameters as given. Using conductors having coated strands, different stranding type, and especially, other temperatures, change the resistance.

Formula for temperature change: $R_2 = R_1 (1 + \alpha (T_2 - 75))$ where: $\alpha_{cu} = 0.00323$, $\alpha_{AL} = 0.00330$.

Conductors with compact and compressed stranding have about 9 percent and 3 percent, respectively, smaller bare conductor diameters than those shown. See **Table 5A** for actual compact cable dimensions.

The IACS conductivities used: bare copper = 100%, aluminum = 61%.

Class B stranding is listed as well as solid for some sizes. Its overall diameter and area is that of its circumscribing circle.

(FPB): The construction information is per NEMA WC8-1976 (Rev 5-1980). The resistance is calculated per National Bureau of Standards Handbook 100, dated 1966, and Handbook 109, dated 1972.

Table 8, the column for area square inch shows **two** dimensions **0.013** or **0.017** for a #8 bare conductor. The third column in Table 8 lists "Stranding" "Quantity", for a #8 quantity **1** = 0.013 square inch. The quantity **1** is for **solid** conductor (1 strand). #8 conductor quantity **7** = 0.017 square inch. The quantity **7** is for stranded conductor (7 strands).

Now it's decision time again; which dimensions do we use 0.013 or 0.017? The question asks for the area of square inch for a #8 bare conductor installed in a **raceway**.
    Code Section 310.3: Where installed in **raceways**, conductors of size #8 and larger shall be **stranded**.
    The answer for a #8 bare copper conductor in a raceway is **0.017 square inch**.

COMPACT ALUMINUM CONDUCTORS

A new Table **5A** was added to the 1987 Code which lists the dimensions for Aluminum building wire.

This Table lists Aluminum **bare conductor**** (compact conductor), also aluminum conductors with type THW, THHN, and XHHW insulations. If the exam question asks for area square inch for an **aluminum** conductor be sure to check this new Table 5A.

Definition :   Compact stranding is the result of a manufacturing process where the standard conductor is **compressed** to the extent that the interstices (voids between strand wires) are virtually eliminated.

Table 5A. ▶ Aluminum Building Wire Nominal Dimensions* and Areas

Bare Conductor			Type THW and THHW		Type THHN		Type XHHW		
Size AWG or kcmil	Number of Strands	Diam. Inches	Approx. Diam. Inches	Approx. Area Sq. In.	Approx. Diam. Inches	Approx. Area Sq. In.	Approx. Diam. Inches	Approx. Area Sq. In.	Size AWG or MCM
8	7	.134	.255	.0510	—	—	.224	.0394	8
6	7	.169	.290	.0660	.240	.0452	.260	.0530	6
4	7	.213	.335	.0881	.305	.0730	.305	.0730	4
2	7	.268	.390	.1194	.360	.1017	.360	.1017	2
1	19	.299	.465	.1698	.415	.1352	.415	.1352	1
1/0	19	.336	.500	.1963	.450	.1590	.450	.1590	1/0
2/0	19	.376	.545	.2332	.495	.1924	.490	.1885	2/0
3/0	19	.423	.590	.2733	.540	.2290	.540	.2290	3/0
4/0	19	.475	.645	.3267	.595	.2780	.590	.2733	4/0
250	37	.520	.725	.4128	.670	.3525	.660	.3421	250
300	37	.570	.775	.4717	.720	.4071	.715	.4015	300
350	37	.616	.820	.5281	.770	.4656	.760	.4536	350
400	37	.659	.865	.5876	.815	.5216	.800	.5026	400
500	37	.736	.940	.6939	.885	.6151	.880	.6082	500
600	61	.813	1.050	.8659	.985	.7620	.980	.7542	600
700	61	.877	1.110	.9676	1.050	.8659	1.050	.8659	700
750	61	.908	1.150	1.0386	1.075	.9076	1.090	.9331	750
1000	61	1.060	1.285	1.2968	1.255	1.2370	1.230	1.1882	1000

* Dimensions are from industry sources

Note 1 mentioned to see Annex C for maximum number of conductors and fixture wires, **all of the same size,** permitted in a conduit or tubing.

Annex C is part of the requirements of the Code.

When conductors are **all the same size** (area sq. in.) you can turn to Annex C and determine the size of conduit required. There are 12 Tables so always check the heading of the Table to make sure you have selected the **correct** Table.

Table C1•	Electrical Metallic Tubing (EMT)	Conductors and Fixture Wires
Table C1A	Electrical Metallic Tubing (EMT)	**Compact Conductors**
Table C2•	Electrical **Non**metallic Tubing (ENT)	Conductors and Fixture Wires
Table C2A	Electrical **Non**metallic Tubing (ENT)	**Compact Conductors**
Table C3•	Flexible Metallic Conduit (greenfield)	Conductors and Fixture Wires
Table C3A	Flexible Metallic Conduit (greenfield)	**Compact Conductors**
Table C4•	Intermediate Metallic Conduit (IMC)	Conductors and Fixture Wires
Table C4A	Intermediate Metallic Conduit (IMC)	**Compact Conductors**
Table C5•	Liquidtight Flexible **Non**metallic Conduit (Type FNMC-B**) Conductors and Fixture Wires	
Table C5A	Liquidtight Flexible **Non**metallic Conduit (Type FNMC-B**) **Compact Conductors**	
Table C6•	Liquidtight Flexible **Non**metallic Conduit (Type FNMC-A**) Conductors and Fixture Wires	
Table C6A	Liquidtight Flexible **Non**metallic Conduit (Type FNMC-A**) **Compact Conductors**	
Table C7•	Liquidtight Flexible Metallic Conduit	Conductors and Fixture Wires
Table C7A	Liquidtight Flexible Metallic Conduit	**Compact Conductors**
Table 8•	Rigid Metallic Conduit	Conductors and Fixture Wires
Table 8A	Rigid Metallic Conduit	**Compact Conductors**
Table 9•	Rigid PVC Conduit Schedule **80**	Conductors and Fixture Wires
Table 9A	Rigid PVC Conduit Schedule **80**	**Compact Conductors**
Table 10•	Rigid PVC Conduit Schedule **40** and **HDPE**	Conductors and Fixture Wires
Table 10A	Rigid PVC Conduit Schedule **40** and **HDPE**	CompactConductors
Table 11•	**Type A** Rigid PVC Conduit	Conductors and Fixture Wires
Table 11A	**Type A** Rigid PVC Conduit	**Compact Conductors**
Table 12•	**Type EB** PVC Conduit	Conductors and Fixture Wires
Table 12A	**Type EB** PVC Conduit	**Compact Conductors**

•This table is for **concentric stranded** conductors only. Tables "A" are for compact conductors.

*Types RHH, RHW, and RHW-2 **without** outer covering.

Definition :   **Compact stranding** is the result of a manufacturing process where the standard conductor is **compressed** to the extent that the interstices (voids between strand wires) are virtually eliminated.

**CONDUIT FILL EXAMPLES
CONDUCTORS ALL THE SAME SIZE**

1. How many #12 THHN conductors can you install in a 3/4" EMT?

Table 4 - 3/4" EMT 40% fill = .213 sq.in.
Table 5 - #12 THHN = .0133 sq.in.   .213/.0133 = **16 conductors**
Table C1 of the Appendix also shows 16 conductors.

2. How many #10 TW conductors can you install in a 1" rigid metal conduit?

Table 4 - 1" rigid metal conduit 40% fill = .355 sq.in.
Table 5 - #10 TW = .0243 sq.in.   .355/.0243 = **14 conductors**
Table C8 of the Annex also shows 14 conductors.

3. How many #6 RHW* conductors can you install in a 1 1/2" IMC?

Table 4 - 1 1/2" IMC 40% fill = .890 sq.in.
Table 5 - #6 RHW* = .0726 sq.in.   .890/.0726 = **12 conductors**
Table C4 of the Annex also shows 12 conductors.

4. How many #4 XHHW conductors can you install in a 2" flexible metal conduit?

Table 4 - 2" flexible metal conduit 40% fill = 1.307 sq.in.
Table 5 - #4 XHHW = .0814 sq.in.   1.307/.0814 = **16 conductors**
Table C3 of the Annex also shows 16 conductors.

5. How many #1/0 THWN conductors can you install in a 3" rigid PVC conduit, schedule 80?

Table 4 - 3" rigid PVC conduit schedule 80 @40% fill = 2.577 sq.in.
Table 5 - #1/0 THWN = .1855 sq.in.   2.577/.1855 = 13**.89** or **14 conductors**

Remember Note 7 stated: Where the calculated number of conductors, **all of the same size**, includes a decimal fraction, the next higher whole number shall be used where this decimal is **0.8** or larger.

Table C9 of the Annex also shows 14 conductors.

When conductors are **all the same size** you can use Tables 4 and 5 or Annex C Tables.

BOX FILL

Count the conductors using 314.16(B) (1) through (5)
•Each conductor counts as one
•Pigtails and jumpers don't count
•Clamps count as one
•Studs count as one
•Hickeys count as one
•Switch or receptacle (device) counts as two
•Equipment grounding counductors count as one
*an additional one is counted for isolated grounding wires

A box containing wires of different sizes:
•Counting the clamps, fixture studs, or hickeys is based on the largest conductor in the box.
•Counting the device is based on the largest conductor connected to a device.
•Counting the green or bare wire is based on the largest green or bare wire present in the box.

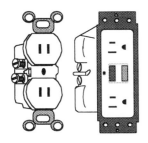

Even though a GFCI receptacle is larger than a standard duplex receptacle and a dimmer switch is larger than a standard single pole switch the Code still counts them as the same size device in calculating box fill.

Table 314.16(B) lists the volume of free space within the box for each conductor in cubic inches.

Pull and junction boxes for raceways containing conductors #4 or larger are sized per section 314.28. Over 600 volts per section 314.70.

CONDUIT FILL

•Table 1 shows the percent of fill
•A nipple is 24" or less in length and can be filled 60%
•Round up to the next conductor at .8 and larger
•Table 4 lists cross-section area (100%) and 40% fill over 2 wires in a conduit
•Table 5 lists the area square inch of an insulated conductor
•Table 5A is for Compact Aluminum area square inch
•Table 8 is for a bare conductor area square inch
•Annex C Tables are for conductors all of the same size

•When conductors are all the same size you can use Tables 4 and 5 or Annex C Tables.

CHAPTER 4 TEST 1 BOX & RACEWAY FILL

1. A conduit body contains the following conductors. Three #12 THHN conductors running through the fitting. Two #12 THHN conductors which enter the fitting and are spliced in the fitting to two #12 THHN conductors which leave the fitting. What is the minimum cubic inch capacity that the manufacturer must have marked on the conduit body?

(a) 13.50 cubic inches   (b) 15.75 cubic inches   (c) 16.5 cubic inches   (d) 18 cubic inches

2. What size rigid metal conduit is required to contain the following compact aluminum conductors: four #1/0 THHN, and three #250 kcmil THHN?

(a) 2"   (b) 2 1/2"   (c) 3"   (d) 3 1/2"

3. A two gang metal box containing nonmetallic cable clamps along with a switch and receptacle is installed in the kitchen of a dwelling unit. The switch is connected to a piece of #14 from a 15 amp circuit and the receptacle is connected to a piece of #12 on a 20 amp circuit. The wiring method is nonmetallic sheathed cable with a ground. The minimum cubic inch capacity box permitted by Code is _____ cubic inches.

(a) 21.5   (b) 22   (c) 23   (d) 24

4. 3" Intermediate Metal Conduit has a total square inch area of _____ square inches.

(a) 7.475   (b) 7.499   (c) 7.922   (d) 8.846

5. What is the minimum cubic inch capacity necessary to contain 2 pieces of #14-2 and one piece of #12-2 romex with ground, assuming the box has cable clamps.

(a) 14 cubic inch   (b) 15 cubic inch   (c) 16 cubic inch   (d) 17 cubic inch

CHAPTER 4   TEST 2   BOX FILL

1. The volume required for two #12 TW grounding conductors and two #12 TW conductors in a box would be _____ cubic inches.

(a) 9   (b) 6.75   (c) 6   (d) 4.5

2. What is the cubic inch capacity required for a device box containing one duplex receptacle, cable clamps and two #12-2 with ground nonmetallic sheathed cables (romex)?

(a) 13.5 cu.in.   (b) 15.75 cu.in.   (c) 16 cu.in.   (d) 18 cu.in.

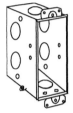

3. What size octagon box is required for 4 - #12 and 3 - #14 conductors?

(a) 1 1/4"   (b) 1 1/2"   (c) 2"   (d) 2 1/8"

4. What is the minimum cubic inch allowed for the box shown below? The box contains three cable clamps, two - #12-2 w/grd romex cables to the duplex receptacle and one- #12-2 w/grd romex cable to the single-pole switch.

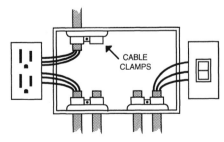

CABLE CLAMPS

(a) 34 cu.in.   (b) 31.5 cu.in.   (c) 27 cu.in   (d) none of these

CHAPTER 4   TEST 3   BOX FILL

1. A metal device box contains cable clamps, six #12 conductors, and one single-pole switch. Which of the following is the minimum size box permitted?

(a) 12 cubic inch   (b) 13 1/2 cubic inch   (c) 15 cubic inch   (d) 20.25 cubic inch

2. When counting the number of conductors in a box, a conductor running through the box is counted as _____ conductor(s).

(a) not counted   (b) one   (c) two   (d) count only if ungrounded

3. How many #12 conductors are permitted in a 3" x 2" x 1 1/2" box?

(a) 5   (b) 4   (c) 3   (d) 2

4. What size box is required for the following?

1 - #14 ungrounded conductor (black)
1 - #14 grounded conductor   (white)
1 - #14 grounding conductor   (green)
2 - #14 fixture wires

(a) 4 cubic inch   (b) 6 cubic inch   (c) 8 cubic inch   (d) 10 cubic inch

5. What size box is required for the twelve #10 THW conductors listed below?

4 - #10 THW (black)
4 - #10 THW (white)
4 - #10 THW (green)

(a) 27.5 cubic inch   (b) 30 cubic inch   (c) 22.5 cubic inch   (d) 20.25 cubic inch

6. How many #12 conductors can you install in a 3" x 2" x 2 1/2" device box containing cable clamps and a duplex receptacle?

(a) 5   (b) 4   (c) 3   (d) 2

CHAPTER 4   TEST 4   RACEWAY FILL

1. What is the minimum dimension for "X" in the box shown below?

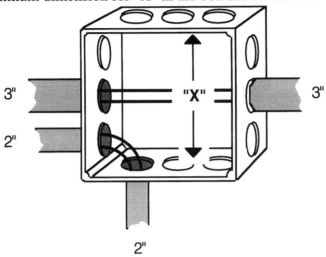

3"

"X"

3"

2"

2"

(a) 10"   (b) 12"   (c) 24"   (d) 26"

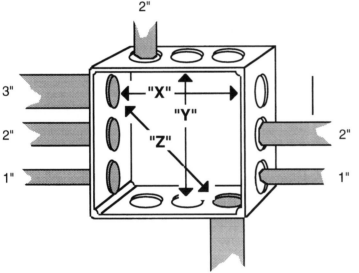

2"

3"

"X"

"Y"

2"

"Z"

1"

3"

2. The box shown to the left:

X = ____ inches

Y = ____ inches

Z = ____ inches

3. The size of the pull box shown to the right should not be less than ____.

(a) 12" x 14"
(b) 16" x 18"
(c) 22" x 22"
(d) 24" x 24"

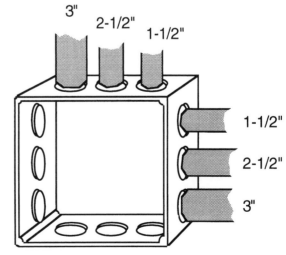

3"

2-1/2"

1-1/2"

1-1/2"

2-1/2"

3"

CHAPTER 4 TEST 5 RACEWAY FILL

1. What is the total cross sectional area of a 2" Intermediate Metal conduit?

(a) 2.150   (b) 3.630   (c) 1.456   (d) 2.223

2. When bare conductors are permitted by other sections of the Code, the dimensions for bare conductors in _____ shall be permitted.

(a) Table 310.16   (b) Table 8, Chapter 9   (c) Table 310.17   (d) Table 9, Chapter 9

3. The approximate area in square inches of a #14 RHH conductor without outer covering is _____ square inches.

(a) 0.0209   (b) 0.0353   (c) 0.026   (d) 0.163

4. The area of allowable fill of a 1 1/4" rigid steel conduit nipple is _____ square inches.

(a) 1.394   (b) 1.526   (c) .610   (d) .916

5. What size PVC schedule 40 conduit is required for the following conductors?

10 - #12 THW
12 - #10 TW
 6 - #8 THHN
 8 - #6 THWN

(a) 2"   (b) 2 1/2"   (c) 3"   (d) 3 1/2"

6. If six #14 TW conductors at .0139 square inches each, and eight #8 THWN conductors at .0366 inches each, were installed in an 18" conduit between two cabinets, the minimum size PVC schedule 80 conduit, permitted by the Code, would be _____ in diameter (trade size).

(a) 3/4"   (b) 1"   (c) 1 1/4"   (d) 1 1/2"

CHAPTER 4 TEST 6 RACEWAY FILL

1. How many #6 XHHW conductors can be installed in a 2" EMT conduit?

(a) 11   (b) 16   (c) 21   (d) 22

2. The internal diameter of a 1" trade size flexible metal conduit is _____ inch.

(a) 1   (b) 1.105   (c) .327   (d) 1.020

3. An existing 2" rigid steel conduit contains ten #8 THHN conductors, how many #8 XHHW conductors can be added to this existing raceway?

(a) 23   (b) 22   (c) 27   (d) none of these

4. How many #12 THW conductors can be installed in a 1 1/2" PVC schedule 40 conduit?

(a) 15   (b) 16   (c) 23   (d) 44

5. What size IMC conduit is required to install all of the following conductors?

4 - #14 THW
2 - #12 RHW (without outer cover)
2 - #14 RHH (with outer cover)
6 - #14 THHN
3 - #12 stranded bare grounding conductors

(a) 1/2"   (b) 3/4"   (c) 1"   (d) 1 1/4"

6. If half of the permitted fill for a 1 1/4" rigid steel conduit between two cabinets located 20" apart is occupied, how many #14 THHN conductors can you add?

(a) 38   (b) 45   (c) 47   (d) 51

CHAPTER 4 TEST 7 RACEWAY FILL

1. How many #6 XHHW conductors can you install in a 1 1/2" liquidtight flexible metal conduit?

(a) 9   (b) 12   (c) 13   (d) 21

2. What percent fill is permitted for one cable in a conduit?

(a) 53%   (b) 38%   (c) 40%   (d) 35%

3. How many #14 TW conductors can be installed in a 1/2" rigid PVC schedule 80 conduit nipple 18" long?

(a) 5   (b) 6   (c) 7   (d) 9

4. What length of nipple may utilize 60% cross-sectional conductor fill?

(a) 30"   (b) 25"   (c) 24"   (d) none of these

5. The cross-sectional area of a 1" Type A rigid PVC conduit is _____ square inches.

(a) .52   (b) 1.049   (c) 1.084   (d) .34

6. What is the area square inch of a #8 bare conductor installed in a 2" raceway?

(a) .34   (b) .86   (c) 0.013   (d) 0.017

7. How many #12 THHN conductors can you install in a 2" EMT conduit nipple?

(a) 48   (b) 49   (c) 77   (d) 151

8. How many #12 RHW conductors with outer covering can you install in a 1" rigid steel conduit?

(a) 6   (b) 7   (c) 8   (d) 10

CHAPTER 4 TEST 8 RACEWAY FILL
---

1. How many #10 RHW conductors with outer covering can be installed in a 1 1/2" rigid steel conduit 20" in length installed between two junction boxes?

(a) 28   (b) 36   (c) 37   (d) 41

2. How many #14 FEP wires can be installed in a 3/4" flexible metal conduit?

(a) 19   (b) 16   (c) 15   (d) 21

3. What size cable tray width is required for six #500 kcmil THW conductors, four #750 kcmil THW conductors, and six #1000 kcmil THW conductors?

(a) 18"   (b) 24"   (c) 30"   (d) 36"

4. How many #2/0 THW conductors can be installed in a 4" x 4" wireway?

(a) 10   (b) 12   (c) 13   (d) 15

5. 1 1/2" liquidtight flexible nonmetallic Type LFNC-B conduit 30" long, the allowable fill would be _____ square inches.

(a) .829   (b) .807   (c) .792   (d) .611

6. How many #12 RHW copper conductors (without outer cover) can be installed in a 1" schedule 80 PVC conduit 20" long?

(a) 8   (b) 13   (c) 15   (d) 16

7. How many square inches of a 1 1/2" EMT nipple 18" long does eight #8 THW conductors take up in the nipple?

(a) .3496   (b) .4448   (c) .6832   (d) none of these

8. How many #14 THHN conductors can be installed in a 3/4" PVC schedule 40 nipple?

(a) 15   (b) 12   (c) 23   (d) 31

CHAPTER 4 TEST 9 RACEWAY FILL

1. A gutter measures 6" x 6". How many #500 kcmil THHN conductors can you install?

(a) 10   (b) 11   (c) 12   (d) 15

2. What is the maximum number of #14 THHN conductors permitted in 3/8" flexible metal conduit?

(a) 0   (b) 2   (c) 3   (d) 4

3. How many #1/0 XHHW conductors can be installed in a cellular concrete floor raceway having a total of 10 square inches?

(a) 10   (b) 15   (c) 22   (d) 25

4. If ten #8 RHW conductors with outer covering were installed in a 2" rigid steel conduit, how many #8 XHHW conductors could you add to this raceway?

(a) 8   (b) 11   (c) 12   (d) 13

5. The allowable area to be filled of a 2" Type A rigid PVC conduit is ____ square inches, if it contains three or more conductors.

(a) 2.067   (b) 3.36   (c) 0.8268   (d) 1.459

6. The following conductors are to be installed in a single conduit. What is the total area of square inches required for these conductors?

6 - #12 RHW without outer cover
4 - #14 RHH with outer cover
8 - #12 THW
4 - #6 XHHW
1 - #8 bare copper

(a) 0.671   (b) 0.759   (c) 0.7978   (d) none of these

CHAPTER 5

COOKING EQUIPMENT DEMAND FACTORS

Demand Factor: The ratio of the maximum demand of a system, or part of a system, to the total connected load of a system or the part of the system under consideration.

INTRODUCTION When an exam question asks for the **minimum** size conductor or service size, you must apply all the **demand factors** that can be applied to the calculation. If you forget one demand, then you never reach the **minimum**.

A demand factor is a reduction in conductor size. When calculating demand factors, you should think of the lowest amount, smallest size, the **minimum** permitted is your best deal, as copper is money $$$.

Starting in this Chapter with Cooking Equipment Demands and following in the next two chapters with feeder-service demands in dwelling and commercial occupancies, we will be applying the various demand factors allowed to the equipment.

The Code permits a demand factor (reduction) to be used in certain areas of a system. Lighting, receptacles, cooking equipment, clothes dryers, fastened in place appliances, are some of the loads the Code allows a demand factor to be applied to.

The reason for allowing these demand factors, **all** the lights won't be on at the **same** time, nor will **all** the receptacles be **fully** loaded at the **same** time, etc.

Example: Section 220.60. Electric heat and air conditioning shouldn't **both** be on at the **same** time, the Code allows the **smallest** load to be omitted in the feeder or service calculation.

Throughout Article 220 you are permitted a demand factor on certain parts of the system.

T.220.55 DEMAND LOADS HOUSEHOLD COOKING EQUIPMENT

Table 220.55. Demand loads for household electric ranges, wall-mounted ovens, counter-mounted cooking units, and other household cooking appliances over **1 3/4 kw** rating. 1 3/4 kw = 1750 watts.

The first column of Table 220.55 shows **Number of Appliances**. The column lists 61 and over, a student once asked "How can I get 61 ranges in one kitchen in my house"? Table 220.55 as well as all the demand factors are applied to the **feeder or service** loads. The **service** will carry **all** the appliances. Example, a 60 unit apartment complex, each unit has an electric range, the service will carry this load. Whereas the **branch circuit** would carry the load for one unit.

When calculating demand factors, remember they are for feeder and service loads, the **only** demand factor permitted for a **branch circuit** is Note 4 to Table 220.55.

CHAPTER 5   COOKING EQUIPMENT DEMAND FACTORS

Table 220.55. Demand Factors and Loads for Household Electric Ranges, Wall-Mounted Ovens, Counter-Mounted Cooking Units, and Other Household Cooking Appliances over 1-3/4 KW Rating. Column C to be used in all cases except as otherwise permitted in Note 3 below.

NUMBER OF APPLIANCES	COLUMN A (Less than 3-1/2 kW Rating)	COLUMN B (3-1/2 kW to 8-3/4 kW Rating)	COLUMN C MaximumDemand (KW) (See Notes) (Not over 12 kW Rating)
1	80%	80%	8 kW
2	75%	65%	11 kW
3	70%	55%	14 kW
4	66%	50%	17 kW
5	62%	45%	20 kW
6	59%	43%	21 kW
7	56%	40%	22 kW
8	53%	36%	23 kW
9	51%	35%	24 kW
10	49%	34%	25 kW
11	47%	32%	26 kW
12	45%	32%	27 kW
13	43%	32%	28 kW
14	41%	32%	29 kW
15	40%	32%	30 kW
16	39%	28%	31 kW
17	38%	28%	32 kW
18	37%	28%	33 kW
19	36%	28%	34 kW
20	35%	28%	35 kW
21	34%	26%	36 kW
22	33%	26%	37 kW
23	32%	26%	38 kW
24	31%	26%	39 kW
25	30%	26%	40 kW
26-30	30%	24%	15 kW plus 1 kW
31-40	30%	22%	for each range
41-50	30%	20%	25 kW plus 3/4
51-60	30%	18%	kW for each
61 & over	30%	16%	range

Column C (Not over 12 kw Rating). Example, one 12 kw range would have a **maximum demand** of 8 kw.

•Note: Above Column C, **MAXIMUM DEMAND** (REDUCTION) is the largest amount of kw you would have to use in the calculation, it could be **less** than the maximum demand from Col. C.

Example:
1 - 12 kw range = 8 kw maximum demand from Column C
1 - 11 kw range = 8 kw maximum demand from Column C
1 - 10 kw range = 8 kw maximum demand from Column C
1 - 9 kw range = 8 kw maximum demand from Column C
1 - 8 kw range = **6.4 kw** maximum demand from Column **B @ 80%**

Note 3 below Table 220.55 reads: Over 1 3/4 kw through 8 3/4 kw. In **lieu** of the method provided in Column C, it shall be permissible to add the nameplate ratings of all ranges rated more than 1 3/4 kw but not more than 8 3/4 kw and multiply the sum by the demand factors specified in Column A or B for the given number of appliances.

With an 8 kw range, now you have a **choice** (in lieu of) either Column C @ 8 kw or per Note 3, Column B @ 6.4 kw (8kw x 80%). Your "best deal" is the lowest amount, the minimum **6.4 kw**.

Always **compare** Column's A and B against Column C and select the **lowest** kw demand.

Example: What is the demand load for twenty 8 kw household ranges?

(a) 160 kw   (b) 44.8 kw   (c) 35 kw   (d) 50 kw

Solution: This question is often answered incorrectly. The connected load (nameplate) would be 20 ranges x 8 kw = 160 kw. Using Column B for 20 appliances shows a demand of 28%, 160 kw x 28% = 44.8 kw. Always **compare** Column C (which is the **maximum demand**, the largest amount required) Column C for 20 appliances = **35 kw**. So why use 44.8 kw for 20 - 8 kw ranges? Always choose the lowest (minimum) kw. •Note the maximum demand for 20 - **12 kw** ranges would still be 35 kw so why would you want to use 44.8 kw for 20 - 8 kw ranges?
   The reason a designer went to Table 220.55 was to select the **best demand** permitted by the Code.

Column B = 44.8 kw or 44,800w/240v = 187 amps required in the service conductor sizing.

Column C = 35 kw or 35,000w/240v = 146 amps required in the service conductor sizing. Copper is dollars $$$. Select the "best deal" permitted by the Code when calculating demand factors.

When an appliance will fit in more than one column, solve the calculation in each column, then choose the column with the **smallest** value.

Example: What is the demand on the service for 25 - 8.5 kw ranges?

Solution: 25 x 8.5 kw = 212.5 kw x 26% Column B = 55.25 kw, now check Column C. Column C shows the correct answer of **40 kw** as the maximum reduction the Code allows for this cooking equipment. Always solve Column B first, then check Column C, and the **smallest** value will be the correct answer.

Always compare the options you may have, and select the **smallest** value permitted by the Table.

A DEMAND IS A REDUCTION FROM THE NAMEPLATE - CONNECTED LOAD

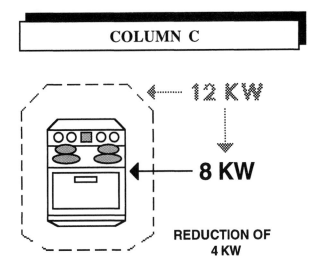

Column C allows a demand of 8 kw for **one** 12 kw or less appliance. A reduction of 4 kw.

Column C maximum demand changes with the **number** of appliances.

Example: What is the demand load on the service for **two** 12 kw ranges?

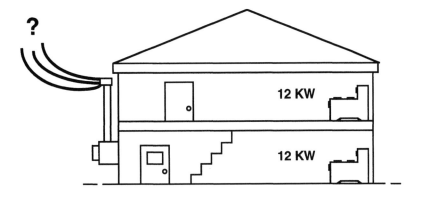

Solution: 2 appliances Column C = **11 kw demand.**

COLUMN A LESS THAN 3 1/2 KW

Example: What is the demand load on the service for 4 - 3 kw counter-mounted cooktops?

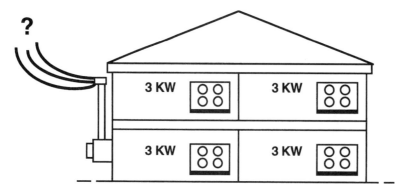

Solution: 4 appliances Column A demand **66%**, 4 x 3 kw = 12 kw x 66% = **7.92 demand**.

COLUMN B   3 1/2 TO 8 3/4 KW RATING

Example: What is the demand load on the service for six 5 kw wall-mounted ovens?

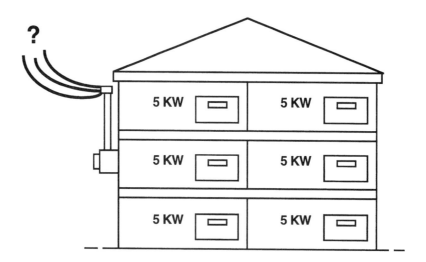

Solution: 6 appliances Column B demand **43%**, 6 x 5 kw = 30 kw x 43% = **12.9 demand**.

DEMANDS WHEN MIXING COLUMNS

Example: What is the demand load on the service for two 3 kw cooktops and two 5 kw ovens?

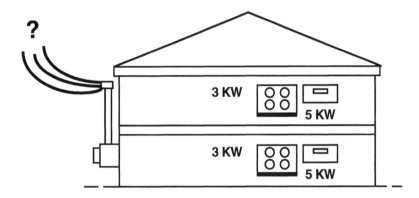

Solution: 2 appliances Column A demand = 75%, 2 x 3 kw =   6 kw x 75% = 4.5 kw
2 appliances Column B demand = 65%, 2 x 5 kw = 10 kw x 65% = 6.5 kw
4.5 kw + 6.5 kw = **11 kw demand**.

Example: What is the feeder demand for a 12 kw range and a 4 kw cooktop?

Solution: 1 appliance Column B demand = 80%, 4 kw x 80% = 3.2 kw
1 appliance Column C   = 8   kw

3.2 kw + 8 kw = 11.2 kw, but the maximum demand required from Column C for 2 appliances is only **11 kw**. The answer is **11 kw demand**; the lowest kw permitted.

Why use 11.2 kw for a 12 kw range and a 4 kw cooktop, Column C requires only an 11 kw demand for **TWO 12 kw ranges**. Always compare Column C with Columns A and B.

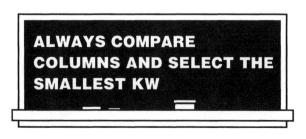

ALWAYS COMPARE
COLUMNS AND SELECT THE
SMALLEST KW

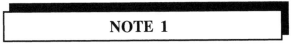

Note 1. EQUAL SIZES over 12KW through 27KW

Over 12 kw through 27 kw ranges all of the **same** rating. For ranges individually rated **more** than 12 kw but not more than 27 kw, the maximum demand in **Column C** shall be **increased 5%** for each additional kw of rating or **major fraction** thereof by which the rating of individual ranges **exceeds** 12 kw.

A student in class once asked me, "What if the range is rated **over** 27 kw"? Remember, Table 220.55 is for **HOUSEHOLD** cooking equipment. A 27 kw range would be 27,000w/240v = 113 amps. I haven't seen too many residential kitchens with a 113 amp branch circuit to the range!

Note 1 states for **each** kw above 12 kw, Column C demand is to be **increased** 5% for each kw over 12.

Example: What is the demand for a 14 kw range?

Solution: 14 kw is **2 kw** above 12 kw, 2 kw x 5% = 10%. Column C demand for one range is 8 kw. **Increase** 8 kw by 10%. 8 kw x 10% = .8 kw, 8 kw + .8 kw = **8.8 kw demand**.

A better way to increase Column C would be to take 8 kw times 110% or 8 kw x 1.10. 8 kw x 110% = **8.8 kw**. Or 8 kw x 1.10 = **8.8 kw.**

When working these calculations I have a simple format (shown below) that I follow. 14 kw - 12 kw = 2 kw x 5% = 10%. I **circle** the number of appliances (which in this case is 1) this reminds me to go to Column C demand for **1** appliance which is 8 kw. Now 8 kw shall be increased by 10%. Use this format, it will keep you from forgetting what to do next!

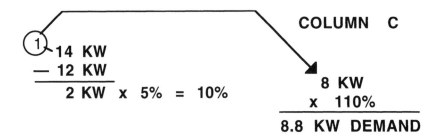

Example: What is the demand for two 14 kw ranges?

Solution: 14 kw - 12 kw = 2 kw x 5% = 10%. Column C for **two** appliances = 11 kw.
11 kw x 1.10 = **12.1 kw demand**.

Example: What is the demand for 4 - 15 kw ranges?

Solution: 15 kw - 12 kw = 3 kw x 5% = 15%. Column C for **four** appliances = 17 kw.
17 kw x 1.15 = **19.55 kw demand**.

Example: What is the demand for 20 -16 kw ranges?

Solution: 16 kw - 12 kw = 4 kw x 5% = 20%. Column C for **twenty** appliances = 35 kw.
35 kw x 1.20 = **42 kw demand**.

Example: What is the demand for 30 - 17 kw ranges?

Solution: 17 kw - 12 kw = 5 kw x 5% = 25%. Column C for **thirty** appliances = 45 kw (15kw + 30kw).
45 kw x 1.25 = **56.25 kw demand**.

Example: What is the demand for 50 - 18 kw ranges?

Solution: 18 kw - 12 kw = 6 kw x 5% = 30%. Column C for **fifty** appliances = 62.5 kw (25kw +.75kw
x 50 ranges = 37.5) Column C = 25 kw + 37.5 kw = 62.5 kw.
62.5 kw x 1.30 = **81.25 kw demand**.

Example: What is the demand for 60 - 20 kw ranges?

Solution: 20 kw - 12 kw = 8 kw x 5% = 40%. Column C for **sixty** appliances = 70 kw (25kw + .75
x 60 ranges = 45 kw) Column C = 25 kw + 45 kw = 70 kw.
70 kw x 1.40 = **98 kw demand**.

USE THE FORMAT FOR
RANGES LARGER THAN
12 KW

NOTE 2 UNEQUAL SIZES OVER 8 3/4 KW

Note 2. Over 8 3/4 kw through 27 kw ranges of **unequal** ratings. For ranges individually rated **more** than 12 kw and of **different** ratings but none exceeding 27 kw, an **AVERAGE VALUE** of rating shall be computed by adding together the ratings of all ranges to obtain the total connected load **(USING 12 KW for any range rated LESS than 12 kw)** and dividing by the total number of ranges; and then the maximum demand in **Column C** shall be **increased** 5 percent for each kw or **MAJOR FRACTION THEREOF** by which this **AVERAGE VALUE** exceeds 12 kw.

Note 2 states to add all the ranges together to get a **total** kw connected load (using 12 kw for any range rated less than 12 kw). Now divide the **total kw** connected load by the **total number of ranges**. This number is called the **average value**. If the average value is .5 and larger, round up to the next higher whole number. Example, 220 kw/16 ranges = 13.75 kw average value. Change the 13.75 kw to **14 kw average value**.

Once the **average value** is determined, you work the calculation just as you did in Note 1. For each kw over 12 kw increase Column C by 5%.

Example: What is the demand load for three 9 kw ranges, four 14 kw ranges, and five 15 kw ranges?

Solution: **First step**, any range rated less than 12 kw, raise it to 12 kw.

$$
\begin{array}{l}
\quad\;\; \mathbf{12} \\
3 - \cancel{9}\,\text{kw} = 36\text{ kw} \\
4 - 14\text{ kw} = 56\text{ kw} \\
\underline{5 - 15\text{ kw} = 75\text{ kw}} \\
\overline{12} \qquad \overline{167\text{ kw}}
\end{array}
$$

167 kw/12 ranges = 13.9 or **14 kw average value**.

Now we have 12 - 14 kw ranges. Work the calculation just as you did in Note 1.

14 kw - 12 kw = 2 kw x 5% = 10%. Column C for **12** ranges = 27 kw.

27 kw x 1.10 = **29.7 kw demand**.

Remember when using Note 2, any range rated **less** than 12 kw, raise it to 12 kw.

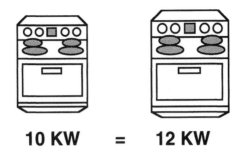

10 KW   =   12 KW

Example: What is the demand load for two 10 kw ranges, six 15 kw ranges, and seven 16 kw ranges?

Solution:

~~12~~
2 - ~~10~~ kw = 24 kw
6 - 15 kw = 90 kw
7 - 16 kw = 112 kw
15   226 kw   226 kw/15 ranges = 15.06 or **15 kw average value**.

Now we have 15 -15 kw ranges. Work the calculation just as you did in Note 1.
15 kw - 12 kw = 3 kw x 5% = 15%. Column C for 15 ranges = 30 kw.
30 kw x 1.15 = **34.5 kw demand**.

Example: What is the demand load for two 15 kw ranges and three 16 kw ranges?

Solution:

2 - 15 kw = 30 kw
3 - 16 kw = 48 kw
5   78 kw   78 kw/5 ranges = 15.6 or **16 kw average value**.

Now we have 5 - 16 kw ranges.
16 kw - 12 kw = 4 kw x 5% = 20%. Column C for 5 ranges = 20 kw.
20 kw x 1.20 = **24 kw demand**.

**USE .5 AND LARGER TO
ROUND UP THE
AVERAGE VALUE**

NOTE 3

All Note 3 does is grant you permission to use Columns A and B instead of Column C. We covered this on pages 158 and 159.

NOTE 4   BRANCH CIRCUIT

Note 4 is for a **BRANCH CIRCUIT** load. It shall be permissible to compute the **branch circuit** load for **one** range in accordance with Table 220.55. The branch circuit load for **ONE** wall-mounted oven or **ONE** counter-mounted cooking unit shall be the **NAMEPLATE RATING** of the appliance. The branch circuit load for a counter-mounted cooking unit and not more than two wall-mounted ovens, all supplied from a single branch circuit and located in the same room, shall be computed by adding the nameplate rating of the individual appliances and treating this **TOTAL** as equivalent to **ONE RANGE**.

HOUSEHOLD COOKING EQUIPMENT

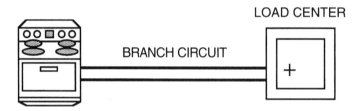

NOTE 4. This is the **only** place in the Code that permits a demand factor on a **branch circuit**. Up till now we have been calculating the demand factor for **feeder and service loads**.

On the exam, when the question mentions **BRANCH CIRCUIT** or **NOTE 4**, you must follow the rules of Note 4.

The first sentence states you can apply the same demand to **one** range as you did with a feeder. Example, for the branch circuit, one 12 kw range has a demand of 8 kw from Column C.

The second sentence of Note 4 states, if you have only **ONE** oven or **ONE** cooktop, there is **NO DEMAND**. You must use the **nameplate rating**.

The next sentence states, if you have **more** than **ONE** cooktop or oven you add them together and treat them as **ONE RANGE**.

Example: What is the branch circuit demand for one 4 kw cooktop and two 4 kw ovens?

Solution: 4 kw + 4 kw + 4 kw = 12 kw. Treat as one 12 kw range. Column C = **8 kw demand**.

The exam question can ask for the feeder-service demand or the branch circuit demand.

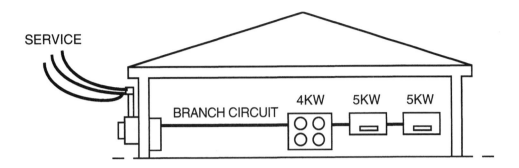

Example: What is the demand for the **service** for one 4 kw cooktop and two 5 kw ovens?

Solution: 3 appliances Column B = 55% demand. 4 kw + 5 kw + 5 kw = 14 kw x 55% = **7.7 kw demand**.

Example: What is the demand for the **branch circuit** for one 4 kw cooktop and two 5 kw ovens?

Solution: Note 4. You shall add the appliances together at nameplate rating and treat the total as **ONE RANGE**.

4 kw + 5 kw + 5 kw = 14 kw. We can't use Column B because Column B is for appliances rated 3 1/2 kw to 8 3/4 kw. Since we now have one 14 kw range we must apply **Note 1**.

  14 kw - 12 kw = 2 kw x 5% = 10%. Column C for **ONE** range = 8 kw demand.
  8 kw x 1.10 = **8.8 kw branch circuit demand**.

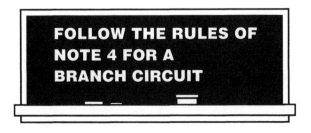

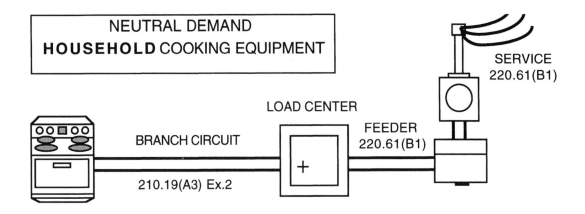

NEUTRAL DEMAND
HOUSEHOLD COOKING EQUIPMENT

SERVICE
220.61(B1)

LOAD CENTER

BRANCH CIRCUIT

FEEDER
220.61(B1)

210.19(A3) Ex.2

NEUTRAL DEMAND HOUSEHOLD COOKING EQUIPMENT

Section 220.61(B1) states, for a feeder supplying **household** electric ranges, wall-mounted ovens, and counter-mounted cooking units the maximum unbalanced load shall be considered as **70 PERCENT** of the load on the ungrounded conductors, as determined in accordance with Table 220.55 for ranges.

Section 240.23. Change in Size of Grounded Conductor. Where a change occurs in the size of the ungrounded conductor, a similar change shall be permitted to be made in the size of the grounded conductor.

Example: What is the feeder **neutral** demand for five 12 kw ranges?

Solution: Column C for five ranges = 20 kw demand for the ungrounded (hot) conductor. The neutral (grounded conductor) demand is **70%** of 20 kw = **14 kw neutral demand**.

Neutral **branch circuit**. Section 210.19(A3) ex.2: The neutral conductor of a 3-wire branch circuit supplying a household electric range, a wall-mounted oven, or a counter-mounted cooking unit shall be permitted to be smaller than the ungrounded conductors where the maximum demand of a range of 8 3/4 kw or more rating has been computed according to Column C of Table 220.55, but shall have an ampacity of not less than 70 percent of the branch circuit rating and shall not be smaller than **#10**.

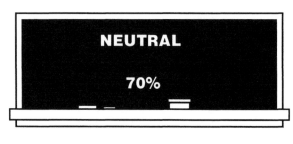

NEUTRAL

70%

SINGLE-PHASE RANGES ON A THREE-PHASE SYSTEM

This calculation is asked on a MASTER exam, not Journeyman.

Section 220.55: Where two or more single-phase ranges are supplied by a 3-phase, 4-wire feeder, the total load shall be computed on the basis of twice the maximum number between any two phases.

Annex D Example D5A shows a calculation for 10 single-phase ranges on a three-phase 4-wire feeder.

At first, this type of calculation appears to be difficult. I have a format I teach in class for single-phase ranges on a three-phase system, and I feel after working two of these examples it will become an easy calculation to solve.

For **10** ranges, find the best balance per phase:

A PHASE   B PHASE   C PHASE
4 ranges   3 ranges   3 ranges

Take the largest number of ranges on one phase (4 on A PHASE) times the number of connections (two). 4 ranges x 2 = **8 appliances**. This is the advantage of a 3-phase over a single-phase, instead of calculating 10 appliance loads, you now have **8** appliance loads.

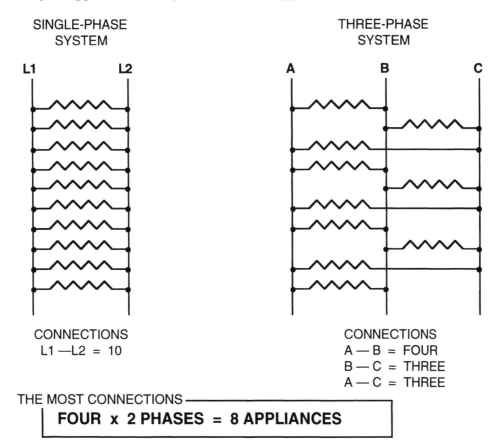

SINGLE-PHASE
SYSTEM

THREE-PHASE
SYSTEM

CONNECTIONS
L1 —L2 = 10

CONNECTIONS
A — B = FOUR
B — C = THREE
A — C = THREE

THE MOST CONNECTIONS
FOUR x 2 PHASES = 8 APPLIANCES

Example: 30 single-phase ranges at 12 kw each are supplied by a 3-phase, 4-wire, 120/208v feeder. What is the demand on the feeder for these ranges?

Solution:

A PHASE	B PHASE	C PHASE
10 ranges	10 ranges	10 ranges

   10 ranges x 2 = **20** appliances. Column C **20** appliances = **35 kw demand**.

Example: 38 - 15 kw single-phase ranges, served by a 4-wire, three-phase 208/120v system are installed in a condominium complex. Determine the demand on the feeder.

Solution:

A PHASE	B PHASE	C PHASE
13 ranges	13 ranges	12 ranges

   13 ranges x 2 = **26** appliances. Column C **26** appliances = 41 kw demand (15 kw + 26 kw).
   15 kw - 12 kw = 3 kw x 5% = 15%. Column C 41 kw x 1.15 = **47.15 kw demand**.

Example: Calculate the demand on the 4-wire, 3-phase, 208/120v feeder supplying the following 35 single-phase ranges:

12 - 14 kw ranges
12 - 12 kw ranges
11 - 8 kw ranges

A PHASE	B PHASE	C PHASE	
12 ranges	12 ranges	11 ranges	12 ranges x 2 = 24 appliances.

   Since the ranges are of **unequal** value we must apply Note 2 and find the **average value**.

12 - 14 kw = 168 kw
12 - 12 kw = 144 kw
11 - 8̶ kw = 132 kw   (change the 8 kw to 12 kw)
―――――――――――――――――
35   444 kw   444 kw/35 = 12.68 or **13 kw average value**.

   Now we have 24 - 13 kw ranges. Column C 24 appliances = 39 kw demand.
   13 kw - 12 kw = 1 kw x 5% = 5%. Column C 39 kw x 1.05 = **40.95 kw demand**.

NOTE 5

Note 5. This Table also applies to household cooking appliances rated over 1 3/4 kw and used in **INSTRUCTIONAL PROGRAMS**.

(FPN): See Table 220.56 for commercial cooking equipment.

Example: A 12 kw range in a school building, if the range is in the **kitchen**, Table 220.56 for **commercial** cooking equipment would apply. If the same range was put in the **home economics classroom** (instructional program) Table 220.55 would apply.

Table 220.56 does not allow a demand for **one** range, the demand is 100% = **12 kw**.

Table 220.55 demand from Column C for **one** 12 kw range is **8 kw**.

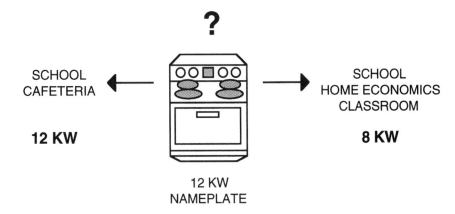

COMMERCIAL COOKING EQUIPMENT

Section 220.56. Kitchen Equipment - Other than Dwelling Unit(s). It shall be permissible to compute the load for commercial electric cooking equipment, dishwasher booster heaters, water heaters, and other kitchen equipment in accordance with Table 220.56. These demand factors shall be applied to all equipment which has either thermostatic control or intermittent use as kitchen equipment. They shall not apply to space heating, ventilating or air-conditioning equipment.

However, in no case shall the feeder demand be less than the sum of the largest two kitchen equipment loads.

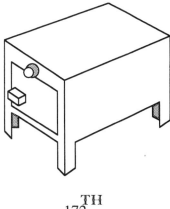

CHAPTER 5   COOKING EQUIPMENT DEMAND FACTORS

Table 220.56
Feeder Demand Factors for Kitchen Equipment —
Other than Dwelling Unit(s)

Numbers of Units of Equipment	Demand Factors Percent
1	100
2	100
3	90
4	80
5	70
6 & Over	65

This Table allows a demand factor for **3 or more** kitchen equipment loads other than a dwelling.

Example: The kitchen equipment in a restaurant consists of one 12 kw range and one 3 kw dishwasher. What is the demand on the feeder?

Solution: No demand factor is permitted for **2** units of equipment. The load would be calculated at 100% which is the nameplate connected load. 12 kw + 3 kw = **15 kw**.

Example: A school cafeteria kitchen has the following equipment, one 14 kw range, one 6 kw oven, two 2 kw deep fat fryers, one 5 kw booster water heater, and one 3 kw dishwasher. What is the feeder demand for this kitchen equipment?

Solution: Total connected load = 32 kw x 65% demand for 6 units of equipment = **20.8 kw demand on the feeder.**

Example: What is the Code requirement for the minimum feeder demand on the following restaurant kitchen equipment?

1 - 16 kw range
1 - 2 kw potato peeler
1 - 3 kw deep fat fryer

Solution: 16 kw + 2 kw + 3 kw = 21 kw x 90% = 18.9 demand **BUT!!!**

  The second paragraph of Section 220.56 states: In **NO** case shall the feeder demand be **LESS** than the sum of the **LARGEST TWO** kitchen equipment loads.

  Two largest loads = 16 kw + 3 kw = **19 kw minimum feeder demand permitted**.

Summary

As with any exam question it requires the careful reading of each **word.**

BRANCH CIRCUIT   HOUSEHOLD   NEUTRAL   UNEQUAL

COMMERCIAL

HOME ECONOMICS CLASSROOM   FEEDER   1ø on 3ø   SERVICE   OVER 1 3/4 KW

•There is NO 70% for a commercial range, only a household range per section 220.61(B1).

•A 12 kw range in a school has a 12 kw demand in the kitchen and an 8 kw demand in the classroom.

•A branch circuit has a different demand than a service per Note 4.

Don't forget Tom Henry has 12 *VIDEO'S* that cover all the chapters in this book and more!

Tom Henry's 12 *VIDEOS FOR ELECTRICAL EXAMS*

CHAPTER 5 TEST 1   COMMERCIAL & HOUSEHOLD COOKING

1. The following equipment is installed in a small delicatessen: One 4.5 kw water heater, one 9 kw booster heater, one 4.6 kw fryer, one 12 kw grill and three 10 kw pizza ovens, each with its own thermostatic controls. What is the computed feeder demand load?

(a) 32.86 kw   (b) 37.12 kw   (c) 39.07 kw   (d) 42.07 kw

2. The feeder demand load for four 14 kw residential ranges is _____.

(a) 17 kw   (b) 18.7 kw   (c) 20.4 kw   (d) 22.6 kw

3. What is the ampere load demand for a 20 kw household electric range rated @ 240 volts?

(a) 46.7 amps   (b) 54.7 amps   (c) 66.4 amps   (d) 86.9 amps

4. What is the neutral load for twenty - 12kw ranges used in a school home economic class room?

(a) 24.5 kw   (b) 35 kw   (c) 156 kw   (d) 109.2 kw

5. A dwelling unit has three ovens rated 8kw, 6kw, and 3.5kw, a 6kw cooktop and a 3.5kw counter mounted broiler. The calculated feeder demand load is ____.

(a) 12.2 kw   (b) 18.6 kw   (c) 27.3 kw   (d) 29.7 kw

6. The feeder demand for one 12 kw, two 14 kw and one 17 kw ranges is ____.

(a) 12.1 kw   (b) 14.2 kw   (c) 18.7 kw   (d) 22.6 kw

CHAPTER 5 TEST 2 HOUSEHOLD COOKING EQUIPMENT

1. What is the feeder demand for one 15 kw range?

(a) 15 kw   (b) 12 kw   (c) 9.2 kw   (d) none of these

2. What is the demand load for a branch circuit to a 5 kw oven?

(a) 4 kw   (b) 5 kw   (c) 8 kw   (d) 12 kw

3. What is the feeder demand for six 4 kw ovens?

(a) 24 kw   (b) 21 kw   (c) 10.32 kw   (d) 10.8 kw

4. What is the demand load on the service for five 16 kw ranges?

(a) 21 kw   (b) 24 kw   (c) 25.2 kw   (d) 35 kw

5. In an apartment, what is the demand load for thirty 8 kw ranges?

(a) 240 kw   (b) 57.6 kw   (c) 45 kw   (d) 15 kw

6. What is the feeder demand for a 12 kw range and a 5 kw cooktop in a residence?

(a) 8 kw   (b) 12 kw   (c) 11 kw   (d) 17 kw

7. What is the neutral demand for six 12 kw residential ranges?

(a) 12 kw   (b) 14.7 kw   (c) 16.8 kw   (d) 21 kw

8. What is the minimum size branch circuit conductor for a neutral on a 12 kw rated household range?

(a) #12   (b) #10   (c) #8   (d) #6

CHAPTER 5   TEST 3   HOUSEHOLD COOKING EQUIPMENT

1. A 12 kw range has a branch circuit demand of _____ amps. 115/230v single-phase.

(a) 34.8   (b) 33.3   (c) 50   (d) 52.1

2. If the kitchen in a new residence has a 6 kw counter-mounted cooking unit and one 4 kw wall-mounted oven, the minimum feeder demand would be _____ kw.

(a) 12   (b) 10   (c) 8   (d) 6.5

3. A 13.55 kw range would require a conductor with an ampacity of _____ amps. 220/110v single-phase.

(a) 30   (b) 40   (c) 50   (d) 60

4. A feeder supplying two 4 kw wall-mounted ovens and a 5 kw counter-mounted cooking unit in a dwelling shall have a minimum demand of _____ kw.

(a) 8.4   (b) 8.8   (c) 7.15   (d) none of these

5. What is the demand load for the following ranges?
6 - 9 kw
4 - 12 kw
10 - 15 kw

(a) 35 kw   (b) 36.75 kw   (c) 38.5 kw   (d) none of these

6. 35 apartments, each has a 12 kw range 120/240v single-phase. What is the neutral demand for the service?

(a) 50 amps   (b) 146 amps   (c) 208 amps   (d) 416 amps

CHAPTER 5 TEST 4 HOUSEHOLD COOKING EQUIPMENT

1. In a residence, two 5 kw wall-mounted ovens and a 4 kw counter-mounted cooktop are supplied by the same feeder. The minimum feeder neutral demand would be _____ kw.

(a) 8.8   (b) 6.16   (c) 5.39   (d) 7.7

2. What is the demand on the service for two 14 kw ranges and three 15 kw ranges?

(a) 20 kw   (b) 22 kw   (c) 23 kw   (d) none of these

3. What is the demand on the service for 50 - 14 kw ranges?

(a) 25 kw   (b) 37.5 kw   (c) 62.5 kw   (d) 68.75 kw

4. The minimum demand load for 15 - 3.5 kw ranges in an apartment complex would be _____ kw.

(a) 9.6   (b) 16.8   (c) 30   (d) none of these

5. In a residence, what is the minimum branch circuit load in amps for one 5 kw counter-mounted cooktop and one 8 kw wall-mounted oven? 120/240v single-phase.

(a) 28 amps   (b) 35 amps   (c) 36.6 amps   (d) none of these

6. What is the demand for four 3 kw cooktops and four 5 kw ovens on the same feeder?

(a) 23 kw   (b) 17.92 kw   (c) 16 kw   (d) none of these

CHAPTER 5   TEST 5   COMMERCIAL & HOUSEHOLD COOKING

1. Calculate the feeder demand for 55 - 14 kw ranges in an apartment building.

(a) 66.25 kw   (b) 72.875 kw   (c) 138.6 kw   (d) 770 kw

2. What is the feeder demand for twenty 8.5 kw household ranges?

(a) 170 kw   (b) 47.6   (c) 35 kw   (d) 36 kw

3. What is the demand load for a 16 kw range? 115/230v single-phase.

(a) 9.6 amps   (b) 8 amps   (c) 41.7 amps   (d) 50 amps

4. The demand for 45 - 12 kw ranges in an apartment complex would be _____ kw.

(a) 25   (b) 33.75   (c) 58.75   (d) 97.2

5. The demand load for twenty-eight 14 kw residential ranges rated 115/230v single-phase would be _____ kw.

(a) 94.08   (b) 392   (c) 47.3   (d) none of these

6. What is the demand load on the service for the following ranges?

4 - 9 kw
5 - 14 kw
6 - 16 kw

(a) 33 kw   (b) 30 kw   (c) 214 kw   (d) none of these

CHAPTER 5 TEST 6   COMMERCIAL & HOUSEHOLD COOKING

1. What is the feeder demand for the following equipment in a restaurant?

3 - 6 kw booster heaters
1 - 5 kw dishwasher
3 - 3 kw deep fat fryers

(a) 32 kw   (b) 24 kw   (c) 20.8 kw   (d) none of these

2. A school building has six 12 kw ranges in the home economics classroom. The service demand for these ranges would be _____ kw.

(a) 46.8   (b) 21   (c) 30.96   (d) 72

3. In an apartment building, what is the demand load on a three-phase service for 46 - 15 kw ranges 208/120v single-phase?

(a) 54.05 kw   (b) 51.75 kw   (c) 47 kw   (d) 45 kw

4. A restaurant has a 15 kw range, a 5 kw oven, a 4 kw dishwasher, and a 3 kw booster heater. What is the feeder demand for this group of kitchen equipment?

(a) 17 kw   (b) 13.5 kw   (c) 20 kw   (d) 21.6 kw

5. The demand load for five 9 kw ranges, four 12 kw ranges, and seven 16 kw ranges would be _____ kw, in a multi-family building.

(a) 220   (b) 200   (c) 34.1   (d) 13.75

6. In a dwelling duplex, each unit has a 15 kw range. What is the service demand for these two ranges?

(a) 12.65 kw   (b) 30 kw   (c) 11 kw   (d) 17.25 kw

CHAPTER 5 TEST 7   COMMERCIAL & HOUSEHOLD COOKING

1. A cafeteria in a school building has the following equipment in the kitchen:

2 - 12 kw ranges
1 - 3 kw dishwasher
1 - 5 kw booster heater
2 - 4 kw ovens

The demand on the service would be _____ kw for this equipment.

(a) 21   (b) 23   (c) 26   (d) 30

2. In a 50 unit condominium, each unit has a 14 kw range 208/120v single-phase. What is the demand on a three-phase service for these ranges?

(a) 68.75 kw   (b) 50 kw   (c) 53.9 kw   (d) 49 kw

3. The minimum branch circuit demand for one 6 kw counter-mounted cooktop and one 8 kw wall-mounted oven in a dwelling would be _____ kw.

(a) 8.4   (b) 8.8   (c) 11.2   (d) 14

4. What is the Code requirement for a commercial kitchen feeder supplying a 16 kw range, a 3 kw deep fat fryer, and a 2 kw potato peeler?

(a) 18.9 kw   (b) 19 kw   (c) 21 kw   (d) 16.8 kw

5. What is the neutral demand for 15 - 12 kw ranges used in a school home economics classroom?

(a) 180 kw   (b) 117 kw   (c) 30 kw   (d) 21 kw

6. What is the feeder neutral demand for 30 - 4 kw counter-mounted cooktops in an apartment building?

(a) 45 kw   (b) 20.16 kw   (c) 28.8 kw   (d) 120 kw

CHAPTER 6

DWELLING SERVICE CALCULATIONS

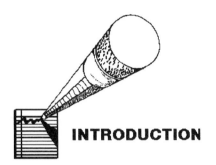

INTRODUCTION

Section 230.42(A). Service-entrance conductors shall be of sufficient size to carry the loads as computed in **Article 220.**

Dwelling Unit: One or more rooms for the use of one or more persons as a housekeeping unit with space for eating, living, and sleeping, and permanent provisions for cooking and sanitation.

When the exam question asks for the **minimum** size service to a dwelling, several rules and demand factors apply.

For a one-family dwelling, the service disconnecting means shall have a rating not less than **100 amps** per section 230.79(C).

For a dwelling the Code lists only **3** rules you **shall have** when sizing the service.

1. Section 220.12. Lighting Load for Listed Occupancies. A unit load of not less than that specified in Table 220.12 for occupancies listed therein shall constitute the **minimum** lighting load for each square foot of floor area. The floor area for each floor shall be computed from the **outside dimensions** of the building, apartment, or other area involved. For **dwelling unit(s)**, the computed floor area shall **not** include open porches, garages, or unused or unfinished spaces not adaptable for future use.

2. Section 220.52(A). In each dwelling unit the feeder load shall be computed at **1500 volt-amperes** for **each** 2-wire small appliance branch circuit required by Section 210.11(C1) for small appliances supplied by 15 or 20 ampere receptacles on 20 ampere branch circuits in the kitchen. Where the load is subdivided through two or more feeders, the computed load for each shall include not less than 1500 volt-amperes for each 2-wire branch circuit for small appliances. These loads **shall be** permitted to be **included** with the general lighting load and subjected to the **demand factors permitted in Table 220.42** for the general lighting load.

3. Section 220.52(B). A feeder load of not less than **1500 volt-amperes** shall be included for each 2-wire **laundry branch circuit** installed as required by Section 210.11(C2). It **shall be** permissible to **include** this load with the general lighting load and subject it to the **demand factors provided** in Table 220.42.

These are the 3 items you **shall have** in a dwelling:

1. 3va for each square foot of living area
2. 2 small appliance circuits at 1500va each
3. 1 laundry circuit at 1500va

A demand factor from Table 220.42 is permitted for all three items.

Table 220.12.

Table 220.12.   General Lighting Loads by Occupancies

Type of Occupancy	Unit Load per Sq. Ft. (Volt-Amperes)
Armories and Auditoriums	1
Banks	3-1/2 [b]
Barber Shops and Beauty Parlors	3
Churches	1
Clubs	2
Court Rooms	2
* Dwelling Units[a]	3
Garages — Commercial (storage)	1/2
Hospitals	2
* Hotels and Motels, including apartment houses without provisions for cooking by tenants.	2
Industrial Commercial (Loft) Buildings	2
Lodge Rooms	1-1/2
Office Buildings	3-1/2 [b]
Restaurants	2
Schools	3
Stores	3
Warehouses (storage)	1/4
In any of the above occupancies except one-family dwellings and individual dwelling units of two-family and multi-family dwellings:	
Assembly Halls and Auditoriums	1
Halls, Corridors, Closets, Stairways	1/2
Storage Spaces	1/4

[a]See 220.14(J)
[b]See 220.14(K)

Dwelling unit **minimum** of 3va per square foot of **living area**.

The 3va per square foot is to cover **both** lighting and receptacles.

In a dwelling there is NO limit to the number of receptacles installed on a branch circuit. Rightfully so, as you are NOT adding any more load to the circuit. By installing more receptacles you are providing more convenience receptacles. The [a] in the notes below Table 220.12 refers you to 220.14(J) which states that no other load is required. The 180 va applies to **other than a dwelling** as the other outlets indicates in 220.14(L).

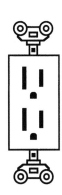

Example: What is the minimum size service for a 800 sq.ft. house?

Solution:
800 sq.ft. x 3va	= 2400va
2 small appl. x 1500 va	= 3000 va
1 laundry	= 1500va
	6900va

The 6900va total is subject to a demand factor from Table 220.42:

Table 220.42. Lighting Load Feeder Demand Factors

Type of Occupancy	Portion of Lighting Load to Which Demand Factor Applies (volt-amperes)	Demand Factor Percent
Dwelling Units	First 3000 or less at	100
	From 3001 to 120,000 at	35
	Remainder over 120,000 at	25
* Hospitals	First 50,000 or less at	40
	Remainder over 50,000 at	20
* Hotels and Motels — Including	First 20,000 or less at	50
Apartment Houses without	From 20,001 to 100,000 at	40
Provision for Cooking by Tenants	Remainder over 100,000 at	30
Warehouses	First 12,500 or less at	100
(Storage)	Remainder over 12,500 at	50
All Others	Total Volt-amperes	100

* The demand factors of this table shall not apply to the calculated load of feeders or services supplying areas in hospitals, hotels, and motels where the entire lighting is likely to be used at one time, as in operating rooms, ballrooms, or dining rooms.

Table 220.42:
First 3000va @ 100%   = 3000va
Remaining 3900va x 35% = 1365va
                   4365va   4365va/240v = 18.1 amps

Circuits required:

General lighting 800 sq.ft. x 3va = 2400va/120v = 20 amps. This requires two 15 amp 2-wire circuits or **one** 20 amp 2-wire circuits. Note: Section 220.42, The demand factors listed in Table 220.42 shall **not** be applied to determine the number of **branch circuits** required.

Total circuits required:
General lighting	= 1
Small appliance	= 2
Laundry	= 1
Bathroom	= 1
	5 total

4.365 kva and five 2-wire circuits, **minimum** size service for this house would be **100 amps**.

The Code does **not** require a dwelling to have **electric** appliances. The dwelling may have gas appliances instead of electric.

If the dwelling has electrical appliances such as a water heater, clothes dryer, range, dishwasher, electric heat, etc., then we have Code rules and demand factors that would apply.

The dwelling can be calculated using either of two methods of calculation.

1. General Method (Standard Method)
2. Optional Method

Article 220 is divided into four parts:

A. Branch Circuits.
B. Feeders.
C. Optional Method.
D. Farm Loads.

The General Method of calculation for the service starts at Section 220.12.
The Optional Method of calculation for the service starts at Section 220.82.

The basic difference between the two methods of calculation is with the General Method you would have **several** demand factors to apply throughout the calculation. With the Optional Method you simply add all the equipment at nameplate and apply only **one** demand factor. The Optional Method does require a minimum 100 amp service.

For a dwelling some of the requirements are the same for both the General or Optional Method of calculation. Both require 3va per square foot for the general lighting, two small appliance circuits, one laundry circuit, and you are permitted to omit the **smaller** load either heat or air conditioning. The General Method permits a demand factor for the general lighting load from Table 220.42, the Optional Method applies only one demand factor at the end of the calculation.

GENERAL METHOD OF CALCULATION

Section 220.50. Motor loads shall be computed in accordance with Sections 430.24, 430.25, and 430.26 and with 440.6 for hermetic refrigerant motor compressors.

Section 430.24. Conductors supplying two or more motors shall have an ampacity equal to the sum of the full-load current rating of all the motors **plus 25 percent** of the highest rated motor in the group.

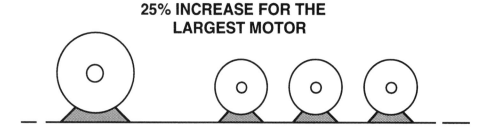

25% INCREASE FOR THE LARGEST MOTOR

Regardless of the number of motors connected on the feeder, only **one** motor, the **largest in F.L.C.** is to be increased 25%. A motor load rated in hp or F.L.C. from the motor tables, not the kw of an appliance such as a dishwasher, as this load is **not** all motor load. Part of the dishwasher is heating elements, clock, timer, controls, etc. When applying the **largest** motor rule make sure you are calculating **motor load** which will be the hp or F.L.C. rating.

Generally in a dwelling the largest motor is the air conditioning unit.

A 3 hp single-phase 230v motor F.L.C. = 17 amps x 25% **= 4.25 amps**.

A 5 hp single-phase 230v motor F.L.C. = 28 amps x 25% = **7 amps**.

This additional 25% is added to the total when calculating the service size.

When calculating the service size for a dwelling, if the largest motor is the air conditioning, but Section 220.60 allows you to **omit** the smaller load. Example, electric space heat = 10kw. 10,000w/230v = 43 amps which is larger than a 5 hp A/C motor at 28 amps x 125% = 35a. In calculating the service size you can omit the **smaller** load, the A/C motor. But you also omitted the largest motor rule 25%. This rule must be applied to the **next** largest motor in the calculation in hp or F.L.C.

OMIT THE *SMALLER* LOAD EITHER HEAT OR AIR CONDITIONING

Section 220.53. Appliance load - Dwelling Unit(s). It shall be permissible to apply a demand factor of 75% to the nameplate-rating load of **four or more** appliances fastened in place, served by the same feeder in a one-family, two-family, or multifamily dwelling.

This demand factor shall **not** be applied to electric ranges, clothes dryers, space heating equipment, or air-conditioning equipment.

220.53

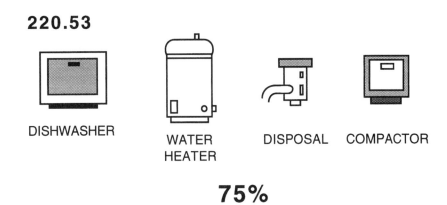

DISHWASHER   WATER HEATER   DISPOSAL   COMPACTOR

75%

A demand factor of **75%** may be applied to **four or more,** fastened in place, appliance loads.

Fastened in place appliance loads would include garbage disposer, dishwasher, water heater, well pump, compactor, vent fan, etc. These appliances cannot be easily moved due to plumbing connections or are built into the cabinets, etc. These appliances might be plug and cord connected for convenience of servicing.

220.53 does not allow the demand factor to be applied to ranges, dryers, heat or A/C equipment. The reason is, ranges have their own demand factor from Table 220.55. Clothes dryers are to be 5kw minimum per section 220.54, Table 220.54 does allow a demand factor for five or more dryers. Heat and A/C is calculated at 100%.

Definitions:

Appliance, fixed: An appliance which is fastened or otherwise secured at a specific location.

Appliance, portable: An appliance which is actually moved or can easily be moved from one place to another in normal use.

Appliance, stationary: An appliance which is not easily moved from one place to another in normal use.

FASTENED IN PLACE APPLIANCES 75% FOR *FOUR OR MORE*

Section 220.54. Electric Clothes Dryers - Dwelling Unit(s). The load for household electric clothes dryers in a dwelling unit(s) shall be **5000 watts** (volt-amperes) or the nameplate rating, whichever is **larger**, for each dryer served. The use of the demand factor in Table 220.54 shall be permitted.

220.54
CLOTHES DRYERS

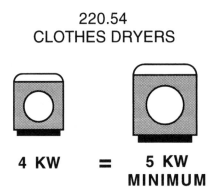

4 KW   =   5 KW
MINIMUM

Example: What is the demand for a 4kw household clothes dryer?

Solution: 220.54 **Minimum of 5kw.**

Example: What is the demand of a 6kw clothes dryer?

Solution: 220.54 Nameplate is larger = **6kw.** Table 220.54 **one** dryer = 100%.

Section 220.61(B1). For a feeder supplying household electric ranges, wall-mounted ovens, counter-mounted cooking units, and **electric dryers,** the maximum unbalanced load shall be considered as **70%** of the load on the ungrounded conductors, as determined in accordance with Table 220.55 for ranges and **Table 220.54 for dryers.**

Example: What is the demand on the feeder **neutral** for a 5kw clothes dryer?

Solution: 220.61(B1)   5kw x 70% = **3.5kw or 3500 watts.**

CLOTHES DRYER
5 KW MINIMUM

Table 220.54

Table 220.54
Demand Factors for Household Electric Clothes Dryers

Number of Dryers	Demand Factor Percent
1-4	100%
5	85%
6	75%
7	65%
8	60%
9	55%
10	50%
11	47%
12-22	% = 47 - (number of dryers - 11)
23	35%
24-42	% = 35 - (0.5 x (number of dryers - 23)
43 and over	25%

Table 220.54 allows a demand factor for **five or more HOUSEHOLD** clothes dryers.

Table 220.54
CLOTHES DRYERS

85%

Clothes dryers make good exam questions as you have several steps to remember.

Example: What is the feeder neutral demand for ten 4kw clothes dryers?

Solution: The first step is to raise the 4kw up to a minimum of 5kw. Now you have ten 5kw dryers. 10 x 5kw = 50kw. Table 220.54 shows a 50% demand factor for ten dryers. 50 kw x 50% = 25kw, this would be the demand for the ungrounded (hot) conductor, the question asks for the feeder **neutral** demand. 25kw x 70% = **17.5kw neutral demand**.

Table 220.55 Household Cooking Equipment was covered in Chapter 5.

Section 220.60. Noncoincident Loads. Where it is unlikely that two dissimilar loads will be in use simultaneously, it shall be permissible to **omit** the **smaller** of the two in computing the total load of a feeder.

In a dwelling, an example would be electric space heat and air conditioning. Both should not be operating at the same time.

220.60

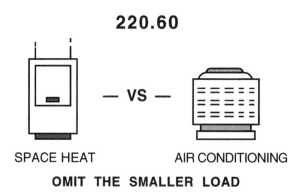

SPACE HEAT   AIR CONDITIONING

OMIT THE SMALLER LOAD

Example: A dwelling has 10kw electric space heat and a 5 hp 230v air conditioning load. What is the demand load on the service for this equipment?

Solution: Table 430.248: 5 hp, 230v = 28 amps x 230v = 6440va. Omit the air conditioning at 6440, the demand would be the larger load, the heat = **10kw**.

OMIT THE *SMALLER* LOAD EITHER HEAT OR AIR CONDITIONING

Section 220.61(B2). Feeder neutral load. We have already calculated for **household** cooking equipment at **70%** and **household** clothes dryers at **70%**. The next part of this article is not limited to just household, it applies to any neutral load **above 200 amps** except for *nonlinear loads* (harmonics).

For 3-wire DC or single-phase AC, 4-wire, 3-phase, and 5-wire, 2-phase systems, a **further** demand factor of **70%** shall be permitted for that **portion** of the unbalanced load in **excess of 200 amperes**. There shall be **no** reduction of neutral capacity for that **portion** of the load which consists of nonlinear loads such as electric-discharge lighting, data processing, or similar equipment, and supplied from a 4-wire, wye-connected 3-phase system.

An example of nonlinear loads would be fluorescent, mercury vapor or other HID lamps. This creates the third harmonic condition we covered in Chapter 2 on Ampacity. The third harmonic components of the phase currents are in phase with each other and add together in the neutral instead of cancelling out thus becoming a heat factor.

Example: What is the demand for a neutral load of 500 amperes?

Solution: 220.61(B2)   First 200 amps @ 100%   = 200 amps
                                    Remaining 300 amps x 70% = <u>210 amps</u>
                                                           410 amps

The neutral is reduced from 500 amps to **410 amps**.

Example: What is the demand for a neutral load of 1000 amperes, of which 600 amperes consists of electric-discharge lighting?

Solution: First 200 amps @ 100%   = 200 amps
               Remaining 200 amps x 70% = 140 amps
               Electric-discharge @ 100% = <u>600 amps</u>
                                     940 amps

The neutral is reduced from 1000 amps to **940 amps**.

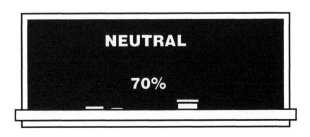

Annex D Example No. D1 (a) One-Family Dwelling

  The dwelling has a floor area of 1500 sq.ft. exclusive of unoccupied cellar, unfinished attic, and open porches. Appliances are a 12kw range and a 5.5kw, 240v dryer.

1500 sq.ft. x 3va	= 4500va
Small appliance 2 x 1500va	= 3000va
Laundry 1 x 1500va	= 1500va
	9000va

Table 220.42 demand factor:

First 3000va @ 100%	= 3000va
Remaining 6000va @ 35%	= 2100va
	5100va net load general lighting and appliances

12kw range (Table 220.55)	= 8000va
5.5kw dryer	= 5500va
	18,600va

  18,600va/240v = 77.5 amps. Service shall be a minimum of 100 amps per section 230.79(C).

Neutral for Feeder and Service:

Lighting and small appliance load	= 5100va
Range load 8000va x 70% (220.61B1)	= 5600va
Dryer load 5500va x 70% (220.61B1)	= 3850va
	14,550va

  14,550va/240v = 60.6 amperes neutral load.

GENERAL METHOD FOR SINGLE DWELLING UNIT

I use the following format that I designed when I'm calculating service loads. The format is laid out in 9 steps.

STEP 1 - Table 220.12   Lighting load of 3va x the total square footage of living area. Use outside dimensions.

STEP 2 - 220.52(A,B)   Small appliance 2 x 1500va.
Laundry 1 x 1500va.

STEP 3 - Table 220.42   Apply general lighting demand to the total of Steps 1 and 2.

STEP 4 - 220.60   Compare electric space heat against the A/C load. Omit the smaller.

STEP 5 - 220.53   Fastened in place appliances 75% demand for four or more.

STEP 6 - 220.54   Clothes dryers 5kw minimum. Table 220.54 demand factor for 5 or more. Neutral demand 70% on feeders.

STEP 7 - Table 220.55   Household cooking equipment demand factor. Neutral 70%.

STEP 8 - 220.50   Largest motor in F.L.C. to be increased 25%.

STEP 9 -   Size the service by dividing the total volt-amperes by the line voltage and apply Table 310.15(B6) for service size and service conductor size. Table 250.66 for sizing the grounding electrode conductor.

CHAPTER 6   DWELLING SERVICE CALCULATIONS

The following example is how I lay out my calculation on paper. I calculate the neutral load as I'm working the line load.

Example: Size the minimum service for the following dwelling.

1500 sq.ft. living area
5 hp single-phase 240v A/C load
10 kw electric space heating 240v
14 kw range 240/120v
4 kw water heater 240v
4 kw clothes dryer 240/120v
2 kw dishwasher 120v
1/2 hp compactor 120v
1/3 hp disposal 120v
1 hp pool pump 240v

Solution:	LINE	NEUTRAL
1500 sq.ft x 3 va	4500va	4500va
Small appliance 2 x 1500va	3000va	3000va
Laundry 1 x 1500va	1500va	1500va
	9000va	9000va
Table 220.42 Lighting demand:		
First 3000va @ 100%	3000	3000
Remaining 6000va @ 35%	2100	2100
	5100	5100

5 hp A/C 28a x 240v = 6720va (smaller than 10kw heat)

	LINE	NEUTRAL
10 kw heat	10000	0
4 kw water heater (220.53=75%)	3000	0
2 kw dishwasher (220.53=75%)	1500	1500
1/2 hp compactor •9.8a x 120v = 1176va x 75% (220.53)	882	882
1/3 hp disposal 7.2a x 120v = 864va x 75% (220.53)	648	648
1 hp pump 8a x 240v = 1920va x 75% (220.53)	1440	0
4 kw dryer = 5kw minimum	5000	3500
14 kw range (Table 220.55 Note 1)	8800	6160
•Largest motor 9.8a x 120v = 1176va x 25%	294	294
	36,664va	18,084va

LINE = 36,664va/240v = 153 amps   Table 310.15(B6)   Use 175 amp service   #1/0 copper

NEUTRAL = 18,084va/240v = 75 amps

GROUNDING ELECTRODE CONDUCTOR   Table 250.66 = #6 copper

Example: Calculate the minimum size service for the following dwelling.

1000 sq.ft. living area
3 hp A/C 230v
6 kw heat 230v
4 kw cooktop 230/115v
5 kw oven 230/115v
6 kw dryer 230/115v
4.5 kw water heater 230v
1/2 hp disposal 115v
1200va dishwasher 115v
3/4 hp pool pump 230v

Solution:	LINE	NEUTRAL
1000 sq.ft. x 3va	3000	3000
Small appliance 2 x 1500va	3000	3000
Laundry 1 x 1500va	1500	1500
	7500	7500
Table 220.42 Lighting demand:		
First 3000va @ 100%	3000	3000
Remaining 4500va @ 35%	1575	1575
	4575	4575

3 hp A/C 230v x 17a = 3910va (smaller than 6kw heat)

	LINE	NEUTRAL
6 kw heat	6000	0
4 kw cooktop (Col.B - 2 appl. @ 65%)	2600	1820
5 kw oven (Col.B - 2 appl. @ 65%)	3250	2275
6 kw dryer @ 100%	6000	4200
4.5 kw water heater @ 75%	3375	0
1/2 hp disposal •9.8a x 115v =1127va @ 75%	845	845
1200va dishwasher @ 75%	900	900
3/4 hp pool pump 6.9a x 230v = 1587va @ 75%	1190	0
•Largest motor 9.8a x 115v = 1127va x 25%	282	282
	29017	14897

LINE = 29,017va/230v = 126 amps   Table 310.15(B6)   Use 150 amp service   #1 copper

NEUTRAL = 14,897va/230v = 64.7 amps

GROUNDING ELECTRODE CONDUCTOR   Table 250.66 = #6

OPTIONAL METHOD FOR SINGLE DWELLING UNIT

Starting at 220.82 we can disregard the General Method of calculation rules, now we must follow the rules for the Optional Method.

The **"General Calulated Load"**, is everything except electric heat or A/C load. Simply add everything together at **nameplate**, apply the demand factor from section 220.82(B) to **"General Load"**, now add either the heat or A/C load per section 220.82(C) to the "General Calculated Load" total.

Annex D Example No. D2(a). Optional Calculation for One-Family Dwelling.

Dwelling has a floor area of 1500 sq.ft. exclusive of unoccupied cellar, unfinished attic, and open porches. It has a 12 kw range, a 2.5 kw water heater, a 1.2 kw dishwasher, 9 kw of electric space heating installed in five rooms, a 5 kw clothes dryer, and a 6 ampere 230 volt room air-conditioning unit.

Air conditioner kva is 6a x 230v/1000 = 1.38 kva.

1.38 kva is less than 40% of the connected load of 9 kw of space heating; therefore, the air conditioner load need not be included in the service calculation (see section 220.60).

1500 sq.ft. x 3va	= 4.5
Small appliance 2 x 1500va	= 3.0
Laundry 1 x 1500va	= 1.5
Range	= 12.0
Water heater	= 2.5
Dishwasher	= 1.2
Clothes dryer	= 5.0
	29.7 kva

220.82(B) Demand:

First 10 kva of **"General Load"** at 100%	= 10.0
Remainder of **"General Load"** 19.7 kva @ 40%	= 7.88
	17.88 kva total of "General Load"

9 kw heat @ 40%	= 3.6
	21.48 kva total load

21,480va/240v = 89.5 amperes. Use 100 amp service.

OPTIONAL METHOD FORMAT-SINGLE DWELLING UNIT

The following format is for the Optional Method of Calulation; a total of 8 steps.

STEP 1 - 220.82(B1)   3 volt-amperes per square foot.

STEP 2 - 220.82(B2)   Small appliance 2 x 1500va. Laundry 1 x 1500va.

STEP 3 - 220.82(B3)   Calculate **all** appliances at **nameplate rating**.

STEP 4 -   Total Steps 1, 2 and 3. This total is called **"General Load".**

STEP 5 - 220.82(B)   Apply 220.82(B) to **"General Load"**. First 10 kva @ 100%. Remainder of **"General Load"** @ 40%.

STEP 6 - 220.82(C4,5)   Compare A/C load at 100% against **space heat** at 65%, or **less** than four separately controlled heat units at 65%, or **four or more** separately controlled heat units at 40%.

STEP 7 - 220.60   Omit the smaller load either heat or A/C. **Add** the **largest** load either heat or A/C to the Step 5 total.

STEP 8 -   Size the service by dividing the total volt-amperes by the line voltage. Apply Table 310.15(B6) for service size (100 amp minimum). Table 250.66 for sizing the grounding electrode conductor.

Optional Method Example: Size the service for the following dwelling.

1500 square foot living area
5 hp single-phase 240v A/C load
10 kw electric space heating 240v
14 kw range 240/120v
4 kw water heater 240v
4 kw clothes dryer 240/120v
2 kw dishwasher 120v
1/2 hp compactor 120v
1/3 hp disposal 120v
1 hp pool pump 240v

	LINE
1500 sq.ft. x 3va	4500
Small appliance 2 x 1500va	3000
Laundry 1 x 1500	1500
14 kw range	14000
4 kw water heater	4000
4 kw clothes dryer	4000
2 kw dishwasher	2000
1/2 hp compactor 9.8a x 120v = 1176va	1176
1/3 hp disposal 7.2a x 120v = 864va	864
1 hp pool pump 8a x 240v = 1920va	1920

36,960va total "other load"

220.82(B) Demand Factor:

First 10 kva **General Load** @ 100%	10000
Remaining 26,960va **General Load** @ 40%	10784
A/C 5 hp 28a x 240v = 6720va	6720
•Omit heat 10kw x 65% = 6.5kw or 6500w, A/C is larger	

27,504va total load

27,504va/240v = 114.6 amps   Table 310.15(B6)   Use 125 amp service   #2 copper.

There is **no** Optional Method for calculating the neutral, it would be calculated from the General Method of calculation.

Example: Using the Optional Method calculate the minimum service size for the following dwelling.

30' x 60' outside dimensions (living area)
24' x 30' garage
6' x 20' open porch
The dwelling has the following equipment:
12 kw total heat 240v (six - 2000w separately controlled units)
4.5 kw air conditioning unit 240v
4.5 kw water heater 240v
1500w dishwasher 120v
6 kw clothes dryer 240/120v
4 kw cooktop 240/120v
5 kw oven 240/120v

	LINE
1800 sq.ft. x 3va (30' x 60')	5400
Small appliance 2 x 1500va	3000
Laundry 1 x 1500va	1500
4.5 kw water heater	4500
1500w dishwasher	1500
6 kw clothes dryer	6000
4 kw cooktop	4000
5 kw oven	5000

30,900va total "General Load"

220.82(B) Demand Factor:

First 10 kva **General Load** @ 100%	10000
Remaining 20,900va **General Load** @ 40%	8360
Heat 12000 @ 40%	4800

•Omit A/C load @ 4500, heat is the larger.

23,160va total load

23,160va/240v = 96.5 amps   Table 310.15(B6)   Use 100 amp service   #4 copper

Single dwelling summary

As you can see by now, the General Method of calculation with several demand factors is the more difficult to calculate. With the Optional Method, you have only one demand factor to apply, 100 amp minimum, no neutral calculation, and a smaller service size are some of the points to remember.

The 5 kw minimum for a clothes dryer and the 25% for the largest motor are rules that come under Article 220 Part III, which is the General Method of calculation, only the rules specified in Part IV Section 220.82 apply to the Optional Method.

MULTIFAMILY DWELLING

Multifamily Dwelling: A building containing **three or more** dwelling units.

The service calculation for the multifamily dwelling is **NOT** simply the sum of the single dwelling unit loads because of the demand factors that can be applied.

Example: A ten unit apartment, each dwelling unit has a 5 kw clothes dryer. The demand required for the service would **not** be, 10 units x 5 kw = 50 kw. Table 220.54 allows a demand factor of 50%, 50 kw x 50% = **25 kw** demand on the service.

Example: A 20 unit apartment, each unit has a 12 kw range, the feeder to this unit would have a demand of 8 kw. The demand required for the service is **not** 8 kw x 20 units = 160 kw. Table 220.55 Column C **maximum demand** is only **35 kw**.

Table 220.42 allows a further demand factor of 25% for lighting and receptacle loads **over 120,000va**.

Table 220.42.   Lighting Load Feeder Demand Factors

Type of Occupancy	Portion of Lighting Load to Which Demand Factor Applies (volt-amperes)	Demand Factor Percent
Dwelling Units	First 3000 or less at	100
	From 3001 to 120,000 at	35
	Remainder over 120,000 at	25

The largest motor increase of 25% applies to only **one** motor on the service, **not** the largest motor in each unit.

If the multifamily dwelling has the laundry in each unit the 1500va would be included in the general lighting and subject to Table 220.42 demand factors. If the multifamily dwelling has **laundry facilities on premises** available to all tenants (laundromat) the 1500va would **not** be applied in the general lighting load. The laundry load would become **"house load"**, 1500va x the number of units added to the total service load. House load is at **nameplate**, no demand factors are applied to house load.

House load can be the parking lot lights, hallway lights, pool equipment, recreation room, laundromat, etc.

Clothes dryers in a **laundromat** would no longer have a demand factor from Table 220.54, as this Table is for **household** clothes dryers not commercial usage.

220.61(B2) Neutral load over 200 amps can be reduced **70%**.

GENERAL METHOD - MULTIFAMILY DWELLING

STEP 1 - Table 220.12   Lighting load of 3 volt-amps x the total square footage of each unit x the total number of units.

STEP 2 - 220.52(A,B)   Small appliance 2 x 1500va x total number of units.•Laundry 1 x 1500va x total number of units.•If **laundry on premises**, omit laundry in this Step and apply at Step 9.

STEP 3 - Table 220.42   Apply general lighting demand to the total of Steps 1 and 2.

STEP 4 - 220.60   Compare electric space heat against A/C load. Omit the smaller.

STEP 5 - 220.53   Fixed appliances x total number of units x 75%.

STEP 6 - 220.54   Clothes dryers 5 kw minimum. Table 220.54 demand factor for five or more dryers. Neutral demand 70%.

STEP 7 - Table 220.55   Household cooking equipment demand. Neutral demand 70%.

STEP 8 - 220.50   Largest motor in F.L.C. to be increased 25% (one motor only).

STEP 9 -   Include any houseloads at nameplate. •If laundry is on premises add 1500va x total number of units to service load.

STEP 10 -   Size the service by dividing the total volt-amps by the line voltage and select 75°C conductors from Table 310.16.

STEP 11 -   Neutral load over 200 amps can be reduced 70% if not nonlinear loads.

Example: Use the General Method of calculation to determine the demand load on the service for a 25 unit apartment complex. 240/120v single-phase. Each apartment unit has the following:

900 square foot living area
3 hp A/C unit 240v
3 kw electric space heat 240v
8 kw range 240/120v
4 kw water heater 240v
1.2 kw dishwasher 120v
1/2 hp compactor 120v
5 kw clothes dryer 240/120v

	LINE	NEUTRAL
900 sq.ft. x 3va x 25 units	67500	67500
Small appliance 2 x 1500va x 25 units	75000	75000
Laundry 1 x 1500va x 25 units	37500	37500
	180000	180000

Table 220.42 Lighting Demand:		
First 3000va @ 100%	3000	3000
Next 117,000va @ 35%	40950	40950
Remaining 60,000va @ 25%	15000	15000
	58950	58950

	LINE	NEUTRAL
3 hp A/C 17a x 240v = 4080va x 25 units (omit heat)	102000	0
4 kw water heater 4kw x 25 units x 75%	75000	0
1.2 kw dishwasher 1.2kw x 25 units x 75%	22500	22500
1/2 hp compactor 9.8a x 120v = 1176va x 25 units x 75%	22050	22050
5 kw clothes dryer 5kw x 25 units = 125 kw x 34% T.220.54		
T.220.54 (25 dryers - 23 = 2 x .5 = 1 -35 = 34%)	40625	28438
8 kw range T.220.55 Col.C for 25 appliances = 40kw	40000	28000
•Largest motor 3 hp 17a x 240v = 4080va x25%	1020	0
	364,020va	161,250va

LINE = 364,020va/240v = **1517 amps**

NEUTRAL = 161,250va/240v = 672 amps•

•220.61(B2) Neutral load over 200 amps: First 200 amps @ 100% = 200 amps
                                           Next 472 amps @ 70% = 330 amps
                                                  530 amps neutral

Example: Use the General Method of calculation to determine the demand load on the service for a 30 unit condominium. The service is 4-wire, three-phase, 208/120v. Each condo unit has the following: (assume laundry on premises)

1100 sq.ft. living area
4 kw wall oven 208/120v
5 kw cooktop 208/120v
4.5 kw water heater 208v
1.5 kw dishwasher 120v
1.2 kw trash compactor 120v
5 hp heat pump 208v single-phase

	LINE	NEUTRAL
1100 sq.ft. x 3va x 30 units	99000	99000
Small appliance 2 x 1500va x 30 units	90000	90000
	189000	189000
Table 220.42 Lighting Demand:		
First 3000va @ 100%	3000	3000
Next 117,000 @ 35%	40950	40950
Remaining 69,000 @ 25%	17250	17250
	61200	61200
5 hp heat pump 30.8a x 208v = 6406va x 30 units	192180	0
4.5 kw water heater 4.5kw x 30 units x 75%	101250	0
1.5 kw dishwasher 1.5kw x 30 units x 75%	33750	33750
1.2 kw compactor 1.2kw x 30 units x 75%	27000	27000
4 kw oven x 30 units = 120kw x 18% (Col.B 60 appl.)	21600	15120
5 kw cooktop x 30 units = 150kw x 18% (Col.B 60 appl.)	27000	18900
•Largest motor 5 hp 30.8a x 208v = 6406va x 25%	1602	0
Laundry on premises 1500va x 30 units	45000	45000
	510582	200970

$$\text{LINE} = \frac{510,582\text{va}}{208\text{v x }1.732} = 1417 \text{ amps}$$

$$\text{NEUTRAL} = \frac{200,970}{208\text{v x }1.732} = 558 \text{ amps•}$$

Neutral load over 200 amps: First 200 amps @ 100% = 200 amps
Next 358 amps @ 70% = 251 amps
451 amps neutral

OPTIONAL METHOD - MULTIFAMILY DWELLING

STEP 1 - 220.84(C1)   Lighting load of 3 volt-amps x the total square footage of each unit x the total number of units.

STEP 2 - 220.84(C2)   Small appliance 2 x 1500va x total number of units. •Laundry 1 x 1500 va x total number of units. •If **laundry on premises**, omit laundry in this STEP and apply at STEP 7.

STEP 3 - 220.84(C3)   Calculate **all** appliances at nameplate x number of units.

STEP 4 - 220.84(C5)   Compare electric space heat against A/C load. Omit the smaller.

STEP 5 -   Total STEPS 1 through 4 for a total volt-amp load.

STEP 6 - Table 220.84   The demand factor percentage is based on the total number of units. Apply this demand percentage to the total va in STEP 5.

STEP 7 -   Include any houseloads at nameplate. •If laundry is on premises add 1500va x total number of units to service load.

STEP 8 -   Size the service by dividing the total volt-amps by the line voltage and select 75°C conductors from Table 310.16. •Neutral calculation is by General Method of calculation only.

Example: Use the Optional Method of calculation to determine the demand load on the service for a 25 unit apartment complex. 240/120v single-phase. Each apartment unit has the following:

900 sq.ft. living area
3 hp A/C unit 240v
3 kw electric space heat 240v
8 kw range 240/120v
4 kw water heater 240v
1.2 kw dishwasher 120v
1/2 hp compactor 120v
5 kw clothes dryer 240/120v

	LINE
900 sq.ft. x 3va x 25 units	67500
Small appliance 2 x 1500va x 25 units	75000
Laundry 1 x 1500va x 25 units	37500
3 hp A/C 17a x 240v = 4080va x 25 units	102000
•omit heat @ 3kw, A/C load is larger	
8 kw range x 25 units	200000
4 kw water heater x 25 units	100000
1.2 kw dishwasher x 25 units	30000
1/2 hp compactor 9.8a x 120v = 1176va x 25 units	29400
5 kw clothes dryer x 25 units	125000
	766400va total load

Table 220.84 Demand:
25 units = 35%   766,400va x 35% = 268,240va

LINE = 268,240va/240v = **1118 amps**.

NEUTRAL is calculated by General Method.

Example: Use the Optional Method of calculation to determine the demand load on the service for a 30 unit condominium. The service is 4-wire, three-phase, 208/120v. Each condo unit has the following: (assume laundry on premises)

1100 sq.ft. living area
4 kw wall oven 208/120v
5 kw cooktop 208/120v
4.5 kw water heater 208v
1.5 kw dishwasher 120v
1.2 kw trash compactor 120v
5 hp heat pump 208v single-phase

	LINE
1100 sq.ft. x 3va x 30 units	99000
Small appliance 2 x 1500va x 30 units	90000
4 kw oven x 30 units	120000
5 kw cooktop x 30 units	150000
4.5 kw water heater x 30 units	135000
1.5 kw dishwasher x 30 units	45000
1.2 kw compactor x 30 units	36000
5 hp heat pump 30.8a x 208v = 6406va x 30 units	192180
	867,180va total load

Table 220.84 Demand:

30 units = 33% 867,180va x 33% =	286169
Laundry on premises 1500va x 30 units	45000
	331,169va total demand

$$\text{LINE} = \frac{331,169va}{208v \times 1.732} = \textbf{919 amps}$$

NEUTRAL is calculated by General Method.

MOBILE HOME

550.18 Calculations

Example General Method: A mobile home floor is 70' x 10' and has two small appliance circuits, a 1000va 240v heater, a 200va 120v exhaust fan, a 400va 120v dishwasher, and a 7000va electric range.

	LINE	NEUTRAL
70' x 10' x 3va	2100	2100
Small appliance 2 x 1500va	3000	3000
Laundry 1 x 1500va	1500	1500
	6600	6600
Lighting Demand:		
First 3000va @ 100%	3000	3000
Remaining 3600va @ 35%	1260	1260
	4260	4260
1000va heater	1000	0
200va fan	200	200
400va dishwasher	400	400
7000va range x 80%	5600	5600
	11460va	10460va

LINE = 11,460va/240v = 47.75 amps   Use 50 amp supply cord.

550.31 Mobile Home Park Calculated Load

Example: What is the demand on the service for a mobile home park with 32 lots at 16,000va each?

Solution: Table 550.31: 32 lots x 16 kva = 512 kva x 24% (T.550.31) = 122.88 kva demand.

ummary   As with any exam question it requires the careful reading of each **word.**

BRANCH CIRCUIT

DWELLING UNIT

NEUTRAL

DRYER

OPTIONAL METHOD

OTHER LOAD

MULTIFAMILY

SMALL APPLIANCE

OMIT A/C or HEAT

MOBILE HOME

LAUNDRY

75% 4 or MORE

HOUSE LOAD

MINIMUM SIZE

LAUNDRY ON PREMISES

TABLE 220.42 DEMAND

NAMEPLATE

5 kw MINIMUM

Don't forget Tom Henry has 12 _VIDEO'S_ that cover all the chapters in this book and more!

Tom Henry's 12 VIDEOS FOR ELECTRICAL EXAMS

CHAPTER 6   TEST 1   DWELLINGS

1. The number of 20 amp branch circuits required for a dwelling unit is ____.

(a) 5   (b) 4   (c) 3   (d) 2

2. A dwelling with a floor area of 1400 square feet, exclusive of unoccupied cellar, unfinished attic and open porches, has a general lighting load of ____ va.

(a) 1400   (b) 2800   (c) 4200   (d) 4800

3. What is the minimum number of 15 amp branch circuits required for the general lighting load for a 2200 sq.ft. single family dwelling?

(a) 2   (b) 3   (c) 4   (d) 5

4. A 4.5 kw clothes dryer in a dwelling will add an additional ____ amps to the demand on the service neutral. 115/230 service voltage.

(a) 14   (b) 15   (c) 20   (d) 22

5. In a residence, using the optional method of calculation, the air-conditioning load would be calculated at ____ percent.

(a) 100   (b) 75   (c) 65   (d) 40

6. A dwelling measures 60' x 30' outside dimensions. The walls are one foot thick, what is the required general lighting load?

(a) 4872va   (b) 5400va   (c) 2700va   (d) 3640va

CHAPTER 6   TEST 2   DWELLINGS

Using the general method of calculation, calculate the service size for a dwelling unit with 1452 sq.ft. of living area. The service is 230/115v single-phase with the following equipment:

9.6 kw electric heat 230v
5 hp A/C unit 230v
1200va dishwasher 115v
1/2 hp disposal 115v
4.5 kw water heater 230v
4.0 kw clothes dryer 230/115v
15 kw range 230/115v

```
┌─────────────────────────────────────────┐
│        CHAPTER 6   TEST 3   DWELLINGS     │
└─────────────────────────────────────────┘
```

1. What is the demand on the service for a 5 hp A/C unit single-phase 230 volts and a 5 kw space heat furnace 230 volts?

(a) 5 kw   (b) 6440va   (c) 11,440va   (d) 3250va

2. A dwelling has a total of 2400 sq.ft. which includes a 10' x 20' carport. What is the general lighting load?

(a) 7200va   (b) 7800va   (c) 6600va   (d) 4500va

3. A dwelling has 2500 sq.ft. How many 15 amp branch circuits are required for the general lighting?

(a) 2   (b) 3   (c) 4   (d) 5

4. A residential service has an A/C load of 3800va and a space heat load of 6 kw. What does this add to the demand on the service? Use the optional method of calculation.

(a) 3900va   (b) 3800va   (c) 6000va   (d) 9800va

5. The neutral demand load required on the service for a 4.5 kw clothes dryer 240/120v would be _____ amps.

(a) 13.13   (b) 14.0   (c) 14.58   (d) 18.75

6. In a duplex, each unit requires a 100 amp main panel, the 200 amp service would require a minimum _____ THW copper conductor.

(a) #1   (b) #1/0   (c) #2/0   (d) #3/0

CHAPTER 6   TEST 4   DWELLINGS

Using the optional method of calculation, determine the minimum service size required for a dwelling with 2500 sq.ft. living area, 864 sq.ft. garage, and a porch area of 500 sq.ft. 230/115v single-phase with the following equipment:

12 kw total for electric heat (six separately controlled units) 230v
5 hp A/C unit 230v
14 kw electric range 230/115v
4.5 kw clothes dryer 230/115v
5 kw water heater 230v
1/3 hp compactor 115v
750va blender 115v
3/4 hp pool pump 230v
1200va dishwasher 115v

CHAPTER 6 TEST 5 DWELLINGS

1. A 60 unit apartment complex, each apartment has a 4.5 kw clothes dryer 240/120v. Using the general method of calculation for a dwelling, what is the demand on the service for these dryers?

(a) 67.5 kw (b) 270 kw (c) 75 kw (d) 300 kw

2. A 40 unit condo, each condo has a 4.5 kw water heater 230v. Using the general method of calculation, what is the demand on the service for these water heaters?

(a) 180 kw (b) 135 kw (c) 126 kw (d) 150 kw

3. The demand load on the service for the "house load" of ten - 1500va washers and ten - 5 kw clothes dryers in a 10 unit apartment would be _____ kw.

(a) 15 (b) 30 (c) 50 (d) 65

4. Using a 3 hp A/C unit 230v single-phase, and a 6 kw electric space heat furnace in a dwelling, which would be calculated on the service demand using the optional method of calculation?

(a) A/C (b) furnace (c) either (d) both

5. What is the feeder neutral demand for six - 4.5 kw clothes dryers 240/120v? Use general method of calculation.

(a) 27 kw (b) 15.7 kw (c) 21 kw (d) 18.9 kw

6. The demand load for ten - 1.5 kw dishwashers in a ten unit apartment would be _____ kw. Use optional method of calculation.

(a) 15 kw (b) 11.25 kw (c) 6.45 kw (d) 10.5 kw

Using the general method of calculation for a multifamily dwelling, determine the service demand for a 20 unit apartment building. 230/115v single-phase. Each unit has the following:

850 sq.ft. living area
3 hp A/C unit 230v
3 kw electric space heat 230v
4.5 kw clothes dryer 230/115v
1.5 kw dishwasher 115v
1/4 hp compactor 115v
10 kw range 230/115v

CHAPTER 6   TEST 7   DWELLINGS

1. A twenty unit apartment building, each unit has a 4 kw clothes dryer. These dryers add _____ kw to the service demand. Use optional method for multifamily dwelling.

(a) 30.4   (b) 75   (c) 35   (d) 28

2. A 30 unit apartment building, each unit has a 1500va dishwasher. Use the general method for a dwelling, the dishwashers add _____ kw to the service demand.

(a) 45   (b) 31.5   (c) 14.85   (d) 33.75

3. A six unit apartment, each unit has a 4.5 kw clothes dryer. Using the optional method for a multifamily dwelling, these six dryers would have a combined connected load of _____ kw.

(a) 27   (b) 11.88   (c) 13.2   (d) 20.25

4. Calculate the neutral demand on the service @ 230/115v for the following:

15 - 750 sq.ft. apartments
15 - 12 kw ranges
30 - small appliance circuits
15 - laundry circuits

(a) 238 amps   (b) 254 amps   (c) 275 amps   (d) none of these

5. 35 apartments, each unit has a 5 kw water heater. What is the demand on the service for these water heaters? Use optional method multifamily dwelling.

(a) 175 kw   (b) 52.5 kw   (c) 131.25 kw   (d) none of these

6. A 60 unit apartment, each unit has a 4 kw cooktop and a 5 kw oven. What is the demand on the service for the cooking equipment? Use optional method multifamily.

(a) 540 kw   (b) 97.2 kw   (c) 86.4 kw   (d) 129.6 kw

CHAPTER 6   TEST 8   DWELLINGS

Using the optional method of calculation for a multifamily dwelling, determine the service demand for a 24 unit apartment building. 208/120v three-phase service. Each unit has the following: (laundry on premises)

900 sq.ft. living area
6 kw central space heat 208v single-phase
3 hp A/C unit 208v single-phase
4 kw cooktop
3 kw oven
4.5 kw water heater
1.2 kw dishwasher

```
CHAPTER 6   TEST 9   DWELLINGS
```

1. A dwelling has 2,200 sq. ft. of habitable space and the following equipment: 6 kw range top, two 4 kw wall ovens, 4.5 kw water heater, 5 kw dryer, 1.2 kw dishwasher, 15 kw of heat supplied from 11 pieces of baseboard heat. Using the optional calculation, what is the minimum size service entrance conductor permitted?

(a) 108 amps   (b) 110 amps   (c) 112 amps   (d) 120 amps

2. A dwelling unit has a floor area of 1850 sq. ft. with the following appliances and equipment. 10 kw range, 4.5 kw clothes dryer, 1/2 hp 120v fan motor for the oil heater and air conditioning, 23 ampere 240v air conditioner. Using the standard calculation, what is the service size at 120/240v?

(a) 102 amps   (b) 106 amps   (c) 108 amps   (d) 112 amps

3. An apartment building has 12 dwelling units each with 1640 sq. ft. of space plus the following equipment: 12 kw range, 5 kw water heater, 5 kw dryer, 10.5 kw of heat supplied from 5 pieces of baseboard heat. Using the optional calculation, what is the minimum size service permitted for this building at 120/240v?

(a) 859 amps   (b) 1,074 amps   (c) 1,110 amps   (d) 2,096 amps

4. Using the optional calculation for twenty 1,000 sq.ft. apartments with 8kw ranges, 1ø 3 hp A/C units with laundry facilities available on the premises, what would be the demand load in kilowatts?

(a) less than 100   (b) 100-150   (c) 150-200   (d) 300-400

5. What is the ampacity required for a 2000 sq.ft. single-family dwelling 240/120v service with the following equipment: 12.5kw range, 10kw central A/C, 4.5kw water heater, 1.2 kw dishwasher, and a 5kw clothes dryer? Use optional method of calculation.

(a) 109 amps   (b) 117 amps   (c) 123 amps   (d) 141 amps

6. Using the optional calculation for a single-family dwelling 240 volt single-phase having 1800 sq. ft. with a 10 kw range, 4.5 kw water heater, 1.2 kw dishwasher, four separately controlled electric room heaters with a combined load of 10 kw, a 5 kw clothes dryer, the calculated load is _____ amps.

(a) 87.63   (b) 92.67   (c) 100.42   (d) 118.32

CHAPTER 7

COMMERCIAL SERVICE CALCULATIONS

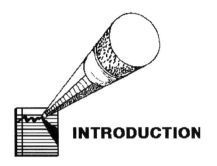

INTRODUCTION

Commercial service calculations are generally asked on a Master exam, not Journeyman.

This Chapter will include:

•Continuous Loading

•Paralleling Conductors

•Panelboard Sizing

•Three-phase Services

Prepare for the exam properly with *Tom Henry's* personally hi-lited looseleaf Code book "The Ultimate".

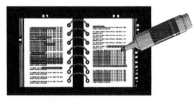

Over 1500 of the most frequent referenced areas of the Code are hi-lited for quick reference!

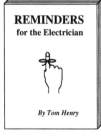

68 TABS ARE INSTALLED FOR YOU!

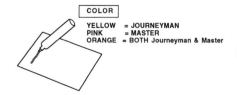

COLOR

YELLOW = JOURNEYMAN
PINK = MASTER
ORANGE = BOTH Journeyman & Master

PERSONALLY HI-LITED!

Commercial calculations are referred to as **other than a dwelling** or **nondwelling** and have different demand factors to apply.

The general method of calculation can be applied to any occupancy. The optional method of calculation can be applied only to a dwelling, restaurant or a **school building**.

When calculating the overcurrent device for a commercial building the lighting load must be **increased** 25% for continuous loading on the lighting.

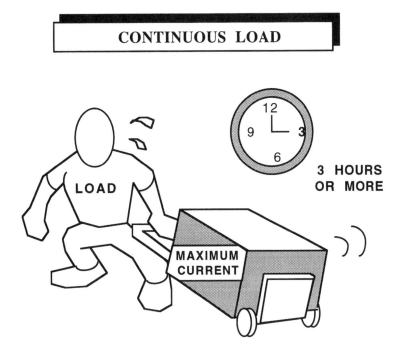

CONTINUOUS LOAD

LOAD

MAXIMUM CURRENT

3 HOURS OR MORE

Continuous load: A load where the maximum current is expected to continue for three hours or more.

215.2(A1) and 230.42(A1) Where a feeder or service supplies continuous loads or any combination of continuous and noncontinuous loads, the **rating of the overcurrent device** shall not be less than the noncontinuous load plus 125% of the continuous load.

The **only** lighting loads that are normally **not** continuous loads would be a dwelling or a hotel or motel **sleeping room**. The other occupancies shown in Table 220.12 such as banks, hospitals, offices, restaurants, schools, stores, etc. would be continuous loads as the lighting would operate for three hours or more. The lighting load is required to be increased by 25%.

Article 100 Definition of ampacity: The current in amperes a conductor can carry **continuously** under the conditions of use without exceeding its temperature rating.

The minimum feeder conductor size, without any adjustment or correction factors, shall have an allowable ampacity **equal to or greater** than the noncontinuous load plus **125% of the continuous load.**

FEEDER - CONTINUOUS LOAD - EXAMPLES

Example: A 50 amp continuous load x 125% = 62.5 amps requires a 70 amp overcurrent device. The feeder conductors are required to have an ampacity of at least 62.5 amps, this would be a #4 wire at 60°C which has an ampacity of 70.

70 amp BREAKER

ON   OFF   #4 TW = 70 AMPACITY   CONTINUOUS LOAD X 125%

Example: An 80 amp continuous load x 125% = 100 amps. The overcurrent device would be 100 amps. The feeder conductors are required to have an ampacity of at least 100 amps, this would be a #1 TW wire.

100 amp

#1 TW = 110 AMPACITY   CONTINUOUS LOAD X 125%

Example: A 100 amp continuous load x 125% = 125 amps. The overcurrent device would be 125 amps and the feeder conductors are required to have an ampacity **equal to or greater than** 125 amps.

125 amp

#1 THW = 130 AMPACITY   CONTINUOUS LOAD X 125%

Example: What is the general lighting demand on the overcurrent device for a 2000 sq.ft. restaurant?

Solution: Table 220.12   2000 sq.ft. x 2va x 125% = **5000va**.

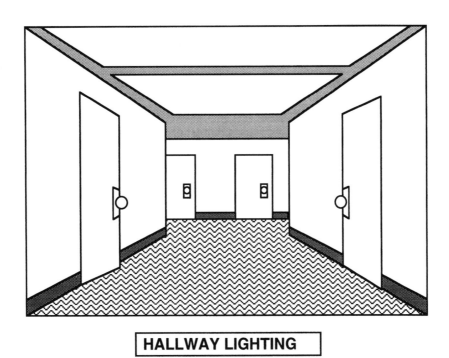

HALLWAY LIGHTING

Example: What is the general lighting demand on the overcurrent device for 1200 sq.ft. of hotel hallways?

Solution: Table 220.12   1200 sq.ft. x .5va x 125% = **750va**.

OFFICE BUILDING

Example: What is the general lighting demand on the overcurrent device for a 15,000 sq.ft. office building?

Solution: Table 220.12   15000 sq.ft. x 3.5va[b] x 125% = 65625va
                               [b] 15000 sq.ft x 1va   = 15000va
                                                                       80625va

[b] (220.14K2) In addition, a unit load of 1 volt-ampere per square foot shall be included for general purpose receptacle outlets when the actual number of general purpose receptacle outlets is unknown.

   Lighting is continuous, **receptacles** are **not** considered a continuous load. Apply the 25% increase only to the lighting.

MOTEL

Example: What is the lighting demand for 50 motel rooms? Each room is 12' x 24'.

Solution: Table 220.12 12' x 24' = 288 sq.ft. x 2va x 50 rooms = <u>28,800va</u>
          Table 220.42 Lighting demand:
          First 20,000va @ 50%   10,000va
          Remaining 8,800va @ 40%   <u>3,520va</u>
                                                 13,520va demand

Section 220.14(E) Outlet for heavy-duty lampholder   600va
        220.14(L) Other outlets   180va

220.14(H1): Where fixed multioutlet assemblies are employed, each 5 feet or fraction thereof of each separate and continuous length shall be considered as one outlet of not less than 180 volt-amperes capacity, except in locations where a number of appliances are likely to be used simultaneously, when each foot or fraction thereof shall be considered as an outlet of not less than 180 volt-amperes.

220.14(G2): A load of not less than 200 volt-amperes per linear foot of show window, measured horizontally along its base, shall be permitted instead of the specified unit load per outlet.

Table 220.42.   Lighting Load Feeder Demand Factors

Type of Occupancy	Portion of Lighting Load to Which Demand Factor Applies (volt-amperes)	Demand Factor Percent
Dwelling Units	First 3000 or less at	100
	From 3001 to 120,000 at............................	35
	Remainder over 120,000 at	25
* Hospitals	First 50,000 or less at	40
	Remainder over 50,000 at	20
* Hotels and Motels — Including Apartment Houses without	First 20,000 or less at	50
	From 20,001 to 100,000 at.........................	40
Provisions for Cooking by Tenants	Remainder over 100,000 at	30
Warehouses	First 12,500 or less at	100
(Storage)	Remainder over 12,500 at	50
All Others	Total Volt-amperes	100

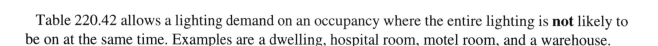

* The demand factors of this table shall not apply to the calculated load of feeders or sevices supplying areas in hospitals, hotels, and motels where the entire lighting is likely to be used at one time, as in operating rooms, ballrooms, or dining rooms.

Table 220.42 allows a lighting demand on an occupancy where the entire lighting is **not** likely to be on at the same time. Examples are a dwelling, hospital room, motel room, and a warehouse.

All others @ 100%, there is **no** demand for offices, banks, churches, restaurants, etc.

For the exam, common sense will help when applying Table 220.42. A lighting demand can be applied to a hotel **sleeping room**, but not to a hotel meeting room, dining room, hallway, parking lot lighting, or where the entire lighting is on at the same time. These loads are normally continuous lighting loads operating for 3 hours or more. Table 220.42 demand would not apply to these loads.

220.14(G2) For show window lighting, a load of not less than 200 volt-amperes shall be included for each linear foot of show window, measured horizontally along its base.

220.44 Receptacle loads - **Other than dwelling units**. In other than dwelling units, receptacle loads calculated in accordance with 220.14(H) and (I) shall be permitted to be made subject to the demand factors given in Table 220.42 or Table 220.44.

Table 220.44
Demand Factors for Nondwelling Receptacle Loads

Portion of Receptacle Load to which Demand Factor Applies (volt-amperes)	Demand Factor Percent
First 10 kVA or less	100
Remainder over 10kVA at	50

Example: An office building has a receptacle load of 50 kva, what is the demand for these receptacles?

Solution: Table 220.44 demand:

    First 10 kva @ 100%   =   10 kva

    Remaining 40 kva @ 50% =   <u>20 kva</u>

                                  30 kva demand

Example: A restaurant has a total of 75 receptacles, what is the demand for these receptacles?

Solution: 75 receptacles x 180va each = 13,500va

    Table 220.44 demand:

    First 10 kva @ 100%   =   10,000va

    Remaining 3500va @ 50% =   <u>1,750va</u>

                                11,750va demand

NONDWELLING

OVER 10 KVA LOAD		OVER 55 RECEPTACLES

APPLY TABLE 220.44

220.56 Kitchen Equipment - Other than Dwelling Unit(s). We covered this subject in Chapter 5 Cooking Equipment.

600.5(A) Each commercial building and each commercial occupancy accessible to pedestrians shall be provided at an accessible location outside the occupancy, with at least one outlet for sign or outline lighting use. The outlet(s) shall be supplied by a 20-ampere branch circuit which supplies no other load. Exception: Service hallways or corridors shall not be considered outside the occupancy to pedestrians.

220.14(F) Computed Load. The load for the required branch circuit installed for the supply of exterior signs or outline lighting shall be computed at a minimum of 1200 volt-amperes.

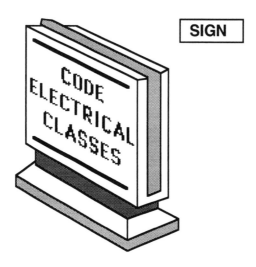

• If the exam calculation question mentions "accessible to pedestrians", then you would include the **1200va** for the sign. Not all commercial buildings are accessible to pedestrians.

SERVICE AND FEEDER SIZING - COMMERICAL

COMMERCIAL Calculation Format designed by Tom Henry

CONDUCTOR SIZING

STEP 1 - Table 220.12
    •215.2 & 230.42

•Lighting load of _____ va x total square footage. •Continuous feeder or service loads x 125%.

STEP 2 - Table 220.42

Apply lighting demand factor to hotel-motels, hospital, or warehouse. **All other** occupancies @ 100%.

STEP 3 - 220.60

Compare electric heat against A/C load. Omit the smaller load. For a **heat pump** include **both** the heat strips and compressor load.

STEP 4 - 220.14(E)
    220.14(L)
    220.14(H1)
    220.14G2)

Heavy-duty lampholders @ 600va each.
Other outlets @ 180va each.
Multioutlet assemblies each 5 feet @ 180va.
•Show-window lighting each linear foot @ 200va minimum.

STEP 5 - Table 220.44

Apply Table 220.44 demand factor to **receptacle** loads over **10 kva**.

STEP 6 - Table 220.56

Commercial cooking equipment demand factor for **3 or more** units of kitchen equipment.

STEP 7 - 220.50

Largest motor in F.L.C. to be increased 25%.

STEP 8 -

Size the service by dividing the total volt-amperes by the line voltage and select 75°C conductors from Table 310.16. The grounded service conductor shall **not** be smaller than the grounding electrode conductor sized from Table 250.66 per 250.24(C1).

220.88   New restaurants - Optional calculation.

Table 220.88 permits a demand on the service for a new restaurant. A connected load from 0 to 200 kva has a demand of 80% if the restaurant is **all** electric equipment. If some of the equipment is gas supplied a demand of 100% is required. Between 201-325 kva **all electric** has a demand factor of 10% (amount over 200) + 160.0 and 50% (amount over 200) + 200.0 for **not** all electric.

Example: A new restaurant has a connected load of 324 kva all electric equipment. What is the demand on the three-phase 208/120v service?

Solution: 324 -200 kva = 124 kva x 10% = 12.4 kva + 160 kva = 172.4 kva

$$\frac{172,400va}{208v \times 1.732} = 479 \text{ amps} \text{ Use 500 amp service}$$

If the restaurant had **not** all electric equipment :

Solution: 324 kva - 200 kva = 124 kva x 50% = 62 kva + 200 kva = 262 kva

$$\frac{262,000va}{208v \times 1.732} = 727 \text{ amps} \text{ Use 800 amp service}$$

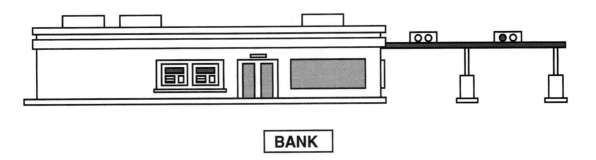

BANK

Example: What is the service demand on the overcurrent device for a 2500 sq.ft. bank 208/120v three-phase service with the following:

15 kw space heat 208v
7.5 hp A/C unit 208v three-phase
40 linear feet of show window lighting 120v

	LINE
2500 sq.ft. x 3.5va x 125%	10938va
2500 sq.ft. x 1va (unknown receptacles)	2500
15 kw heat	15000
7.5 hp A/C 24.2a x 208v x 1.732 = 8718va (omit A/C)	
40 ft. show window 40' x 200va x 125%	10000
	38,438va

LINE: $\dfrac{38,438va}{208v \times 1.732}$ = 107 amps

Example: A restaurant is 4000 sq.ft., service is 208/120v three-phase. What is the demand on the overcurrent device for the restaurant which has the following equipment?

2 - 14 kw ranges 208v three-phase
1 - 5 kw dishwasher 208v three-phase
2 - 3 kw booster heaters 208v three-phase
6 - heavy-duty lampholders 120v single-phase
30 - duplex receptacles 120v single-phase
2 - 4 kw deep fat fryers 208v single-phase
1 - 20 hp heat pump with 15 kw heat strips 208v three-phase

	LINE
4000 sq.ft. x 2va x 125%	10000va
2 - 14 kw ranges = 28000 @ 65% (Table 220.56)	18200
1 - 5 kw dishwasher = 5000 x 65% (Table 220.56)	3250
2 - 3 kw heaters = 6000 x 65% (Table 220.56)	3900
2 - 4 kw fryers = 8000 x 65% (Table 220.56)	5200
6 - heavy-duty lamps @ 600va each	3600
30 - receptacles @ 180va each	5400
1 - 20 hp heat pump 59.4a x 208v x 1.732	21399
15 kw heat strips	15000
Largest motor 21399va x 25%	5350
	91,299va

LINE: $\dfrac{91,299va}{208v \times 1.732}$ = 253 amps   Table 310.16   Use #250 kcmil THW copper

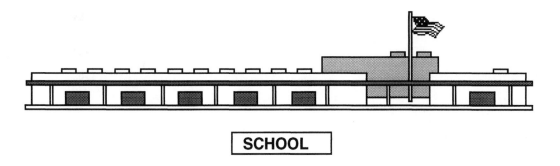

SCHOOL

Example: Use the general method of calculation and determine the demand on the overcurrent device for the following school building. 208/120v single-phase service.

20,000 sq.ft. of classroom
4,000 sq.ft. auditorium
2,000 sq.ft. cafeteria
10 kw outside lighting 120v
5 kw stage lighting 120v
200 receptacles 120v

Cafeteria equipment:

2 - 14 kw ranges 208v
2 - 6 kw ovens 208v
3 - 4 kw fryers 208v
1 - 12 kw water heater 208v
1 - 3 kw dishwasher 208v
1 - 6 kw booster heater 208v
2 - 2 kw toasters 120v
2 - 1/2 hp hood fans 120v
2 - 3/4 hp grill vent fans 120v

4 - 10 hp A/C units 208v
40 kw electric heat 208v

(Solution on next page)

School building continued:

Solution:	LINE
20,000 sq.ft. x 3va x 125%	75000
4,000 sq.ft. x 1va x 125%	5000
2,000 sq.ft. x 2va x 125%	5000
10 kw outside lights 10,000 x 125%	12500
5 kw stage lighting (assume noncontinuous)	5000
200 receptacles 200 x 180va = 36000	
Table 220.44: First 10 kva @ 100% =	10000
Remaining 26 kva @ 50% =	13000
2 - 14 kw ranges = 28 kw x 65% (T.220.56)	18200
2 - 6 kw ovens = 12 kw x 65% (T.220.56)	7800
3 - 4 kw fryers = 12 kw x 65% (T.220.56)	7800
1 - 12 kw water heater = 12 kw x 65% (T.220.56)	7800
1 - 3 kw dishwasher = 3 kw x 65% (T.220.56)	1950
1 - 6 kw heater = 6 kw x 65% (T.220.56)	3900
2 - 2 kw toasters = 4 kw x 65% (T.220.56)	2600
2 - 1/2 hp fans 9.8a x 120v = 1176va x 2 = 2352 va x 65%	1529
2 - 3/4 hp fans 13.8a x 120v = 1656va x 2 = 3312 x 65%	2153
4 - 10 hp A/C units 55a x 208v = 11440va x 4	45760
40 kw heat (omit)	
Largest motor 11440va x 25%	2860
	227,852va

LINE: 227,852va/208v = 1095 amps   Use 1200 amp service

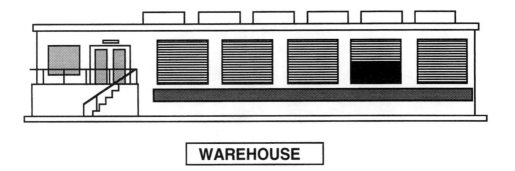

WAREHOUSE

Example: What is the demand on the service for an 80,000 sq.ft. warehouse (noncontinuous lighting), 240/120v single-phase service, with the following:

2 - 7 1/2 hp A/C units 240v
15 kw electric heat 240v
80 duplex receptacles 120v
10 - 3 hp freezer units 240v

	LINE	NEUTRAL
80,000 sq.ft. x .25va	20,000	20,000
80 receptacles 80 x 180va = 14,400va	14,400	14,400
	34,400	34,400
Table 220.42 demand:		
First 12,500va @ 100% =	12500	12500
Remaining 21,900va @ 50% =	10950	10950
2 - 7 1/2 hp A/C units 40a x 240v = 9600va x 2	19200	0
15 kw heat (omit)		
10 - 3 hp freezer units 17a x 240v = 4080va x 10	40800	0
Largest motor 9600va x 25%	2400	0
	85,850va	23,450va

LINE: 85,850va/240v = 358 amps   Table 310.16   #500 kcmil THW copper

NEUTRAL: 23,450va/240v = 98 amps*

Table 250.66 requires a size 0 copper grounding electrode conductor

*250.24(C1) Grounded service conductor (neutral) can **not** be smaller than the grounding electrode conductor.

OFFICE BUILDING

Example: What is the demand on the feeder overcurrent device for a 25' x 30' office, 20' show window, ground floor footage accessible to pedestrians, 3 hp A/C 230v single-phase. Panel is supplied with 230/115v single-phase.

	LINE
750 sq.ft. x 3.5va x 125%	3281
750 sq.ft. x 1va (unknown receptacles)	750
20' show window 20' x 200va x 125%	5000
sign 1200va x 125%	1500
3 hp A/C unit 17a x 230v	3910
Largest motor 3910va x 25%	978
	15,419va total

LINE: 15,419va/230v = 67 amp demand.

Example: What is the minimum power required for the following boat berth receptacles?

15 - 20 amp 120v locations
12 - 30 amp 120v locations
 8 - 50 amp 120v locations

Article 555.12:

15 x 20 amps = 300 amps
12 x 30 amps = 360 amps
 8 x 50 amps = 400 amps
‾‾‾   ‾‾‾‾‾‾‾‾‾‾
35   1060 amps

Table 555.12: For 35 receptacles 60% demand

1060 amps x 60% = **636 amps minimum required**.

OPTIONAL CALCULATION - SCHOOL

Section 220.86 and Table 220.86   Optional Method demand factors for feeders and service conductors.

   At first, Table 220.86 seems confusing, but after working two or three school calculations you will find the optional method to be a very fast and easy calculation.

OPTIONAL method format for a **SCHOOL BUILDING**

STEP 1 - Table 220.86   Divide the total connected load by the total square footage of the school to determine the volt-amperes per square foot.

STEP 2 - Table 220.86   Apply the demand factor from Table 220.86 to the total volt-amps per square foot from STEP 1.

STEP 3 -   Multiply the va demand from STEP 2 times the total square footage of the school for the demand on the service in va.

Example: Using the optional method, what is the demand on the service for a school building with a total connected load of 345 kva and a total square footage of 15,000?

Solution:
First STEP is to divide 345,000va/15,000 sq.ft. = 23 va per square foot.
STEP 2 is to apply the demand factor from Table 220.86 to the 23va:
Connected load up to and including 3va @ 100%
(First 3 va @ 100%) =   3 va
Connected load over 3va and including 20va @ 75%
(Next 17va @ 75%)   =   12.75 va
Connected load over 20va @ 25%
(23va - 20va = 3va over 20) 3va x 25% =   .75 va
                                                  _____
                                                  16.5 va total per square foot

STEP 3 16.5va x 15,000 sq.ft. = **247,500va demand on the service**

Example: Using the optional method, what is the demand on the service for a school building with a total connected load of 247 kva and a total square footage of 26,000?

Solution: 247,000va/26,000 sq.ft. = 9.5va

Table 220.86 demand:
3va @ 100% = 3va
6.5va @ 75% = 4.875va
          7.875va total

7.875va x 26,000 total sq.ft = **204,750va demand on the service**.

Example: Using the optional method, what is the demand on the service for a school building with a total connected load of 500 kva and a total square footage of 20,000?

Solution: 500,000va/20,000 sq.ft. = 25va

Table 220.86 demand:
 3va @ 100% = 3va
17va @ 75%   = 12.75va
 5va @ 25%   = 1.25va
          17va total

17va x 20,000 total sq.ft. = **340,000va demand on the service**.

Example: Using the optional method, what is the demand on the service for a school building with a total connected load of 420 kva and a total square footage of 12,000?

Solution: 420,000va/12,000 sq.ft. = 35va

Table 220.86 demand:
 3va @ 100% = 3va
17va @ 75%   = 12.75va
15va @ 25%   = 3.75va
          19.5va total

19.5va x 12,000 total sq.ft. = **234,000va demand on the service**.

PANELBOARD   SIZING

Sections 210.11(B) and 408.30 require the panelboard to have a busbar ampacity at least equal to the **minimum** calculated load.

Note: Manufacturers refer to light-duty panelboards as **loadcenters**.

Section 240.4(B2,3): If the allowable current-carrying capacity of a conductor (ampacity) does not correspond to the rating of a standard size fuse or breaker, the next larger rating of fuse or breaker may be used where the rating of the fuse or breaker does **not** exceed **800 amps**.

Example: A calculated load of 375 amps is fed by #500 kcmil THW copper conductors. What is the required overcurrent protection size?

Solution: 240.4(B) and 240.6 standard size = **400 amps**.

A violation would be a 1200 amp circuit breaker protecting three #500 kcmil THW copper conductors in parallel per phase (380 x 3 = 1140 ampacity). 240.3(B): The maximum overcurrent device permitted is **1000 amp**.

215.2(A1): Where a feeder supplies **continuous loads**, the rating of the overcurrent device shall not be less than **125%** of the continuous load.

Exception: Where the assembly, including the overcurrent devices protecting the feeder(s), are listed for operation at **100 percent** of their rating, neither the ampere rating of the overcurrent device nor the ampacity of the feeder conductors shall be less than the sum of the continuous load plus the noncontinuous load.

Only a very small percentage of feeder protective devices are **listed** for **continuous load**, and then only in **600 amps or above**. Breakers listed for 100% continuous loading are ventilated to prevent the generation of excessive heat.

Example: What size overcurrent protection is required for a continuous load of 80 amps?

Solution: 80 amps x 125% (215.2A1) = **100 amp overcurrent device** or 100 amp overcurrent device x 80% = **80 amp maximum continuous load**.

As you can see, **80%** of its rating is the **reciprocal** of having a rating of at least **125%** of the continuous load.

EXAMPLES

Example: Size the feeder to this 200 amp *Continuous load*. The equipment is rated at 75°C.

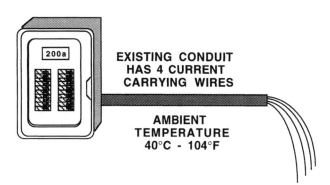

EXISTING CONDUIT HAS 4 CURRENT CARRYING WIRES

AMBIENT TEMPERATURE 40°C - 104°F

The first step is to select the overcurrent device. 200 amp x 125% = 250 circuit breaker.

The feeder conductor shall have an ampacity equal to or greater than 200a x 125% = 250 minimum ampacity required.

A #300 kcmil THW has a normal ampacity of 285 x 80% (T.310.15(B2a) = 228a x .88 (correction factor) = 200.64 or 201 amps, but the #300 kcmil THW with a derated ampacity of 201 would not be protected by a 250 amp breaker nor does it has the required 250 ampacity.

A #350 kcmil THW has a normal ampacity of 310 x 80% (T.310.16B2a) = 248a x .88 (correction factor) = 218.24 or 218 amps. The #350 kcmil THW can be protected at the next higher size breaker above it's *derated* ampacity, which is a 225 amp breaker per section 240.6, but it would not be protected by a 250 amp breaker.

A #400 kcmil THW has a normal ampacity of 335 x 80% (T.310.15B2a) = 268a x .88 (correction factor) = 235.84 or 236 amps. The #400 kcmil THW with a *derated* ampacity of 236 amps can be protected by the next higher size breaker; a 250 amp per section 240.3(B), but it does not have the required 250 ampacity.

A #500 kcmil THW has a normal ampacity of 380 x 80% (T.310.15B2a) = 304a x .88 (correction factor) = 267.52 or 268 amps. The #500 kcmil THW with a derated ampacity of 268 amps is protected with a 250 amp breaker and has the required ampacity of 250 amps for continuous loading.

A #400 kcmil **THHN** has a normal ampacity of 380 x 80% (T.310.15B2a) = 304a x .*91* (correction factor = 276.64 or 277 amps. The #400 kcmil THHN with a derated ampacity of 277 amps is protected by the 250 amp breaker, has the required 250 ampacity, and meets the 75°C termination rating.

The minimum size conductors permitted for the conditions are #500 kcmil THW or #400 kcmil **THHN**.

Shown below is a 76 amp load which would require a #3 THHN conductor which has an ampacity of 110 amps, but can only be loaded to a 60°C ampacity of 85 amps.

The circuit breaker would be the next higher standard size of 80 amps.

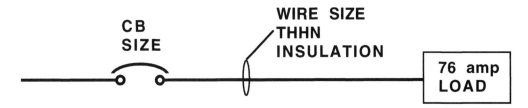

If the load was *continuous*, 76a x 125% = 95 amps. The next higher standard size breaker is a 100 amp. The breaker can only be loaded 80% x 100a = 80 amps. The load is 76 amps so this is sufficient. The #3 THHN has an ampacity of 110 amps, so it will be properly protected using a 100 amp breaker.

If the load was *continuous* with *four current carrying conductors*, the #3 THHN with an ampacity of 110a x 80% (T.310.15B2a) = 88 ampacity. The conductors must be protected at the *derated* ampacity of 88 amps. The next higher standard size breaker is a 90 amp. Since this is a continuous load of 76a x 125% = 95a, a 100 amp breaker is required and can be loaded to 80 amps. Using a required 100 amp breaker does *not* protect the conductors with an ampacity of 88.

A #2 THHN has a normal ampacity of 130 amps x 80% (T.310.15b2a) = 104 ampacity. The 90°C THHN can only be *loaded* to the 60°C ampacity. A #2 TW @ 60°C has an ampacity of 95 amps. A #2 THHN is the smallest THHN conductor permitted for a continuous load and four current carrying conductors.

Ampacities from Table 310.16 are based @ 86°F. A more realistic ambient would be 96-104°F. At this temperature the #2 THHN would be derated twice, 130a x 80% = 104a x .91 (correction factor) = 94.64 or 95 ampacity. A 100 amp breaker would still protect the #2 THHN conductors.

A #2 THHN can only be loaded to the 60°C ampacity. A #2 TW has an ampacity of 95 amps. The actual load is 76 amps.

A #2 THHN is the *smallest* conductor the Code would allow on a 100 amp breaker for a 76 amp continuous with four current carrying conductors and an ambient temperature of 96°F.

THE 90°C THHN CAN ONLY BE LOADED TO THE 60°C AMPACITY

PARALLELING CONDUCTORS

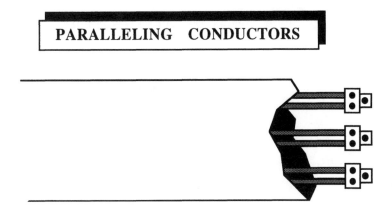

Most exam questions ask the demand on the service or feeder, rather than what size conductor is required. The reason being in the larger commercial services, paralleling conductors enters into the design. Since there can be **more** than **one** correct combination of paralleling, the exam question will ask for the demand on the service.

Example: One #2000 kcmil THW copper has an ampacity of 665, or you could parallel **two** #400 kcmil THW conductors (2 x 335a = 670 ampacity), or you could parallel **three** #4/0 THW conductors (3 x 230a = 690 ampacity) or you could parallel **four** #2/0 THW conductors (4 x 175a = 700 ampacity). As you can see there is more than one correct combination.

The reason for paralleling conductors is that larger conductors cost more per ampere than smaller conductors. Smaller conductors carry more current per circular mil than large conductors.

Example: Table 310.16 #10 TW copper = 30 ampacity   Table 8 #10 = 10,380 circular mils. A conductor **ten** times larger than a #10 from Table 8 would be a **#1/0** with a circular mil area of 105,600. But, from Table 310.16, the ampacity of a #1/0 TW copper is **not** ten times greater than a #10 TW.

It is seldom economical to use conductors larger than 1000 kcmil, because the increase in ampacity is very small in proportion to the increase in circular mil area.

A 1000 kcmil THW copper conductor has an ampacity of 545 amps, **two** #300 kcmil THW copper conductors connected in parallel have an ampacity of 2 x 285a = 570 amps.

Instead of 1000 kcmil of copper, you can parallel **two** 300 kcmil conductors for a total of 600 kcmil of copper. Less copper and more ampacity, but by reducing the overall cross section of conductor by paralleling instead of a single conductor per phase produces **higher resistance** and **greater voltage drop** than the same length as a single conductor per phase. Always make a voltage drop calculation when paralleling conductors.

Example: A three-phase circuit with three #1000 kcmil THW conductors

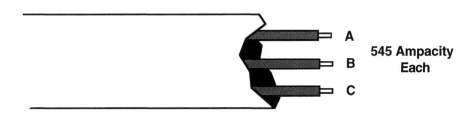

545 Ampacity
Each

Paralleling two #300 kcmil THW conductors per phase, but since we have a total of six current carrying conductors in a raceway, **T.310.15(B2a) would apply.** 2 x 285a = 570 ampacity x **80% (T.310.15B2a) = 456 reduced ampacity**.

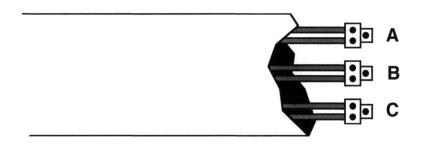

To **avoid** applying T.310.15(B2a) for an ampacity adjustment deration you can install two **separate** conduits.

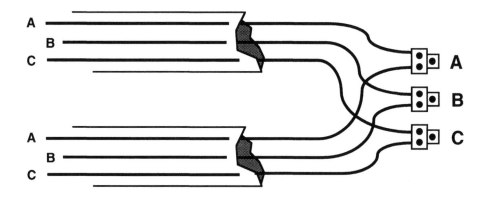

Each conduit now has only 3 current carrying conductors. T.310.15(B2a) would **not** apply. The ampacity would now be 2 x 285a = **570 ampacity**.

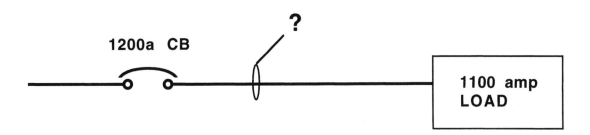

Example: If three #500 kcmil THW conductors were paralleled, the ampacity would be 3 x 380a = 1140 amps. Since you are *over* 800 amps you cannot go to the next higher size unless the conductor ampacity is equal to or higher than the breaker size of 1200 amps per section 240.4(C).

If #500 kcmil **THHN** conductors were used instead of THW, the ampacity in parallel would be 430a x 3 = 1290 ampacity. A 1200 amp overcurrent device can be used and the conductors would be protected at their ampacity. Of course the 90°C THHN conductors could only be *loaded* to the 75°C ampacity of 1140 amps.

Example: The same load only now it's *continuous*.

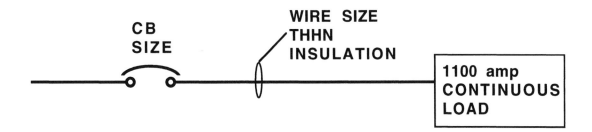

The first step is to determine the breaker size. For example, for a 1100 amp *continuous* load x 125% = 1375 amps. The Code states for continuous loading the overcurrent device shall not be loaded over 80%. In this example we could not select a lower standard size of 1200 amps because of the 80% load limitation required. 1200 amp overcurrent device x 80% = 960 amps maximum continuous load permitted, and the actual load is 1100 amps.

Section 240.6 lists the next higher standard size at 1600 amps. A 1600 amp overcurrent device x 80% = 1280 amps maximum continuous load permitted.

The feeder conductors are required to have an ampacity of at least 1100a x 125% = **1375a.**

The overcurrent device would be a 1600 amp. The THHN minimum size would be 3 - #750 kcmil THHN @ 535a x 3 = 1605 ampacity. The conductors would be protected at 1600 amps. The 90°C THHN conductors could only be loaded to the 75°C ampacity of 475a x 3 = 1425 ampacity. The actual load is 1100 amps. The required ampacity for continuous load is 1375 amps.

310.4 Conductors in Parallel. Aluminum, copper-clad aluminum, or copper conductors of size **#1/0 and larger**, comprising each phase, neutral or grounded circuit conductor, shall be permitted to be connected in parallel (electrically joined at both ends to form a single conductor).

The paralleled conductors in each phase, polarity, neutral, or grounded conductor shall:
1. Be the same length
2. Have the same conductor material
3. Be the same size in circular mil area
4. Have the same insulation type
5. Be terminated in the same manner

Each phase is not required to be the same length, but different lengths in the phases can cause different voltages from phase to phase as with three-phase motors.

Remember, where parallel conductors are installed in separate raceways, the raceways must have the same physical characteristics. The impedance of a circuit in a metal raceway is different from the impedance of the same circuit in a nonmetallic raceway. Using raceways with different characteristics would unbalance currents.

Separate phase conductors should be located close together. All phases and the neutral (and grounding conductor, if used) be installed in each conduit, even when the conduit is nonmetallic.

It is necessary to run the equipment grounding conductor with the circuit conductors to keep the AC impedance of the equipment grounding conductor as low as possible.

Where equipment grounding conductors are run in parallel in multiple raceways, each parallel equipment grounding conductor shall be sized on the basis of the ampere rating of the overcurrent device protecting the circuit conductors in the raceway in accordance with Table 250.122. A **full-sized** equipment grounding conductor is required in **each** raceway enclosing parallel conductors. Each equipment grounding conductor must be capable of carrying full fault currents.

The neutral conductor when installed in parallel would require a **minimum** size of **#1/0** per Section 310.4.

Summary   Table 220.12 is the starting point to use the listed va per square foot required for the occupancy.

•The demand factors for lighting, receptacles, cooking equipment, optional school, etc. must be applied to reach the minimum size.

•The maximum number of receptacles on a branch circuit is limited by the 180 va.

•Always apply the 1.732 for three-phase calculations.

•Continuous loading rules apply in commercial calculations.

Careful reading of a question is always a must!

Question: A 5000 sq.ft. industrial commercial (loft) building with unknown receptacles has a general lighting load of _____ kva.

(a) 10,000   (b) 15,000   (c) 100   (d) 10

Solution: Table 220.12 lists a loft building at 2 va per square foot. 5000 sq.ft. x 2va = 10,000va.

Choice **(a)** is 10,000 which makes it an easy selection, BUT, the question asked for **k**va and not va. The correct answer is **(d)** 10 **k**va.

You must not only read each word carefully, but even each letter carefully.

Before you can answer a calculation question correctly, you must first understand what the question is asking. It is so easy to select the incorrect choice.

By Tom Henry and Tim Henry

          An excellent book for more calculations and electrical designing is the "ELECTRICAL DESIGNING WORKBOOK". A must workbook for electrical students.

Separate chapters and exams on:
•Terminations
•90°C wire
•Continuous loads
•Derating conductors using the variables
••Starting at the beginning with over 375 pages on electrical designing

1. A motel has a connected load of 35 kva, what does this lighting load add to the service demand?

(a) 35 kva   (b) 17.5 kva   (c) 16 kva   (d) 14 kva

2. A 100 unit motel has a total of 4000 square feet of hallways. The hallway lighting load adds _____ va to the demand on the overcurrent device.

(a) 2000   (b) 2500   (c) 3000   (d) 4000

3. A motel has 300 receptacles in addition to those in the rooms. How much do they add to the service demand?

(a) 0 - 10 kva   (b) 10 - 25 kva   (c) 25 - 30 kva   (d) 30 - 40 kva

4. What is the general lighting load on the overcurrent device for an office with a total square footage of 1500?

(a) 6.5 - 7 kva   (b) 7 - 8 kva   (c) 8 - 8.4 kva   (d) 8.4 - 9 kva

5. Where connected to a made electrode, that portion of the grounding electrode conductor which is the sole connection to the grounding electrode shall not be required to be larger than _____ copper.

(a) #8   (b) #6   (c) #4   (d) #2

6. Using the optional calculation for schools, the demand on the service for a connected load of 300 kva and a total of 12,500 sq.ft. would be approximately _____ kva.

(a) 75   (b) 210   (c) 230   (d) none of these

CHAPTER 7 TEST 2 COMMERCIAL

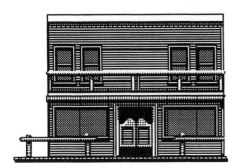

Calculate the demand on the overcurrent device for a store with a total of 3750 square feet. The store has 50 feet of show window, 20 duplex receptacles, 1500va parking lot lighting, 10 kw electric heat, and the store has ground floor footage accessible to pedestrians. Service is 240/120v single-phase.

CHAPTER 7 TEST 3 COMMERCIAL

---

1. A 40,000 sq.ft. office building has how many 20 amp lighting and receptacle circuits when the number of receptacles is unknown? Do not use continuous load factor on lighting.

(a) 0 -25 (b) 26 -50 (c) 51 - 80 (d) 81 - 100

2. An office building has a neutral connected load of 45.6 kva without any household cooking equipment, the ampacity of the conductor for the neutral must be at least _____ amps. 240/120v single-phase service.

(a) 190 (b) 227 (c) 238 (d) none of these

3. A commercial building has a 200 amp service using copper conductors with THW insulation. The minimum size copper grounding electrode conductor would be _____ AWG.

(a) #6 (b) #4 (c) #2 (d) cannot be determined

4. What is the demand for a 20,000 sq.ft. school building with a total connected load of 680 kva? Use optional method of calculation.

(a) 680 kva (b) 385 kva (c) 170 kva (d) none of these

5. A 175 amp fuse is protecting a circuit. What size copper equipment grounding conductor is required?

(a) #10 (b) #8 (c) #6 (d) #4

6. An installation of 40 feet of a fixed multioutlet assembly installed in a continuous length in an office occupancy shall be calculated at _____ amps.

(a) 12 (b) 16 (c) 20 (d) 30

Calculate the demand on the overcurrent device for a 15,000 sq.ft. restaurant, 208/120v three-phase service. Use the general method of calculation. The restaurant has the following:

2 - 35 kw ranges
1 - 15 kw booster heater
1 - 20 kw water heater
1 - 6 kw dishwasher
10 - heavy-duty lampholders
65 - duplex receptacles
20 kva parking lot lighting
4 - 5 hp A/C units 208v three-phase
20 kw electric heat

1. The minimum size service conductors for a restaurant requiring a 200 amp service would be _____ THW.

(a) #2/0　(b) #3/0　(c) #4/0　(d) #250 kcmil

2. What is the minimum demand on the service for 500 duplex receptacles in a hospital?

(a) 28 kva　(b) 35 kva　(c) 50 kva　(d) 75 kva

3. A commercial building has a service voltage of 120/240v single-phase and a connected load of 395 amps, after demands are taken. If the service entrance conductors are paralleled in a single conduit, what is the minimum size conductors permitted?

(a) six #2/0 THW cu　(b) six #3/0 THW cu　(c) six #4/0 THW cu　(d) six #250 kcmil THW cu

4. What is the demand on the overcurrent device for a 20,000 sq.ft. motel with a 750 sq.ft. office, 5000 sq.ft. parking garage, and 2500 sq.ft. of hallway lighting?

(a) 26,719va　(b) 30,719va　(c) 58,719va　(d) 58,907va

5. What is the minimum demand for 120 receptacles in a bank building?

(a) 21.6 kva　(b) 15.8 kva　(c) 10.8 kva　(d) 9 kva

6. The service conductors are #750 kcmil THW aluminum, what size AL grounding electrode conductor is required?

(a) #1/0 cu　(b) #2/0 cu　(c) #3/0 AL　(d) #4/0 AL

CHAPTER 7   TEST 6   COMMERCIAL

Calculate the demand on the overcurrent device for a bank building with 10,000 sq.ft., 208/120v three-phase service. The bank has the following:

12,000va parking lot lighting
200 duplex receptacles
100 feet of fixed multioutlet assemblies
Ground floor footage accessible to pedestrians

1. A 10,000 sq.ft. office building has how many 20 amp lighting and receptacle circuits, when the number of receptacles is unknown? Do not use continuous load factor.

(a) 15   (b) 18   (c) 19   (d) none of these

2. A motel has a service voltage of 120/240 single-phase with a total connected load of 398 amps. The service entrance conductors are paralleled in a single conduit. What is the minimum size THW copper conductors that can be used, in parallel, for this installation?

(a) 3/0   (b) 250 kcmil   (c) 500 kcmil   (d) 1000 kcmil

3. What is the demand on the overcurrent device for a 150,000 sq.ft. warehouse? Lighting is noncontinuous.

(a) 37.5 kva   (b) 25 kva   (c) 12.5 kva   (d) none of these

4. What is the demand for a 25,000 sq.ft. school building with a total connected load of 750 kva? Use optional method of calculation.

(a) 30 kva   (b) 456,250va   (c) 1500 amps   (d) none of these

5. What is the lighting demand on the overcurrent device for a 30,000 sq.ft. office building?

(a) 135,000va   (b) 161,250va   (c) 168,750va   (d) none of these

6. A warehouse has 75 duplex receptacles, what is the minimum demand on the service for these receptacles?

(a) 11,750va   (b) 13,500va   (c) 13,000va   (d) none of these

CHAPTER 7   TEST 8   COMMERCIAL

What is the minimum demand on the overcurrent device for a 100 unit motel, each unit is 12' x 20'. The motel complex has the following:

4000 sq.ft. hallways
Beauty shop 25' x 25'
Office 30' x 50'
12,000 sq.ft. parking garage
Branch bank 30' x 40'

```
CHAPTER 7  TEST 9  COMMERCIAL
```

1. What is the computed load for a store room with the following? 2,300 sq. ft. of floor area, 70 receptacles, 15 feet of show window, a 24 amp (rated-load current motor) three-phase air-conditioner, a 120v 1500 watt water heater. The service is 120/208v wye.

(a) 87 amps   (b) 93 amps   (c) 94 amps   (d) 98 amps

2. A bank branch has 3,755 sq. ft. of floor area, twenty-nine 120v receptacles and 40 kw of electric heat. What is the minimum ampacity of the service conductors at 120/208v three-phase?

(a) 136.75 amps   (b) 168.12 amps   (c) 171.12 amps   (d) 296.39 amps

3. A recreational vehicle park has 25 sites. Each site is equipped with a 20 amp and a 30 amp receptacle. The service will also serve a service building on the premises that will have a computed load of 87 amps. What is the minimum feeder ampacity for the service conductors supplying this vehicle park?

(a) 194 amps   (b) 245 amps   (c) 350 amps   (d) 462 amps

4. A restaurant served by a 208/120v three-phase, 4-wire service has the following kitchen equipment: 2.5kw dishwasher, 2 kw booster water heater, 6 kw water heater, 2 - 12kw ranges, 2 - 5kw deep fryers, 2 - 2kw toasters, 2kw warming oven, (all three-phase loads), 3.2 kva continuous lighting, 67-receptacles 12 kva. The minimum size THW copper feeder to the kitchen panel is _____.

(a) #2   (b) #1   (c) #1/0   (d) #2/0

5. A mobile home park has 26 mobile homes each with a computed load of 22,000 va. What is the ampacity of the service conductors required to serve this park?

(a) 260 amps   (b) 572 amps   (c) 1000 amps   (d) 1750 amps

CHAPTER 8

EXAMS

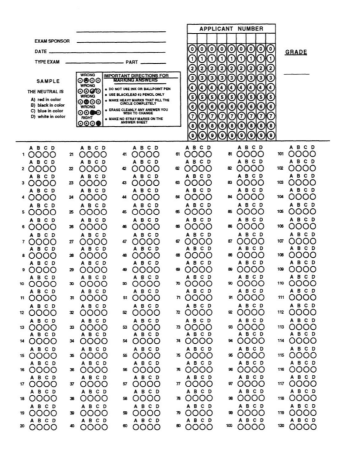

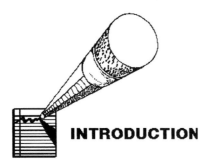

INTRODUCTION

Chapter 8 is a series of full calculation exams. The first exams are for the Journeyman Electrician level, the remaining exams are for the Master Electrician level.

Each exam contains 30 open book calculation questions with a time limit of three hours.

After completing each exam turn to the answer sheets in the back of this book and grade yourself. 75% is passing.

To calculate your grade, simply **divide** the number of **correct** answers by the total number of questions (30). Example: 23 correct answers divided by 30 questions would equal 76.66%.

Don't forget Tom Henry has 12 *VIDEO'S* that cover all the chapters in this book and more!

EXAM SPONSOR ____________________

DATE ____________________

TYPE EXAM ____________________ PART __________

APPLICANT NUMBER								
0	0	0	0	0	0	0	0	0
1	1	1	1	1	1	1	1	1
2	2	2	2	2	2	2	2	2
3	3	3	3	3	3	3	3	3
4	4	4	4	4	4	4	4	4
5	5	5	5	5	5	5	5	5
6	6	6	6	6	6	6	6	6
7	7	7	7	7	7	7	7	7
8	8	8	8	8	8	8	8	8
9	9	9	9	9	9	9	9	9

GRADE

____

SAMPLE

THE NEUTRAL IS

A) red in color
B) black in color
C) blue in color
D) white in color

WRONG A B C D
WRONG A B C D
WRONG A B C D
WRONG A B C D
RIGHT A B C D

IMPORTANT DIRECTIONS FOR MARKING ANSWERS

- DO NOT USE INK OR BALLPOINT PEN
- USE BLACKLEAD #2 PENCIL ONLY
- MAKE HEAVY MARKS THAT FILL THE CIRCLE COMPLETELY
- ERASE CLEANLY ANY ANSWER YOU WISH TO CHANGE
- MAKE NO STRAY MARKS ON THE ANSWER SHEET

JOURNEYMAN CALCULATIONS EXAM

1 A B C D	21 A B C D	41 A B C D	61 A B C D	81 A B C D	101 A B C D
2 A B C D	22 A B C D	42 A B C D	62 A B C D	82 A B C D	102 A B C D
3 A B C D	23 A B C D	43 A B C D	63 A B C D	83 A B C D	103 A B C D
4 A B C D	24 A B C D	44 A B C D	64 A B C D	84 A B C D	104 A B C D
5 A B C D	25 A B C D	45 A B C D	65 A B C D	85 A B C D	105 A B C D
6 A					
7 A					
8 A					
9 A					
10 A					
11 A					
12 A	32	52	72	92	112
13 A B C D	33 A B C D	53 A B C D	73 A B C D	93 A B C D	113 A B C D
14 A B C D	34 A B C D	54 A B C D	74 A B C D	94 A B C D	114 A B C D
15 A B C D	35 A B C D	55 A B C D	75 A B C D	95 A B C D	115 A B C D
16 A B C D	36 A B C D	56 A B C D	76 A B C D	96 A B C D	116 A B C D
17 A B C D	37 A B C D	57 A B C D	77 A B C D	97 A B C D	117 A B C D
18 A B C D	38 A B C D	58 A B C D	78 A B C D	98 A B C D	118 A B C D
19 A B C D	39 A B C D	59 A B C D	79 A B C D	99 A B C D	119 A B C D
20 A B C D	40 A B C D	60 A B C D	80 A B C D	100 A B C D	120 A B C D

JOURNEYMAN EXAM 1 - 30 QUESTIONS - TIME LIMIT 3 HOURS

1. The overcurrent protection of a #10 THW conductor, when there are not more than three conductors in a raceway, and the ambient temperature is 28°C, would be ___ amps.

(a) 30 (b) 25 (c) 20 (d) 16

2. A box contains the following conductors, the minimum cubic inch capacity required is ____.

4 - #14 grounded conductors   4 - #14 ungrounded conductors
4 - #12 grounded conductors   4 - #12 ungrounded conductors
4 - Clamps   8 - #12 equipment grounding conductors

(a) 25.75 (b) 38.50 (c) 54.25 (d) 61

3. How much space remains to be filled without exceeding the percentage allowed when nine #12 XHHW conductors are placed in a 1-inch EMT conduit?

(a) 0.0181 Sq. in.   (b) 0.1831 sq. in.   (c) 0.4497 sq. in.   (d) none of these

4. What size octagon box is required for 5 - #12 and 4 - #14 conductors?

(a) 1 1/4"   (b) 1 1/2"   (c) 2"   (d) 2 1/8"

5. What size dual-element fuse does the Code require for a 2 hp, 208 volt, single-phase motor?

(a) 20 amp   (b) 30 amp   (c) 35 amp   (d) 40 amp

6. Assuming that the area of all the conductors (over 4 conductors) to be installed in a 1" EMT conduit is 0.30 sq. in., which of the following is true?

(a) The conductors' area is greater than the allowable area of tubing fill.
(b) The conductors' area is less than the allowable area of tubing fill.
(c) It is necessary to select another trade size.
(d) It is necessary to change the THW conductors to RHW.

7. When sizing the service conductors for an apartment complex, the minimum demand load in KW for eight 4 KW ranges would be ____KW.

(a) 11.52 (b) 16.96 (c) 32 (d) None of these

8. The ampacity of a #14 THW conductor, when there are <u>six</u> conductors in a conduit and the temperature is _30° C_, would be ___ amps.

(a) 25 (b) 22 (c) 20 (d) 16

9. How many #1 wires can you install in parallel?

(a) 0 (b) 2 (c) 4 (d) 6

10. In a custom house, the demand load (load applied for service calculation) for a 12 kw range and a 4 kw oven is ____ kw.

(a) 11 (b) 11.2 (c) 12 (d) 16

11. You are wiring a house that has 2200 square feet under the roof. The living area accounts for 2000 square feet of this space. The minimum general lighting load for this dwelling would be ___ va.

(a) 6000 (b) 6600 (c) 7700 (d) 8000

12. The ampacity of a #12 TW conductor when there are <u>not</u> more than three conductors in a raceway and the ambient temperature is _36° C_ would be ___ amps.

(a) 25 (b) 22 (c) 20.5 (d) 16

13. The branch circuit conductor supplying a 3/4 hp, 1ø 115 volt motor shall have an ampacity of at least ___.

(a) 13.8 amps (b) 17.25 amps (c) 20 amps (d) 21.3 amps

14. The volume required for two #12 TW grounding conductors and two #12 TW conductors in a box would be ___ cubic inches.

(a) 9 (b) 6.75 (c) 6 (d) 4.5

15. The demand on the service for six - 6 kw ranges in a sixplex apartment would be ____ kw.

(a) 21 (b) 30.96 (c) 15.48 (d) none of these

16. What is the minimum size copper equipment grounding conductor required for a 80 amp circuit breaker?

(a) #12 (b) #10 (c) #8 (d) #6

17. When sizing the service conductors for an apartment complex, the minimum demand load in kw for eight 5 kw ranges would by ___ kw.

(a) 11.52 (b) 16.96 (c) 32 (d) None of these

18. When sizing the service on a dwelling unit, the small appliance load plus laundry load should be computed at ___ va.

(a) 1,500 (b) 3,000 (c) 4,500 (d) 6,000

19. What is the minimum number of 20 amp branch circuits required for a 1500 sq.ft. house?

(a) 3 (b) 4 (c) 5 (d) 6

20. What is the maximum size overload relay permitted for protection against overload for a 1 ø, 2 hp, 208 volt motor?

(a) 15.18 (b) 16.5 (c) 17.16 (d) none of these

21. #2/0 THW copper service conductors would require a grounding electrode conductor of ____.

(a) #6   (b) #4   (c) #3   (d) #2

22. The feeder carrying two single phase, 1 1/2 hp, 230v motors would be required to have a load current rating of ___ amps.

(a) 12   (b) 16   (c) 22.5   (d) 30

23. What is the allowable ampacity of a #12 TW copper conductor in a raceway with an ambient temperature of 75°F?

(a) 20 amps   (b) 25 amps   (c) 27 amps   (d) 30 amps

24. The branch-circuit protection for a 1ø, 115v, 3 hp motor would normally be ___ using dual element time delay fuses.

(a) 35 amps   (b) 40 amps   (c) 60 amps   (d) 90 amps

25. Using the standard method, what would the demand load on the service be for a 1500 sq. ft. house with the following:

> 1-12 kw range
> 1-dryer
> 1-6 kw waterheater
> 1-washer rated 10 amps (full load)

(a) at least 20 but less than 22 kw
(b) at least 22 but less than 24 kw
(c) at least 24 but less than 26 kw
(d) at least 26 but less than 28 kw

26. The ampacity of a #14 THW conductor, when there are six conductors in a conduit and the temperature is 30°C, would be ____ amps.

(a) 25   (b) 22   (c) 20   (d) 16

THE NEXT TWO QUESTIONS (27 - 28) refer to the following diagram and general information

GENERAL NOTE. <u>Circuits 1 and 2 feed a kitchen.</u> **The loads are plugged into the small appliance circuits.**

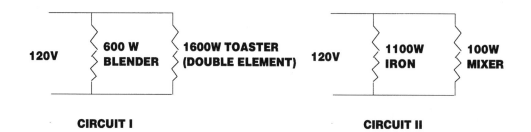

CIRCUIT I   CIRCUIT II

27 Which of the following statements can be inferred from the Circuit I diagram?

(a) **Circuit I does not meet the Code.**
(b) **Circuit I does not meet the Code but will operate.**
(c) **Circuit I does meet the Code but will not operate.**
(d) **Circuit I does meet the Code and will operate.**

28. The total current in Circuit II is ___ ampere(s).

(a) **10.0** (b) **17.5** (c) **9.20** (d) **0.83**

29. The maximum motor-running overload protection would be ___ amps for a 3 hp 1 ø 230V motor.

(a) **15** (b) **20** (c) **22.1** (d) **29.1**

30. The correction factor (C.F.) for 104°F is ___ for a 60°C insulated conductor.

(a) **0.80** (b) **0.82** (c) **0.91** (d) **0.90**

JOURNEYMAN EXAM 2 - 30 QUESTIONS - TIME LIMIT 3 HOURS

1. The branch-circuit load for one 6kw oven would be ____ kw.

(a) 6   (b) 4.8   (c) 4.2   (d) 5

2. If the full load current of a 2 hp, 115v, 1 ø motor with a service factor of 1.2 is 24 amps. What is the maximum motor running overload relay protection?

(a) 24   (b) 27.6   (c) 31.2   (d) 33.6

3. Two 120 volt small appliance circuits are connected, one connected Line one to neutral and one connected Line two to neutral. One line has a 1000 watt load on it and the other line has a 1200 watt load on it. With both loads turned on what would be the wattage in the neutral?

(a) 2200 w   (b) 1200 w   (c) 1000 w   (d) 200 w

4. The total area of 6 - #8 XHHW conductors and 2 - #6 XHHW conductors is ____ square inches.

(a) 0.3026   (b) 0.3265   (c) 0.3295   (d) 0.3802

5. With both loads turned on, what is the current flow in the neutral?

(a) 10 amps   (b) 7 amps   (c) 4 amps   (d) 3 amps

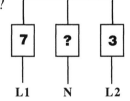

6. The maximum current on the neutral with either Line one or Line two on is ____ amps if the load on Line one to neutral is 9000 watts and the load Line two to neutral is 9500 watts. The voltage is 120/240v.

(a) 75   (b) 77   (c) 79   (d) 154

7. What is the cubic inch capacity required for a device box containing one duplex receptacle, cable clamps and two #12-2 with ground nonmetallic sheathed cables (romex)?

(a) 13.5 cu.in.   (b) 15.75 cu.in.   (c) 16 cu.in.   (d) 18 cu.in.

8. How much space remains to be filled without exceeding the percentage allowed when nine #12 XHHW conductors are placed in a 1" rigid metal conduit?

(a) 0.1297 sq.in.   (b) 0.1831 sq.in.   (c) 0.1921 sq.in.   (d) 0.0181 sq.in.

9. The branch circuit conductor supplying a 10 hp 3 ø 230v motor shall have an ampacity of at least ____ amps.

(a) 38.5   (b) 40.25   (c) 35   (d) 17.5

10. How many #8 TW conductors can be installed in a 1" IMC conduit, 18" long?

(a) 6   (b) 8   (c) 11   (d) 13

11. A toaster and a coffee pot are plugged into the same small appliance circuit rated at 115v. The toaster is 1000w and the coffee pot is rated 800w on 115v. The coffee pot has two windings in parallel, one of which cuts off after the "make" cycle is complete leaving one unit as a "warm" unit. The "warm" winding is 200w. Find the maximum current when both the coffee pot and toaster are turned on together.

(a) 9.6 amps   (b) 10.4 amps   (c) 11.2 amps   (d) 15.65 amps

12. There are seven current carrying #12 THHN conductors run in a conduit where the ambient temperature is 30°C. What is the ampacity of each conductor?

(a) 21   (b) 17.5   (c) 16   (d) 14

13. If 20 amp branch circuits are used exclusively, the number of 20 amp branch circuits for general lighting, small appliances, laundry, and bathroom for an 1800 sq.ft. house with a 240/120v single-phase service would be ____.

(a) 4   (b) 5   (c) 6   (d) 7

14. The approximate area in square inches of a #14 RHH conductor without outer covering is ____ square inches.

(a) 0.206   (b) 0.026   (c) 0.0097   (d) 0.0209

15. What is the total area squares inches for:

4 - #14 TW
3 - #12 THW
12 - #14 RHW without outer covering
14 - #12 TW

(a) .6227   (b) .5175   (c) .6141   (d) none of these

16. The ampacity of a #12 THW conductor when there are not more than three conductors in a raceway and the ambient temperature is 28°C, would be how many amps?

(a) 20   (b) 25   (c) 30   (d) 35

17. A 10 unit apartment building has a 4.5 kw water heater in each unit. What is the demand on the service for these water heaters? Use standard method of calculation.

(a) 45 kw   (b) 50 kw   (c) 33.75 kw   (d) 36 kw

18. A 5 hp, single-phase, 230 volt, wound rotor motor would have nontime delay fuses sized at _____ percent.

(a) 300   (b) 175   (c) 150   (d) 250

19. The overcurrent protection for a #10 RHH conductor in a conduit at 104°F is _____ amps.

(a) 30   (b) 36.4   (c) 40   (d) 20

20. What size dual element time-delay fuse is required for a 15 hp, 230v, three-phase motor?

(a) 75 amp   (b) 80 amp   (c) 85 amp   (d) 90 amp

21. If the full load current of a 2 hp 115v 1ø motor is 24 amps, the branch circuit protection to this motor should not be set at more than _____ amps using dual element time delay fuses.

(a) 30   (b) 40   (c) 60   (d) 80

22. How many #6 XHHW can be installed in a 2" PVC schedule 80 conduit?

(a) 16   (b) 18   (c) 19   (d) 20

23. If the branch circuit is 120v 1ø and a 2 hp motor has a full load current of 24 amps, what is the apparent power?

(a) 2880 va   (b) 10 va   (c) 132 va   (d) 1440 va

24. Under the optional calculation the air conditioning is added to the service at _____.

(a) 125%   (b) full load   (c) 80%   (d) demand load

25. If a dwelling has 1800 sq.ft. and a 12kw range, what size is the approximate service neutral demand load 240/120v?

(a) 5.5 kva   (b) 10.7 kva   (c) 11.0 kva   (d) 13.7 kva

26. In a custom home, two 5kw wall-mounted ovens are supplied by one branch circuit. The demand on the service would be _____ kw.

(a) 10   (b) 8   (c) 6.5   (d) 5

27. The feeder demand for fifteen 3.5kw ovens in an apartment complex would be _____ kw.

(a) 9.6   (b) 16.8   (c) 30   (d) 50

28. What is the feeder ampacity required for two 2 hp 1ø 230v motors?

(a) 48 amps   (b) 54 amps   (c) 60 amps   (d) none of these

29. What is the ampacity of each conductor of a group of nine #14 RHH all in one conduit with an ambient temperature of 45°C?

(a) 25a   (b) 15.225a   (c) 17.5a   (d) 20a

30. What is the feeder neutral demand for six - 4.5 kw clothes dryers 240/120v? Use general method of calculation.

(a) 27 kw   (b) 15.7 kw   (c) 21 kw   (d) 18.9 kw

1. The area of square inch for a #3 bare copper conductor is _____ sq.in.

(a) 0.087 (b) 0.053 (c) 0.260 (d) 0.042

2. The branch circuit protection for a 3 hp single-phase, 208v motor would be _____ amps. Use dual element fuses.

(a) 20 (b) 30 (c) 35 (d) 50

3. A metal conduit contains three #12 RHW copper conductors. The maximum overcurrent device would be _____ amps.

(a) 20 (b) 25 (c) 16 (d) 12

4. What is the area of square inch for a #12 RHW copper conductor with outer covering?

(a) .0353 (b) .026 (c) .0209 (d) .212

5. Each of four #10 RHW conductors in a conduit with an ambient temperature of 104°F have an ampacity of _____ amps.

(a) 24.64 (b) 28 (c) 30 (d) 35

6. A dwelling has 1800 sq.ft. including a 15' x 20' carport. What is the general lighting load?

(a) 5400va (b) 5000va (c) 4800va (d) 4500va

7. The ampacity of a circuit conductor supplying a 14 kw household range should be a minimum of _____ amps @ 220/110 volt.

(a) 30   (b) 40   (c) 50   (d) 60

8. The area of allowable fill of a 1 1/2" EMT conduit nipple is _____ sq.in.

(a) 60%   (b) 1.610   (c) .814   (d) 1.221

9. What is the minimum volume required for a box containing three - #12 THW conductors and three - #10 TW conductors?

(a) 10.5 cu.in.   (b) 12.75 cu.in.   (c) 14.25 cu.in.   (d) 14.5 cu.in.

10. What is the minimum ampacity that a feeder supplying two-25 hp, 208v, three-phase motors, and one-10 hp, 208v, three-phase motor may have?

(a) 164 amps   (b) 181 amps   (c) 200 amps   (d) 218 amps

11. What is the minimum size schedule 80 PVC conduit required for all of the following conductors?

6 - #3 THWN
3 - #8 THW
2 - #10 THW

(a) 2"   (b) 2 1/2"   (c) 1 1/2"   (d) 3"

12. What is the ampacity for a #6 THW copper conductor in a conduit 20" long with 24 other current carrying conductors?

(a) 65a   (b) 52a   (c) 45.5a   (d) 39a

13. A feeder supplying two 4 kw wall-mounted ovens and a 5 kw counter-mounted cooking unit shall have a demand of ____ kw.

(a) 8.4 (b) 7.15 (c) 13 (d) none of these

14. What is the feeder neutral demand for six - 4.5 kw household clothes dryers?

(a) 18.9 kw (b) 21 kw (c) 27 kw (d) 15.7 kw

15. A dwelling has a total of 2500 sq.ft., how many 15 amp circuits are required for the general lighting?

(a) 2 (b) 3 (c) 4 (d) 5

16. How many #8 THW conductors can you install in a 1" rigid steel conduit, 20" in length?

(a) 12 (b) 9 (c) 6 (d) none of these

17. A three-phase, 4-wire lighting circuit has the conductors installed in a raceway in an ambient temperature of 46°C. The raceway has four other current carrying conductors. What is the ampacity of these #10 THW conductors?

(a) 21a (b) 18.38a (c) 20.3a (d) 16.24a

18. If an inverse time circuit breaker of 100 amps is used for branch circuit protection, what is the minimum size copper equipment grounding conductor?

(a) #10 (b) #8 (c) #6 (d) #4

19. An owner wishes to add 12 receptacle outlets to the drawings of his residence. What load will these additional receptacles add to the service load?

(a) 36va   (b) 1200va   (c) 2160va   (d) none of these

20. What is the full load current drawn by a 5 hp, 208v, three-phase motor?

(a) 15.2 amps   (b) 16.7 amps   (c) 19 amps   (d) 20.9 amps

21. The demand load in kw for 15 - 3.5 kw ovens in an apartment complex would be ____ kw.

(a) 9.6   (b) 16.8   (c) 30   (d) none of these

22. The approximate area in square inches of a #14 RHH conductor without outer cover is ____ square inches.

(a) 0.0209   (b) 0.0293   (c) 0.026   (d) 0.0097

23. The demand for 45 - 12 kw ranges in an apartment complex would be ____ kw.

(a) 25   (b) 33.75   (c) 58.75   (d) 97.2

24. What size branch circuit inverse time breaker is required for a 3 hp, 230v, single-phase motor?

(a) 20a   (b) 25a   (c) 30a   (d) 45a

25. What is the area of square inch for a #14 RHH without outer covering conductor?

(a) .163 (b) .0209 (c) .212 (d) .0353

26. What is the percent of allowable fill for two conductors in a conduit?

(a) 40% (b) 80% (c) 53% (d) 31%

27. The overload protection for a 2 hp, 115v, single-phase motor with a 1.15 service factor would be _____ amps.

(a) 31.2 (b) 35.88 (c) 30 (d) 27.6

28. What is the maximum number of #6 XHHW conductors permitted in a 1 1/2" IMC conduit?

(a) 11 (b) 13 (c) 15 (d) 14

29. In a residence using the optional method of calculation the air conditioning would be calculated at _____ percent.

(a) 40 (b) 65 (c) 75 (d) 100

30. The branch circuit demand for one 8 kw range in a residence would be _____ kw.

(a) 12 (b) 8 (c) 6.4 (d) 5.2

1. A 1 1/2" conduit 36" in length contains seven #8 THW current-carrying conductors, what is the ampacity of each conductor?

(a) 50a   (b) 40a   (c) 35a   (d) 30a

2. What is the diameter in inches for a #8 bare aluminum compact conductor?

(a) 0.013   (b) 0.017   (c) 0.146   (d) 0.134

3. What is the ampacity of a 1/2" x 4" copper bus bar?

(a) 1000a   (b) 2000a   (c) 2800a   (d) 3000a

4. What is the demand for 40 - 12 kw ranges in an apartment complex?

(a) 105.6 kw   (b) 480 kw   (c) 55 kw   (d) 12.1 kw

5. Without exceeding the Code, what maximum size running overload protection is needed for a 1 hp, 230v, single-phase motor with a marked service factor of 1.15 and a marked temperature rise of 46°C?

(a) 110%   (b) 120%   (c) 130%   (d) 140%

6. What is the circular mil area of a #2/0 THW copper conductor in a raceway?

(a) .2781   (b) .2332   (c) 0.419   (d) 133,100

7. What is the minimum size EMT conduit permitted which contains the following conductors?

5 - #14 RHH with outer cover
6 - #10 THW
5 - #12 RHW without outer cover
2 - #6 XHHW
1 - #8 bare copper

(a) 1"   (b) 1 1/4"   (c) 1 1/2"   (d) 2"

8. In an apartment building, what is the maximum demand for 28 - 8 kw ranges?

(a) 43 kw   (b) 53.76 kw   (c) 60 kw   (d) none of these

9. The total load of a 15 hp, 208v, three-phase induction motor is closest to _____ va.

(a) 10,000   (b) 11,000   (c) 15,000   (d) 17,000

10. What is the ampacity of a #4 copper, 90°C insulated conductor when the ambient temperature is 120°F?

(a) 67.45a   (b) 76a   (c) 77.9a   (d) 95a

11. What is the minimum branch circuit conductor size for a neutral on a 12 kw rated range?

(a) #12   (b) #10   (c) #8   (d) #6

12. What is the minimum size branch circuit conductor required for a 10 hp, 230v, three-phase induction motor using 60°C insulation?

(a) #10   (b) #8   (c) #6   (d) #4

13. In a residence, what is the minimum branch circuit demand in amperes for one - 6 kw counter-mounted cooking unit and one - 8 kw wall-mounted oven, 230/115v.

(a) 38.3   (b) 52   (c) 60.8   (d) none of these

14. A 1 1/2" PVC schedule 40 conduit contains five - #12 THW conductors. How many #10 RHW conductors with outer covering may be added to this conduit?

(a) 12   (b) 14   (c) 15   (d) 16

15. A cellular metal raceway is 10 square inches in cross section. With special permission, how many #2/0 THHN conductors can you install in this raceway?

(a) 16   (b) 17   (c) 18   (d) 20

16. In a new house, the kitchen has a 6 kw counter-mounted cooking unit and one - 4 kw wall-mounted oven, the demand on the feeder would be ____ kw.

(a) 6.5   (b) 8   (c) 10   (d) 12

17. A dwelling has a floor area of 1500 sq.ft. exclusive of unoccupied cellar, unfinished attic and open porches. It has a 12 kw range. The general lighting load would be ____ va.

(a) 1500   (b) 3000   (c) 4500   (d) 6000

18. Using the general method, two - 4.5 kw residential clothes dryers will add ____ amperes to the demand on the service @ 115/230 volts.

(a) 41.67   (b) 43.48   (c) 37.5   (d) 39.13

19. The area of a #12 RHH without outer covering is _____ square inches.

(a) .0209   (b) .0260   (c) .0353   (d) .0133

20. The branch circuit demand for one - 6 kw counter-mounted cooktop and one - 8 kw wall-mounted oven would be _____ kw.

(a) 14   (b) 12   (c) 9.1   (d) 8.8

21. The feeder conductor for two - 1 hp, 115v, single-phase motors would require an ampacity of _____ amperes.

(a) 32   (b) 36   (c) 40   (d) 16

22. What size disconnecting means is required for a 3 hp, 230v, single-phase motor?

(a) 20 amp   (b) 25 amp   (c) 30 amp   (d) 40 amp

23. What is the maximum number of #14 THW conductors permitted in a 1" PVC schedule 80 conduit?

(a) 13   (b) 14   (c) 15   (d) 19

24. A 12 kw range has a branch circuit demand of _____ amperes. 115/230v.

(a) 34.8   (b) 33.3   (c) 52.1   (d) 50

25. Four #3/0 RHH copper conductors are installed in a PVC raceway with 200 amp overcurrent protection. The equipment grounding conductor must be a minimum of ____ copper.

(a) #1   (b) #2   (c) #4   (d) #6

26. How many #14 THW wires can be installed in a 4" x 1 1/4" octagonal box which contains two cable clamps and one fixture stud?

(a) 6   (b) 5   (c) 4   (d) 3

27. What is the maximum number of #12 THWN conductors that may be installed in a 3/8" flexible metal conduit?

(a) 0   (b) 2   (c) 3   (d) 4

28. The branch circuit below may be loaded to a maximum of ____ amps.

20 amps

(a) 20   (b) 25   (c) 16   (d) 15

29. What is the general lighting load for a single dwelling that measures 1400 sq.ft. inside and has an outside dimension of 1800 sq.ft.?

(a) 4200va   (b) 4500va   (c) 4800va   (d) 5400va

30. The branch circuit below may be loaded to a maximum of ____ amps.

20 amps

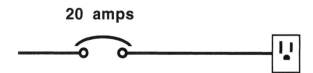

(a) 20   (b) 25   (c) 16   (d) 15

1. A store general lighting branch circuit operates under a continuous load. The branch-circuit rating is 40 amperes. The maximum allowable continuous load on the branch circuit is ____ amperes.

(a) 24   (b) 28   (c) 32   (d) 40

2. Calculate the required service for the following residence:
   1500 sq.ft. floor area
   9kw fixed space heater
   12kw range
   1.2kw dishwasher
   5.5kw clothes dryer
   6 amp 240v air conditioner
   2.5kw water heater

(a) 100 amp   (b) 125 amp   (c) 130 amp   (d) 200 amp

3. Four, single-receptacle, 120v, 15 amp outlets on separate straps are mounted on a 4-gang cover on a single surface-mounted box. The calculated load for this entire assembly shall NOT be less than ____ volt-amps.

(a) 180   (b) 360   (c) 480   (d) 720

4. Refer to the figure below. The required dimensions of sides **A** and **B** of the pull box shown shall be a minimum of ____.

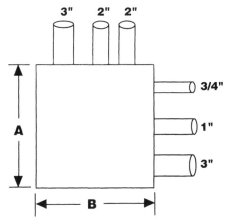

(a) A = 19 3/4"; B = 23"   (b) A = 22"; B = 19 3/4"
(c) A = 24"; B = 21 1/2"   (d) A = 21 1/2"; B = 24"

5. Refer to the figure below. The required size of the bonding jumper is ____.

(a) #3/0   (b) #4/0   (c) #250 kcmil   (d) #300 kcmil

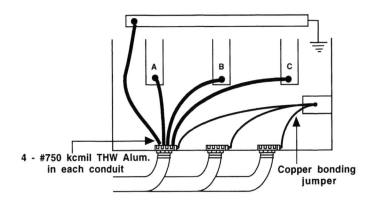

4 - #750 kcmil THW Alum.
in each conduit

Copper bonding
jumper

6. Nine #6 XHHW copper conductors are installed in a raceway in a wet location at an ambient temperature of 110°F. The ampacity of each conductor is ____ amps.

(a) 29   (b) 37   (c) 46   (d) 53

7. A junction box has a 60 cubic inch capacity. The maximum number of #14 conductors permitted to be enclosed within the box is ____.

(a) 12   (b) 27   (c) 30   (d) 32

8. Two motors with a full load current ratings of 10 and 27 amperes are protected by 15 and 40 ampere branch circuit breakers, respectively. The minimum required overcurrent device protecting the feeder which serves these two branch circuits is ____ amperes.

(a) 40   (b) 50   (c) 60   (d) 70

9. GIVEN: A 3-phase, no code letter, wound rotor, 460v, 30 hp motor. What shall be the maximum setting of the motor branch circuit's Short-circuit and Ground-fault protective device using a time-delay fuse?

(a) 40 amp   (b) 60 amp   (c) 70 amp   (d) 90 amp

10. Refer to the figure below. GIVEN: Switch S1 is in the "ON" position, but the light does not come on. Voltage across S1 is measured to be 120 volts. Voltage across L1 is measured to be 0 volts. The light does not come on because ____.

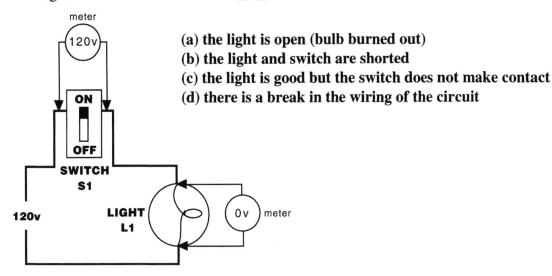

(a) **the light is open (bulb burned out)**
(b) **the light and switch are shorted**
(c) **the light is good but the switch does not make contact**
(d) **there is a break in the wiring of the circuit**

11. A 230v AC transformer arc welder is rated at 20 amperes primary current and has a duty cycle of 70%. The supply conductors to this welder shall have a calculated ampacity of not less than ____ amperes.

(a) **19.2**   (b) **18.7**   (c) **16.8**   (d) **15.3**

12. The minimum size rigid metal conduit required for the installation of the following conductors Two - #500 kcmil THHN, Two - #4/0 THHN, and One - #2/0 THHN. is ____.

(a) **2"**   (b) **2 1/2"**   (c) **3"**   (d) **3 1/2"**

13. Refer to 1 in the figure below. In dwelling units, a multi-wire branch circuit supplying more than one device on the same yoke shall be protected by ____.

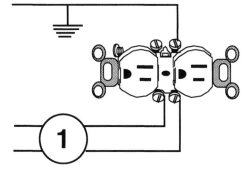

(a) **two (2) single pole circuit breakers, operating independently**
(b) **two (2) single pole circuit breakers, tied together**
(c) **one (1) non-fused disconnect only**
(d) **one (1) fuse only**

14. When using nonmetallic-sheathed cable to wire the diagram shown below, the correct method is illustrated by _____.

(a) Figure A   (b) Figure B   (c) Either A or B   (d) neither A nor B

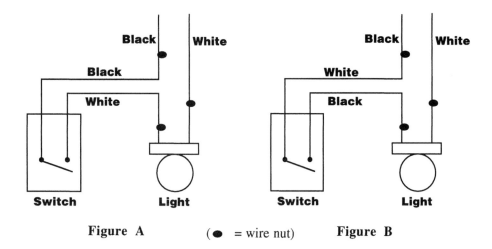

Figure A   (● = wire nut)   Figure B

15. What is the maximum number of #16 Type XF fixture wires allowed in a 3/4" electrical metallic tubing raceway?

(a) 8   (b) 11   (c) 19   (d) 24

16. Two #10 THW and three #8 THHN conductors require a minimum size of _____ for Liquidtight flexible metal conduit.

(a) 1/2"   (b) 3/4"   (c) 1"   (d) 1 1/4"

17. Refer to the figure below, What if anything, is wrong with the circuit?

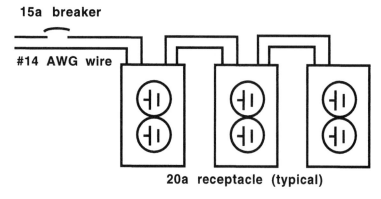

20a receptacle (typical)

(a) This is not a violation of the Code.
(b) The circuit conductors are sized incorrectly.
(c) Six outlets are not allowed on a single branch circuit.
(d) The 20 ampere receptacles are too large for the circuit rating.

18. Refer to the figure below. What is wrong with the ground rod installation?

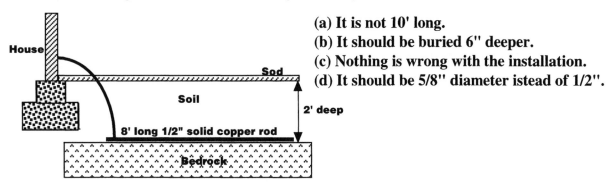

(a) **It is not 10' long.**
(b) **It should be buried 6" deeper.**
(c) **Nothing is wrong with the installation.**
(d) **It should be 5/8" diameter istead of 1/2".**

19. The current on a three-phase motor nameplate is ____.

(a) **the total of the full load running currents in all three supply lines**
(b) **the total of the maximum starting currents in all three supply lines**
(c) **the full load running current at each of the three supply line terminals**
(d) **the maximum starting current at each of the three supply line terminals**

20. An office building has a required general lighting load of 50,000 volt amperes. The general lighting load is supplied by a single phase, 230 volt feeder circuit. The minimum calculated current in the feeder circuit ungrounded (hot) conductors is ____ amperes.

(a) **208**   (b) **217**   (c) **230**   (d) **272**

21. Refer to the figure below. GIVEN: Switch S1 is in the "ON" position, but the light does not come on. Voltage across L1 is measured to be 120 volts. Voltage across S1 is measured to be 0 volts. The light does not come on because ____.

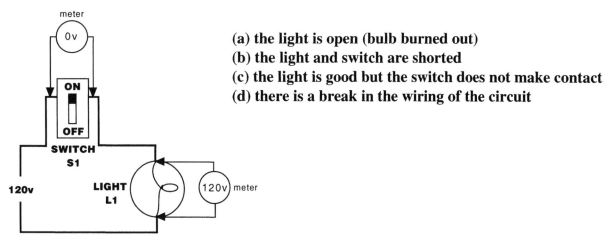

(a) **the light is open (bulb burned out)**
(b) **the light and switch are shorted**
(c) **the light is good but the switch does not make contact**
(d) **there is a break in the wiring of the circuit**

22. Refer to the figures below. A correctly wired 3-way switching circuit is represented by figure
____.

(a) **A**   (b) **B**   (c) **C**   (d) **D**

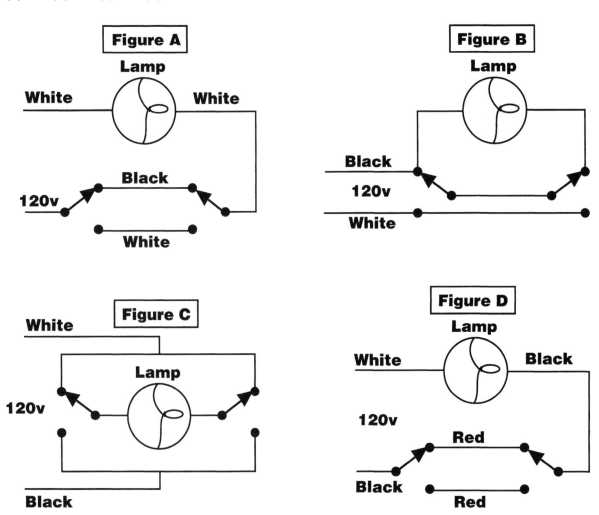

23. The minimum size 20 foot long conductor, tapped from a #500 kcmil THW copper feeder, permitted without overcurrent protection at the tap is ____ THW copper.

(a) **#1** (b) **#2** (c) **#1/0** (d) **#2/0**

24. Nine #8 THHN conductors in a conduit at 30°C. What is the maximum allowable amperage for each conductor?

(a) 33.3   (b) 38.5   (c) 40.0   (d) 55.0

25. Six #12 conductors are spliced in a box which has no grounding wire, clamps or devices and which has a flat cover. What is the minimum size metal octagonal box?

(a) 4" x 1 1/4"   (b) 4" x 1 1/2"   (c) 4" x 2 1/8"   (d) none of these

26. A 30 hp, 3-phase, 460v, induction type, continuous duty motor has a service factor of 1.15 and a temperature rise of 40°C. The maximum rating of the required separate overload device is ____ amperes.

(a) 46   (b) 50   (c) 56   (d) 60

27. A 10 hp, 230v, 3-phase, squirrel cage motor is supplied by the largest allowable inverse-time circuit breaker and by the minimum allowable TW branch circuit conductors run in flexible metal conduit. The minimum size copper equipment grounding conductor required for the motor is ____.

(a) #8   (b) #6   (c) #4   (d) No equipment grounding conductor is required

28. A 2" rigid PVC schedule 80 conduit contains eight -#3 TW conductors. Four additional #3 conductors need to be added in the conduit. All of the conductors will fit in the 2" conduit if all the conductors are Type ____.

(a) TW   (b) THW   (c) RHW   (d) THWN

29. A 30" long intermediate metal conduit nipple contains four THW aluminum conductors. Two of them are #350 kcmil and the two are #500 kcmil. The minimum size of required conduit is _____.

(a) 2 1/2"   (b) 3"   (c) 3 1/2"   (d) 4"

30. Refer to the figure below. This run of 1/2" electrical metallic tubing without couplings is installed between two junction boxes. It contains two 90° bends and one 3-point saddle consisting of one 45° bend and two 22 1/2° bends. At each end of the run is an offset, each consisting of two 30° bends. Which statement below is correct?

(a) This is an approved run because there are only two 90° bends.
(b) This run does NOT meet the National Electrical Code requirements.
(c) This is an approved run because the result of the saddle is still a straight run.
(d) This is an approved run because offsets are not counted in the total number of bends.

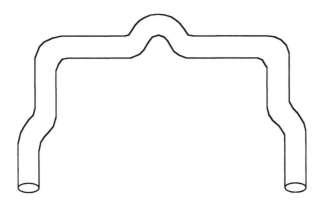

EXAM SPONSOR _____

DATE _____

TYPE EXAM _____ PART _____

APPLICANT NUMBER

0	0	0	0	0	0	0	0	0
1	1	1	1	1	1	1	1	1
2	2	2	2	2	2	2	2	2
3	3	3	3	3	3	3	3	3
4	4	4	4	4	4	4	4	4
5	5	5	5	5	5	5	5	5
6	6	6	6	6	6	6	6	6
7	7	7	7	7	7	7	7	7
8	8	8	8	8	8	8	8	8
9	9	9	9	9	9	9	9	9

GRADE

_____

SAMPLE

THE NEUTRAL IS

A) red in color
B) black in color
C) blue in color
D) white in color

WRONG
(A) (X) (C) (D)
WRONG
(A) (B) (✓) (D)
WRONG
(A) (B) (C) (D)
WRONG
(A) (B) ● (D)
RIGHT
(A) (B) (C) ●

IMPORTANT DIRECTIONS FOR MARKING ANSWERS

- DO NOT USE INK OR BALLPOINT PEN
- USE BLACKLEAD #2 PENCIL ONLY
- MAKE HEAVY MARKS THAT FILL THE CIRCLE COMPLETELY
- ERASE CLEANLY ANY ANSWER YOU WISH TO CHANGE
- MAKE NO STRAY MARKS ON THE ANSWER SHEET

MASTER CALCULATIONS EXAM

1. What is the demand on a three-phase, 4-wire feeder for the following single-phase household ranges?

4 - 12 kw ranges
8 - 16.5 kw ranges

(a) 180 kw   (b) 27 kw   (c) 26.45 kw   (d) 31.05 kw

2. What is the horsepower of a 230 volt, single-phase motor that draws 8 amps, with an efficiency of 40.5%?

(a) 1 hp   (b) 1 1/2 hp   (c) 2 hp   (d) 3 hp

3. What is the minimum demand on the service for 300 duplex receptacles in a hospital?

(a) 20.8 kva   (b) 27 kva   (c) 32 kva   (d) 54 kva

4. What is the efficiency of a three-phase motor whose input is 42 amps on 230v, and whose output is 15 hp?

(a) 66.88   (b) 1.43   (c) 82.8   (d) 1.20

5. If 20% of a 1 1/2" EMT conduit was already occupied by #8 XHHW conductors, what is the maximum number of #8 XHHW's you can add to this conduit?

(a) 7   (b) 8   (c) 9   (d) none of these

6. The demand for ten 1200va dishwashers in a ten unit apartment would be _____ kva. Use the optional method of calculation.

(a) 12   (b) 9   (c) 5.16   (d) none of these

7. The branch circuit protection using dual element fuses would be _____ amperes for a 30 hp, squirrel cage, 460v, three-phase motor.

(a) 70 (b) 80 (c) 100 (d) 125

8. The demand on the feeder for a 16 kw household range 230/115v would be _____ amperes.

(a) 9.6 (b) 8 (c) 41.7 (d) none of these

9. An apartment building with 200 dwelling units, each unit has a 4 kw clothes dryer. The load added to the service after demand factors would be _____ kw. Use general method of calculation.

(a) 200 (b) 250 (c) 800 (d) 1000

10. One 20 hp, 208v, three-phase motor and three - 2 hp, 120v, single-phase motors are connected on the same feeder. The maximum size inverse time breaker for the feeder protection would be _____ amperes.

(a) 150 (b) 175 (c) 200 (d) 225

11. A 60 unit apartment building, each unit has a 4 kw clothes dryer. What is the minimum demand on the feeder? Use optional method of calculation.

(a) 180 kw (b) 75 kw (c) 60 kw (d) 57.6 kw

12. What is the maximum demand on the service for 55 - 16 kw household ranges?

(a) 66.25 kw (b) 79.5 kw (c) 41.25 kw (d) none of these

13. How many #8 RHH conductors without outer covering can be installed in a 1 1/2" ENT (electrical non-metallic tubing) conduit?

(a) 13   (b) 14   (c) 17   (d) 22

14. The minimum ampacity required for a feeder that supplies one - 3 hp, 208v, three-phase motor and one - 2 hp, 208v, three-phase motor would be _____ amperes.

(a) 21   (b) 22   (c) 18   (d) 19

15. What is the demand on a three-phase, 4 - wire feeder for ten - 14 kw single-phase household ranges?

(a) 25 kw   (b) 27.5 kw   (c) 25.3 kw   (d) 34.5 kw

16. The maximum ampacity of a copper #10 RHW is _____ when there are four current-carrying conductors in a conduit and the ambient temperature is 80°F.

(a) 28   (b) 30   (c) 35   (d) 40

17. What is the va to a fully-loaded 5 hp 208v three-phase motor?

(a) 3000 - 4000   (b) 4000 - 5000   (c) 5000 - 6000   (d) 6000 - 7000

18. The approximate area in square inches of a #14 RHH conductor without outer covering is _____ square inches.

(a) 0.0209   (b) 0.0327   (c) 0.0230   (d) 0.0135

19. What is the minimum size branch circuit conductor required for a 10 hp, 230v, three-phase motor? Use 60°C insulation.

(a) #10   (b) #8   (c) #6   (d) #4

20. What is the minimum size PVC schedule 40 conduit required for the following conductors?

6 - #3 THWN
3 - #8 THW
2 - #10 THW

(a) 2"   (b) 2 1/2"   (c) 1 1/2"   (d) 3"

21. What is the ampacity of each conductor of a group of twenty-five #14 copper RHH. All are carrying current and installed in one conduit with an ambient temperature of 45°C?

(a) 25a   (b) 21.75a   (c) 15a   (d) 9.7875a

22. If two-25 hp, 208v, three-phase motors are fed by the same feeder, the feeder conductors would be required to carry a minimum of _____ amperes.

(a) 100   (b) 150   (c) 170   (d) 200

23. Each unit of a six unit all electric apartment complex contains a 4.5 kw clothes dryer. Using the optional method of calculation for multi-family dwellings, these six dryers would have a total connected load of _____ kw.

(a) 11.88   (b) 13.2   (c) 18   (d) 27

24. What is the feeder neutral demand for two - 4 kw wall-mounted ovens and one - 5 kw counter-mounted cooking unit in a dwelling?

(a) 5.005 kw   (b) 7.15 kw   (c) 13 kw   (d) none of these

25. In a 60 unit apartment building each dwelling unit has a 6 kw water heater. What is the demand on the service for these water heaters? Do not use optional method.

(a) 360 kw   (b) 86.4 kw   (c) 270 kw   (d) 189 kw

26. What is the demand for a 25,000 sq.ft. school building with a total connected load of 600 kva? Use optional method.

(a) 402,809va   (b) 418,750va   (c) 526,719va   (d) none of these

27. What is the cross-sectional area of a 2" flexible metal conduit?

(a) 3.629   (b) 3.269   (c) 1.307   (d) 1.452

28. In a 50 unit apartment building each unit has a 14 kw range. What is the demand on the service for these ranges using the optional method of calculation?

(a) 700 kw   (b) 400 kw   (c) 182 kw   (d) 68.75 kw

29. If ten - #8 RHH conductors with outer cover are installed in a 2" PVC schedule 80 conduit, how many #8 XHHW conductors could be added to this conduit?

(a) 8   (b) 9   (c) 7   (d) 11

30. What is the demand load for the following household ranges?

6 - 9 kw
4 - 12 kw
10 -15 kw

(a) 35 kw   (b) 38.5 kw   (c) 54.70 kw   (d) none of these

MASTER EXAM 2 - 30 QUESTIONS - TIME LIMIT 3 HOURS

---

1. What is the demand for 15 kva resistance welder with a 40% duty cycle?

(a) 15 kva   (b) 12 kva   (c) 9.45 kva   (d) 7.5 kva

2. What size cable tray width is required for four - #500 kcmil THW conductors, six - #750 kcmil THW conductors, and eight - #1000 kcmil THW conductors?

(a) 18"   (b) 24"   (c) 30"   (d) 36"

3. The smallest feeder size for one - 10 hp, 208v, three-phase motor and three - 3 hp, 120v, single-phase motors should have a minimum ampacity of _____ amperes.

(a) 72.5   (b) 73.3   (c) 140.5   (d) 141.3

4. The demand load for 32 - 12 kw residential ranges rated 115/230v would be _____ kw.

(a) 107.52   (b) 448   (c) 53   (d) 47

5. If eight - #14 TW, and six - #8 THWN conductors were installed in a 20" rigid steel conduit between two boxes, the minimum size conduit permitted by the Code would be _____.

(a) 3/4"   (b) 1"   (c) 1 1/4"   (d) 1 1/2"

6. The branch circuit protection using dual element fuses would be _____ amperes for a 20 hp, 208v, three-phase motor.

(a) 100a   (b) 110a   (c) 125a   (d) 150a

7. The maximum ampacity for a #3 THWN at 46°C ambient and not more than three conductors in a raceway is _____ amperes.

(a) 70   (b) 75   (c) 80   (d) 82

8. The following motel has:

150 guest rooms 15' x 20' each
3000 sq.ft. of hallways
30' x 40' office

What is the load on the overcurrent device?

(a) 156.375 kva   (b) 98.325 kva   (c) 46.325 kva   (d) 46.625 kva

9. What is the demand on a three-phase, 4-wire feeder for the following single-phase household ranges?

4 - 9 kw
4 - 13.5 kw
4 - 16 kw

(a) 23 kw   (b) 25.3 kw   (c) 150 kw   (d) none of these

10. Three - #8 XHHW conductors are installed in a wet location with an ambient temperature of 104°F. The ampacity of each conductor would be _____ amperes.

(a) 55   (b) 50   (c) 48.4   (d) 44

11. 40 apartments with 950 sq.ft. each. Each five apartments has 130 sq.ft. of hallway. What is the connected lighting load required?

(a) 4 - 6 kva   (b) 75 - 90 kva   (c) 95 - 100 kva   (d) 100 - 110 kva

12. An office building has 150 general purpose outlets. The kva load to be added to the service calculation for the outlets would be _____ kva after demand factors.

(a) 27   (b) 13.5   (c) 18.5   (d) none of these

13. An installation of 60 feet of a fixed multioutlet assembly installed in a continuous length in an office occupancy shall be calculated at _____ amperes.

(a) 15   (b) 18   (c) 20   (d) 25

14. What is the minimum amperes required for the following boat berth receptacles?

30 - 15 amp 120v receptacles
20 - 30 amp 120v receptacles

(a) 525 amps   (b) 420 amps   (c) 630 amps   (d) 1050 amps

15. In a 30 unit apartment building, each dwelling unit has a 1500va garbage disposal. How much do they add to the service demand? Use general method of calculation.

(a) 45,000va   (b) 33,750va   (c) 31,500va   (d) 22,500va

16. What is the maximum demand required for ten - 12 kw ranges located in a school building in the home economics classroom?

(a) 120 kw   (b) 78 kw   (c) 40.8 kw   (d) 25 kw

17. What is the demand on a commercial kitchen feeder supplying a 16 kw range, a 3 kw potato peeler, and a 3.5 kw booster heater?

(a) 20.25 kw   (b) 19.5 kw   (c) 20.5 kw   (d) 23 kw

18. How many #12 RHW conductors without outer covering can be installed in a 1" IMC conduit 18" in length?

(a) 19   (b) 20   (c) 21   (d) 22

19. The maximum overcurrent protection for a #12 THW is _____ when there are three conductors in a conduit and the ambient temperature is 40°C.

(a) 20   (b) 17.6   (c) 14.08   (d) 25

20. The motor running overload protection for a 5 hp, 115v, single-phase motor with a marked service factor of 1.2 would be _____ amps.

(a) 35   (b) 32.2   (c) 64.4   (d) 70

21. What is the ampacity of each of four #6 XHHW copper conductors in a conduit above the dropped ceiling on a 4-wire, three-phase wye circuit where the load is all fluorescent lighting?

(a) 52a   (b) 60a   (c) 65a   (d) 75a

22. A shopping center parking lot has 60 - 150 watt lights. What is the calculated load on the overcurrent device?

(a) 9000w   (b) 11,250w   (c) 15,000w   (d) none of these

23. In a 45 unit apartment building each unit has a 1400va compactor unit 115v single-phase. What is the demand on the service for these compactors? Use optional method.

(a) 17,100va   (b) 63,000va   (c) 16,380va   (d) 17,010va

24. What is the general lighting load for a bank building with a total square footage of 20,000?

(a) 112.5 kva   (b) 107.5 kva   (c) 95 kva   (d) none of these

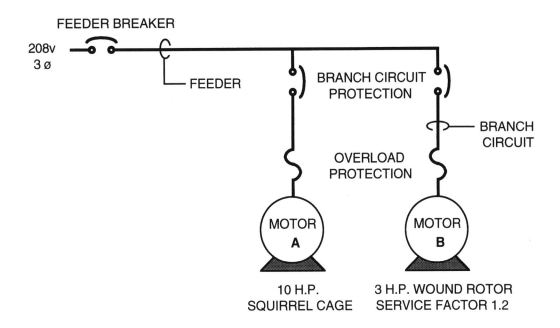

FEEDER BREAKER

208v
3 ø

FEEDER

BRANCH CIRCUIT
PROTECTION

BRANCH
CIRCUIT

OVERLOAD
PROTECTION

MOTOR
A

MOTOR
B

10 H.P.
SQUIRREL CAGE

3 H.P. WOUND ROTOR
SERVICE FACTOR 1.2

FIND:	**MOTOR "A"**	**MOTOR "B"**
25. F.L.C. of motors	_____	_____
26. Overload protection, minimum size	_____	_____
27. Branch circuit conductor size (TW)	_____	_____
28. Branch circuit protection size (breaker)	_____	_____
29. Feeder size (TW)	_____	
30. Feeder protection size (breaker)	_____	

Note - Use TW insulation, maximum size circuit breaker for branch circuit.

MASTER EXAM 3 - 30 QUESTIONS - TIME LIMIT 3 HOURS
---

1. What 75°C conductors are required for two conductors paralleled to carry a 925 amp load?

(a) 2 - 500 kcmil RH   (b) 2 - 600 kcmil THWN   (c) 2 - 700 kcmil RHW   (d) 2 - 750 kcmil THW

2. How many 20 amp, 120 volt, 2-wire circuits are needed for a 40,000 sq.ft. office building with an unknown receptacle load?

(a) 40   (b) 60   (c) 90   (d) 120

3. What is the demand for 16 - 8 kw household ranges?

(a) 128 kw   (b) 50 kw   (c) 35.84 kw   (d) 31 kw

4. What size 60°C conductor is required for a 25 amp load in an ambient temperature of 122°F?

(a) #12   (b) #10   (c) #8   (d) #6

5. A mobile home park has 25 mobile home sites which would require a minimum demand of ____ kva.

(a) 50   (b) 65   (c) 96   (d) 100

6. A 240v, single-phase, 21.85 kw commercial cooking appliance is to be supplied by TW copper branch circuit conductors. Which of the following conductors is the minimum size permitted?

(a) #3   (b) #2   (c) #1   (d) 1/0

7. A single-family dwelling with a 200 amp service supplied with 2/0 THW copper conductors would require a minimum size _____ bonding jumper.

(a) #6 al   (b) #6 cu   (c) #4 al   (d) #4 cu

8. In a 24 unit apartment building each dwelling unit has a 4 kw household clothes dryer. The demand on the feeder neutral for these dryers would be _____ kw. Calculate by using the general method.

(a) 28.9   (b) 42   (c) 120   (d) none of these

9. What is the allowable ampacity of a 4/0 THW al conductor in raceway in free air with an ambient temperature of 23°C?

(a) 230a   (b) 241.5a   (c) 180a   (d) 189a

10. What is the demand load for the following household ranges?

6 - 9 kw
8 - 12 kw
10 - 15 kw

(a) 39 kw   (b) 40.95 kw   (c) 42.9 kw   (d) none of these

11. What is the minimum size rigid steel conduit required to install all of the following conductors?

4 - #10 THW
2 - #12 RHW without outer cover
2 - #14 RHH with outer cover
6 - #14 THHN
3 - #12 bare stranded grounding conductors

(a) 1/2"   (b) 3/4"   (c) 1"   (d) 1 1/4"

12. The branch circuit protection is _____ percent of the full-load current in a DC motor using dual element fuses.

(a) 150   (b) 175   (c) 250   (d) 300

13. What is the feeder demand for the following equipment in a restaurant?

3 - 3 kw deep fat fryers
2 - 4 kw dishwashers
2 - 5 kw booster heaters

(a) 10.8 kw   (b) 15 kw   (c) 17.55 kw   (d) none of these

14. What is the demand load for a 30,000 sq.ft. school building with a total connected load of 750 kva? Use optional method of calculation.

(a) 500 kva   (b) 510 kva   (c) 650 kva   (d) 750 kva

15. A store has a service voltage of 120/240v single-phase with a total connected load of 420 amps. The service entrance conductors are parallel in a single conduit. What are the minimum size THW copper conductors that can be used in parallel?

(a) 4/0   (b) 250 kcmil   (c) 300 kcmil   (d) 500 kcmil

16. What is the feeder neutral demand for five - 12 kw household ranges?

(a) 6.3 kw   (b) 9 kw   (c) 14 kw   (d) 20 kw

17. In a 30 unit apartment building each dwelling unit has a 4 kw cooktop and a 5 kw oven. What is the demand on the service for this cooking equipment? Use optional method of calculation.

(a) 270 kw   (b) 89.1 kw   (c) 62.1 kw   (d) none of these

18. The maximum running overload protection for a 7 1/2 hp, 208v, three-phase motor with a marked temperature rise of 40°C would be _____ amps.

(a) 27.83   (b) 30.5   (c) 31.46   (d) 33.88

19. Twenty-four #12 THW current-carrying conductors are installed in a 20" long conduit. What is the ampacity of each #12 THW conductor?

(a) 25a   (b) 20a   (c) 17.5a   (d) 15a

20. What is the minimum demand on the neutral that has a calculated load of 500 amps of incandescent lighting and 500 amps of fluorescent lighting?

(a) 1000a   (b) 910a   (c) 760a   (d) 500a

21. What is the ampacity of a 1/4" x 6" aluminum bus bar?

(a) 700a   (b) 1000a   (c) 1050a   (d) none of these

22. What is the branch circuit demand load for one 14 kw range rated 115/230v? The range is located in a home economics classroom in a school building.

(a) 61 amps   (b) 38.2 amps   (c) 26.7 amps   (d) none of these

23. How many #14 RHH conductors with outer cover can be installed in a 2" PVC schedule 40 nipple?

(a) 67   (b) 66   (c) 68   (d) 65

24. How many #12 RHH with outer cover can be installed in a 3" x 2" x 1 1/2" device box?

(a) 2   (b) 3   (c) 4   (d) 5

25. In the following drawing of a pull box, the dimension "Y" should not be less than ____ inches.

(a) 15   (b) 18   (c) 20   (d) 24

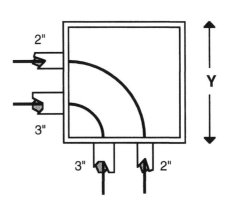

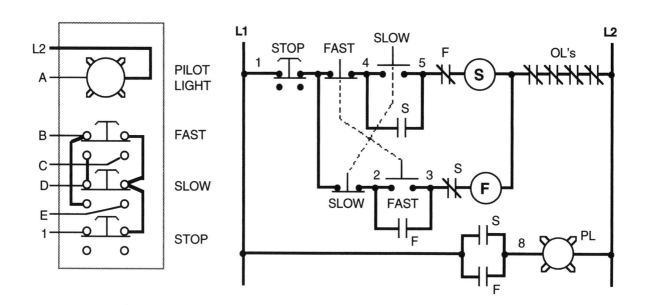

26. "**A**" is actually point _____ on the control diagram.

(a) **L1**   (b) **L2**   (c) **8**   (d) **6**

27. "**D**" is actually point _____ on the control diagram.

(a) **5**   (b) **4**   (c) **3**   (d) **2**

28. "**B**" is actually point _____ on the control diagram.

(a) **4**   (b) **3**   (c) **2**   (d) **L1**

29. "**C**" is actually point _____ on the control diagram.

(a) **4**   (b) **3**   (c) **2**   (d) **L1**

30. "**E**" is actually point _____ on the control diagram.

(a) **4**   (b) **5**   (c) **1**   (d) **2**

1. What size disconnecting means is required for a 7 1/2 hp, 230v, single-phase motor?

(a) 30a   (b) 40a   (c) 50a   (d) 60a

2. What is the minimum size THW copper conductor for a load of 42 amps in a metal conduit containing a total of eight current-carrying conductors? The ambient temperature is 116°F.

(a) #8   (b) #6   (c) #4   (d) #2

3. What is the branch circuit protection required for a 5 hp, 208v, three-phase squirrel-cage motor? Use inverse time breaker.

(a) 35a   (b) 40a   (c) 45a   (d) 50a

4. How many #16 TFFN conductors can be installed in a 1 1/4" EMT conduit?

(a) 43   (b) 55   (c) 76   (d) 83

5. A spot welder supplied by a 60-hertz system makes three hundred 20-cycle welds per hour. What is the duty cycle percent for this welder?

(a) 3.6%   (b) 3%   (c) 2.8%   (d) none of these

6. If 20% of a 1 1/2" PVC schedule 40 conduit 14" long is filled with conductors, what is the remaining allowable area for conductor fill?

(a) 1.026   (b) .7938   (c) .5958   (d) .6840

7. A 25 hp, 460v, three-phase motor is operating in a poorly ventilated location where the ambient temperature reaches 46°C. The raceway contains three current-carrying conductors, and an equipment grounding conductor. What is the minimum size THW copper conductors required for this motor branch circuit?

(a) #10   (b) #8   (c) #6   (d) #4

8. A conduit contains two sets of three-phase conductors, with two neutrals and two equipment grounding conductors. The ambient temperature is 28°C. What is the derating factor if the loads are balanced?

(a) .82   (b) 100%   (c) 80%   (d) 70%

9. What is the branch circuit protection required for a 2 hp, 120v, DC motor using dual element fuses and a marked service factor of 1.2?

(a) 20a   (b) 30a   (c) 35a   (d) 40a

10. What is the maximum demand for 65 - 14 kw household ranges?

(a) 81.125 kw   (b) 73.75 kw   (c) 48.75 kw   (d) 25 kw

11. What is the minimum number of 15 ampere branch circuits required for the general lighting load of a 2200 sq.ft. single-family dwelling?

(a) 2   (b) 3   (c) 4   (d) 5

12.   20 - 800 sq.ft. apartments
      20 - 12 kw ranges
      40 - small appliance circuits
      20 - laundry circuits

Size the neutral conductor to ____ amperes. 230/115v single-phase.

(a) 282a   (b) 317a   (c) 376a   (d) 417a

13. What is the minimum demand on the overcurrent device for the general lighting for a 36,000 sq.ft. office building?

(a) 193.5 kva   (b) 202.5 kva   (c) 214.6 kva   (d) none of these

14. What is the demand load on the service for 34 - 15 kw household ranges when each apartment panel is 208/120v single-phase and the service is 208/120v three-phase?

(a) 34 kw   (b) 39 kw   (c) 44.85 kw   (d) 56.35 kw

15. How many square inches of a 1 1/2" PVC schedule 80 nipple does eight - #8 THW use?

(a) .3496   (b) .4448   (c) .5808   (d) none of these

16. In a 24 unit apartment building each unit has a 4 kw cooktop and a 5 kw oven. What is the demand on the service for this cooking equipment? Use general method.

(a) 61 kw   (b) 56.16 kw   (c) 43.2 kw   (d) none of these

17. A school building has a receptacle load of 25 kva. Using the general method of calculation, what is the demand allowed for these receptacles?

(a) 7.5 kva   (b) 10 kva   (c) 17.5 kva   (d) 25 kva

18. In a motel, the following spaces exist:

50 guest rooms 14' x 20' each
3200 sq.ft. hallway
office 20' x 30'
5,000 sq.ft. parking garage

What is the calculated load on the overcurrent device for these spaces?

(a) 21.55 kva   (b) 22.3 kva   (c) 36.35 kva   (d) none of these

19. In a 75 unit apartment building each unit has a 14 kw household range. What is the demand load for these ranges? Use optional method.

(a) **89 kw** (b) **115 kw** (c) **241.5 kw** (d) **none of these**

20. What size branch circuit protection is required for a 1 hp, 230v, single-phase, wound-rotor motor? Use dual element fuse.

(a) **15a** (b) **20a** (c) **25a** (d) **30a**

21. What is the area of square inches of a #6 bare copper grounding electrode conductor?

(a) **26,240** (b) **0.184** (c) **0.027** (d) **0.146**

22. The ampacity of a #12 THW conductor used with a 15 minute motor on a monorail hoist installed in a raceway containing a total of four current-carrying conductors would be _____ amperes.

(a) **20** (b) **30** (c) **33** (d) **36.96**

23. What is the full-load current for a three-phase, 25 hp, 230v, synchronous motor with a power factor of 80%?

(a) **66.25a** (b) **68a** (c) **53a** (d) **58.3a**

24. What is the va input of a fully loaded three-phase, 208v, 3 hp motor?

(a) **9.6 va** (b) **10.6 va** (c) **2196 va** (d) **3819 va**

25. The smallest feeder size to one-15 hp, 208v, three-phase motor and three-5 hp, 120v, single-phase motors should have an ampacity of _____ amperes.

(a) **226** (b) **228.2** (c) **116.2** (d) **none of these**

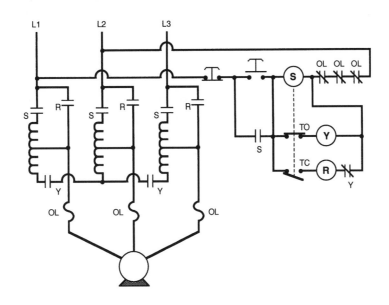

26. This is a _____ type starter.

    (a) full voltage   **(b)** autotransformer   **(c)** reactor   **(d)** resistor

27. What is the sequence of the operation?

    (a) **TO** opens, when **TC** closes   **(b)** R closes, then Y opens

    (c) S closes, then Y closes   **(d)** **TC** closes, then Y opens

28. What is the sequence of operation?

    (a) S energized, then Y   **(b)** Y energized, then S

    (c) S and Y energized simultaneously   **(d)** R energized, then Y

29. What is the sequence of operation?

    (a) S closes before Y closes   **(b)** S closes, then Y closes

    (c) R closes before Y opens   **(d)** Y opens at the same time Y closes

30. Which of the following is true?

    I - When **TO** opens and **TC** closes, R is energized

    II - When R closes, full line voltage is applied to the motor

    III - When Y is closed, Y is open

    (a) I only   **(b) II only**   **(c) III only**   **(d) I, II and III**

MASTER EXAM 5 - 30 QUESTIONS - TIME LIMIT 3 HOURS

1. A building consists of a 25,000 sq.ft. store with lights on continuously for 6 hours a day; a 5,500 sq.ft. restaurant with lights on continuously for 4 hours a day; and a 3,000 sq.ft. auditorium with lights on continuously for 2 hours a day. The service shall be calculated based on a minimum general lighting load of _____ volt-amperes.

(a) 89,000   (b) 101,500   (c) 107,500   (d) 110,500

2. An 18 unit apartment building is supplied by a 208/120v, 3-phase, 4-wire service. Each apartment has a floor area of 950 sq.ft. and contains a 5.5 kw clothes dryer, 12 kw range, and a 1.4 kw dishwasher. The range demand load for the apartment building is _____ kilowatts.

(a) 27 (b) 33   (c) 36   (d) 39

3. Three #500 kcmil THHN conductors are installed in a raceway at 70°F. What is the allowable ampacity of each conductor?

(a) 345   (b) 380   (c) 430   (d) 447

4. Refer to the figure below. The required size of the bonding jumper is _____.

(a) #2/0   (b) #3/0   (c) #250 kcmil   (d) #300 kcmil

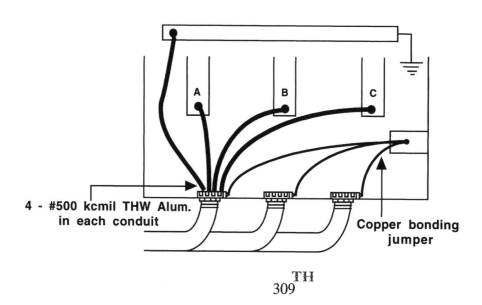

4 - #500 kcmil THW Alum.
in each conduit

Copper bonding
jumper

5. A ladder-type cable tray which is 12" wide, has 4 sides and is made of 3/16" thick aluminum is used as an equipment grounding conductor and is protected by the maximum size overcurrent device required. The minimum size copper equipment bonding jumper required to connect sections of this cable tray is _____.

(a) #1   (b) #2/0   (c) #3/0   (d) #4/0

6. A nonmetallic junction box with a volume of 27 cubic inches contains six #12 conductors. The maximum number of #10 conductors which may be added to the junction box is _____.

(a) 3   (b) 5   (c) 6   (d) 8

7. One 50 hp, wound-rotor, 575v, 3-phase motor and one 7 1/2 hp, 230v, single-phase motors are installed with type TW copper conductors run in conduit. Calculate the minimum size IMC conduit required.

(a) 3/4"   (b) 1"   (c) 1 1/4"   (d) 1 1/2"

8. GIVEN: A 34.25 KVAR capacitor to correct the power factor on a 100 hp, 480v, 3-phase motor. The minimum ampacity of conductors connecting this capacitor to the motor terminals shall be _____ amperes.

(a) 41.2   (b) 55.6   (c) 71.3   (d) 96.3

9. Refer to the figure below of a delta-connected, 3-phase, 4-wire transformer. In a panelboard or switchboard, the highest voltage is measured between the center tap (ground) and Phase _____.

(a) A   (b) B   (c) C   (d) None of these

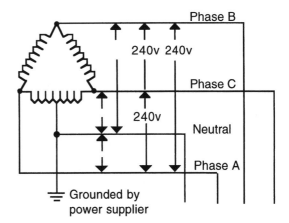

10. The required service ampacity for a mobile home park containg 45 lots is ____ amperes.

(a) 166   (b) 584   (c) 690   (d) 720

11. What size rigid schedule 80 PVC conduit would be required to install the following THW copper conductors? One - #300 kcmil, one - #400 kcmil and two - #500 kcmil.

(a) 2"   (b) 2 1/2"   (c) 3"   (d) 3 1/2"

12. A three-phase squirrel cage induction motor supplied by three wires runs in the counterclockwise direction. The motor may be made to reverse rotation (to clockwise direction) by ____.

(a) reversing the terminal connections of all three supply wires
(b) reversing the terminal connections of any two supply wires
(c) rotating the terminal connections of all three supply wires by one terminal in the clockwise
    direction
(d) rotating the terminal connections of all three supply wires by one terminal in the
    counterclockwise direction

13. A 220 volt, single-phase motor delivers 6.5 mechanical horsepower to a load. An ammeter indicates the motor is drawing 26.5 amperes. The efficiency is ____.

(a) 70%   (b) 78%   (c) 83%   (d) 88%

14. Refer to the figure below. In the gasoline dispensing area, a total of ____ conduit seals are required.

(a) 7   (b) 9   (c) 10   (d) 12

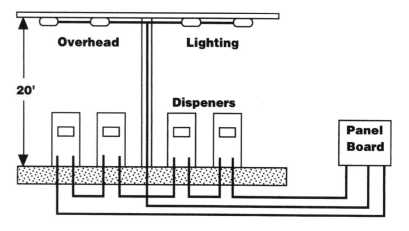

15. An assembly hall contains 10,000 sq.ft., including 500 sq.ft. of corridor. The service is 240/120v single-phase. Twenty heavy-duty lampholders are installed, as are five continuous-use receptacles and an 1800va sign. To supply all loads continuously for 3 hours or more, a minimum of _____ circuit breakers shall be required.

(a) 7   (b) 9   (c) 13   (d) 14

16. Three #500 kcmil THHN conductors are installed in a raceway at 70°C. What is the allowable ampacity of each conductor?

(a) 249   (b) 409   (c) 430   (d) 447

17. The maximum allowable fill area of a 12" wide ladder-type cable tray containing multiconductor cables rated less than 2000 volts and smaller than #4/0 is _____ square inches.

(a) 11   (b) 14   (c) 16.5   (d) 21

18. On the meter skown below, the reading at "X" while on the R X 100 meter scale illustrated would be _____.

(a) 8 ohms
(b) 150 ohms
(c) 800 ohms
(d) 80,000 ohms

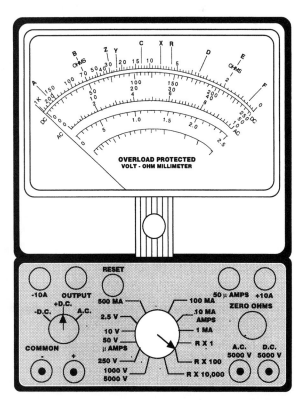

19. A catering business located in a residence requires the installation of:
   Two 3.5 kw ovens
   Two 2.5 kw ranges
   One 2.3 kw warming oven
   One 1.8 kw hot plate
The calculated feeder load for the appliances listed shall be _____ va.

(a) 8,350   (b) 9,500   (c) 10,556   (d) 16,100

20. GIVEN: A 3-phase, 440v, 30 hp synchronous motor with autotransformer starting and code letter H indicated. If the motor is to be operated under continuous load conditions, the branch circuit conductors shall have a minimum ampacity of _____ amperes and the maximum rating of an inverse time circuit breaker in the motor branch circuit shall be _____ percent of full load current.

(a) 32 and 150   (b) 32 and 200   (c) 40 and 400   (d) 63 and 300

21. A mobile home park consists of 30 spaces which accomodate maximum size 12' x 35' mobile homes. The minimum size service provided to the park shall be _____ amperes.

(a) 400   (b) 450   (c) 500   (d) 600

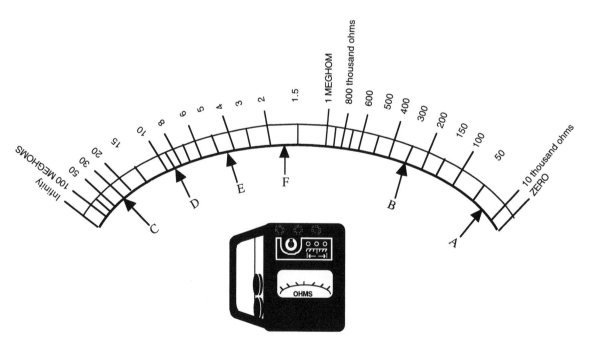

22. The reading at "E" on the megohmmeter scale shown in the illustration is _____.

(a) 45,000 ohms   (b) 450,000 ohms   (c) 4,500,000 ohms   (d) 40,500,000 ohms

23. A single phase, 3-wire service has two ungrounded conductors of size #3/0 THHN aluminum building wire. The neutral conductor is a #2/0 THHN aluminum building wire. The minimum size EMT allowed for the service entrance conductors is ____.

(a) 1 1/4"   (b) 1 1/2"   (c) 2"   (d) 2 1/2"

24. A capacitor rated 32.5 kVA, 3-phase, is used to correct the power factor of a 100 hp, 480v, 3-phase squirrel cage motor. All wires are THW copper. The conductors used to connect the capacitor to the terminals of the motor must be at least ____ copper THW.

(a) #1   (b) #3   (c) #4   (d) #6

25. A commercial kitchen, open from 10:30 am to 1 pm has three-phase, 240v power and contains the following equipment:
   two - 3 kw ovens
   one - 5 kw fryer
   one - 3 kw fryer
   two - 7.5 kw pizza ovens
The required feeder ampacity to serve this equipment is ____ amperes. Do not use the optional method of calculation.

(a) 38.9   (b) 45.3   (c) 59.0   (d) 78.5

26. GIVEN: A motor control circuit requires relay contacts that immediately change position when the relay coil is energized, but are delayed in changing back to the original position when the coil is de-energized. This type of control requires a ____ relay.

(a) overload   (b) control (voltage)
(c) time-delay on energizing   (d) time-delay on de-energizing

27. On typical wiring diagrams for magnetic motor control starters, overload heaters, not overload contacts are shown in series with the ____.

(a) line contacts supplying power to the motor
(b) pilot light that indicates when the motor is running
(c) pilot light that indicates when the motor is stopped
(d) control circuit supplying the coil of the motor starter

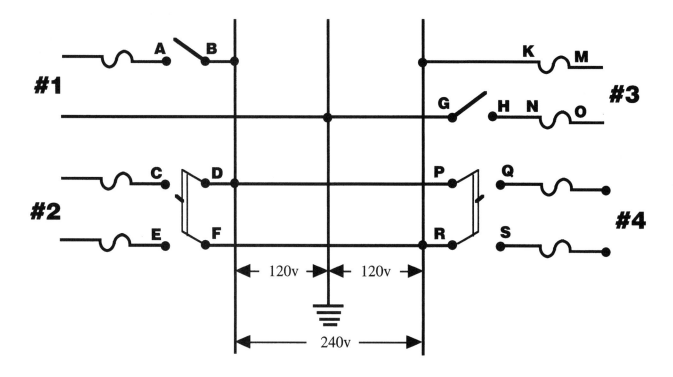

28. Circuit **#3** in the above diagram _____.

(a) supplies 240 volts to the load
(b) would be correctly wired if there were a direct connection instead of a fuse between points "K" and "M"
(c) would be correctly wired if there were a direct connection instead of a fuse between points "N" and "O"
(d) would be correctly wired if the switch and fuse were eliminated and replaced by a direct connection between "G" and "O"

29. Circuit **#4** in the above diagram _____.

(a) is not properly fused as it should have only one fuse in the hot leg
(b) supplies 240 volts to the load
(c) is grounded if, with the switch open, test lamps light when placed between points "P" & "R"
(d) is shorted if, with the switch open, test lamps light when placed between points "P" & "R"

30. Circuit **#1** in the above diagram _____.

(a) supplies 240 volts to the load
(b) is grounded if a pair of test lamps light when placed between point "B" and ground
(c) is not properly fused as it should have a fuse in each leg
(d) supplies 120 volts to the load

CHAPTER 9

ANSWERS

CHAPTER 1   TEST 1   BRANCH CIRCUITS

1. (c) 6'   210.50(C)
2. (b) 6' 6" = 6 1/2'   210.52(E)
3. (d) 12 linear feet   210.62
4. (b) single contact device DEF 100
5. (a) I only   210.23(C)
6. (c) III only   210.5(B) 250.119

CHAPTER 1   TEST 2   BRANCH CIRCUITS

1. (d) 125%   210.20(A)
2. (d) 20 amps   Table 210.24
3. (c) I and III only
4. (d) 20 amps   The **circuit** can be loaded to 20 amps, the A/C load cannot exceed 10a or 50%
5. (d) IV   17 amps exceeds the 80% rating of one plug-cord connected appliance

CHAPTER 2   TEST 1   AMPACITY

1. (a) 13.65a   #12 THHN = 30a x 50% (T.310.15B2a)= 15a x .91 (40°C) = 13.65a
2. (c) 24 amps   #12 THHN = 30a x 80% (310.15B4a = 6 wires) = 24 amps
3. (a) 150.9 amps   #4/0 THWN = 230a x 80% (T.310.15B2a) = 184a x .82 (45°C) = 150.88a
4. (d) not required   Table 310.15(B2a) ex.3 does NOT require derating a nipple nor does 27°C
                                from Table 310.16 require a correction factor
5. (d) 176a   #3/0 THWN = 200a x .88 (104°F) = 176a
6. (a) 10%   310.60 ex.

CHAPTER 2   TEST 2   AMPACITY

1. (c) #4   110.14(C)
2. (b) #6 THWN   50a load/.80 (T.310.15B2a) = 62.5 required ampacity T. 310.16
3. (d) 41.6 amps   T. 310.16 = 40 ampacity x 1.04 correction factor = 41.6a
4. (b) 6   Count 3 black and 3 red wires per 310.15(B4)a and 310.15(B5)
5. (b) 7 amps   Table 400.5(A)
6. (c) 110 amps   T. 310.17 Free Air 125a x .88 = 110

CHAPTER 2 TEST 3 AMPACITY

1. Overcurrent protection for a #10 = **30 amps** *
2. #14 THW ampacity = 20a x 80% (T.310.15B2a) = **16 amps**
3. #12 TW ampacity = 25a x .82 correction factor = **20.5 amps**
4. #12 TW ampacity = 25a x 1.08 correction factor = **27 amps**
5. #12 THHN ampacity = 30a x .82 correction factor = 24.6a x 80% (T.310.15B2a) = **19.68 amps**
6. #10 THW ampacity = 35a x 80% (T.310.15B2a for 6 wires) = **28 amps**

CHAPTER 2 TEST 4 AMPACITY

1. #12 THW ampacity = 25a x .75 correction factor = **18.75a**
2. #10 TW ampacity = 30a x 70% (T.310.15B2a) = **21a**
3. #2/0 THW aluminum ampacity = 135a x 1.05 correction factor = **141.75a**
4. #8 XHHW **wet** location 75°C ampacity = 50a x .82 correction factor = **41a**
5. #14 RHH ampacity = 25a x 45% (T.310.15B2a) = 11.25a x .87 (corr. factor) = **9.7875**
6. **Maximum overcurrent protection** is *30 amp. The asterisk* from Table 310.16 footnote = **30a**

CHAPTER 2 TEST 5 AMPACITY

1. 18" conduit is a **nipple**. 310.15(B2a) ex.3 = **NO DERATING REQUIRED**

2. #10 TW ampacity = 30a x 1.08 correction factor = **32.4a**

3. #3/0 THW ampacity = 200a x 80% (T.310.15B2a) = **160a**

4. T. 310.15(B2a) exception 4 = **65a**

5. #8 XHHW **dry** location 90°C ampacity = 55a x 80% (T.310.15B2a & 310.15B4c) = **44a**

6. Required table ampacity = 25 amp load/.58 correction factor = 43.1 required ampacity.
   Table 310.16 60°C conductor that will carry 43.1 amps is a **#6 TW**.

CHAPTER 3   TEST 1   MOTORS

1. **(a) 17.25a**   F.L.C. 13.8a x 125% (430.22) = 17.25a

2. **(d) 59.4a**   Table 430.250   = 59.4a

3. **(a) 39.1a**   F.L.C. 34a x 115% (430.32A1) = 39.1a

4. **(a) 150%**   Table 430.152 DC motor dual element fuse = 150%

5. **(c) #6 TW copper**   3 hp F.L.C. 18.7a x 125% = 23.375a + 13.2a + 13.2a = 49.775 required ampacity. Table 310.16 TW copper requires a #6. Section 110.5: Use **copper** unless otherwise specified.

6. **(c) 125a**   Largest branch circuit CB = 70a + 28a + 28a = 126 amps. 240.6: Use 125 amp.

CHAPTER 3   TEST 2   MOTORS

1. **(b) 20.875a**   F.L.C. 16.7a x 125% (430.32A1) = 20.875a

2. **(b) #8**   F.L.C. 28a x 125% = 35 required ampacity. Table 310.16 = #8 TW

3. **(b) 54a**   F.L.C. 24a x 125% = 30a + 24a = 54 required ampacity

4. **(c) 35a**   F.L.C. 13.2a x 250% (Table 430.52) = 33a. 240.6: Use 35 amp standard

5. **(a) 50a**   F.L.C. 24a x 125% = 30a + 16.7a = 46.7 required ampacity

6. **(b) 125a**   F.L.C. 65a x 175% (Table 430.52) = 113.75a. 240.6: Use 125a standard

---

CHAPTER 3   TEST 3   MOTORS

FIND:
(a) F.L.C. **motor "A" = 28a**   F.L.C. **motor"B" = 12a**
(b) overloads **motor "A"** = 28a x 115% = **32.2a**   **motor "B"** = 12a x 125% = **15.0a**
(c) conductor **motor "A"** = 28a x 125% = 35a = **#8 TW**   **motor"B"** = 12a x 125% = 15a = **#14 TW**
(d) breaker **motor "A"** = 28a x 250% = **70a CB**   **motor "B"** = 12a x 150% = 18a use **20a CB**
(e) feeder size 28a x 125% = 35a + 12a F.L.C. = 47 required ampacity   Use **#6 TW**
(f) feeder breaker   70a CB + 12a F.L.C. = 82a   Can't go UP on a feeder, drop down to **80a CB**

CHAPTER 3   TEST 4   MOTORS

1. F.L.C. 17a x 115% = **19.55a**
2. Use nameplate (430.6A1) 15a x 115% = **17.25a**
3. F.L.C. 28a x 125% = 35 required ampacity Table 310.16 = **#8 TW**
4. F.L.C. 28a x 125% = 35a + 17a + 17a + 17a = 86 required ampacity Table 310.16 = **#2 TW**
5. F.L.C. 17a x 175% (dual element) = 29.75a 240.6: **30 amps**
6. F.L.C. 28a x 175% (dual element) = 49 240.6: **50 amps**
7. 50a fuse + 17 a + 17a + 17a = 101a 240.6: Drop down to a **100a**

CHAPTER 3   TEST 5   MOTORS

1. F.L.C. 34a x 125% (40°C rise) = **42.5a**
2. F.L.C. 24.2a x 125% = 30.25 required ampacity Table 310.16 = **#8 TW**
3. F.L.C. 34a x 250% = 85a 240.6: **90a**
4. 3ø power = E x I x 1.732 208v x 24.2a x 1.732 = **8718va**
5. F.L.C. 34a x 125% = 42.5a + 24.2a = 66.7 required ampacity Table 310.16 = **#4 TW**
6. 90a CB + 24.2a (all other loads on the **SAME** conductor) = 114.2 Go down to **110a**

CHAPTER 3   TEST 6   MOTORS

1. (b) 80 amps   42a x 175% = 73.5 (240.6) = 80 next higher standard size
2. (c) 25 amps   10.6a x 250% = 26.5a (240.6) = next higher size is 30a, can't go up to 35
3. (a) 20 amps   13.2a x 175% = 23.1a (240.6) = next higher size is 25a, can't go up to 30
4. (b) 40 amps   24a x 175% = 42a (240.6) = next higher size is 45a, can't go up to 50
5. (c) 17.16 amps   13.2a x 130% maximum (430.32C) = 17.16a
6. (b) 21 amps   10.6a x 125% = 13.25a + 7.5a = 20.75 required ampacity
7. (a) #12 THW   13.8a x 125% = 17.25a + 7.5a = 24.75 required ampacity T. 310.16 = #12
8. (c) 60 amp   18.7a x 250% = 46.75a = 50a CB + 16.7a = 66.7a, down to 60a on feeder

CHAPTER 3A   TEST 1   MOTOR CONTROLS

1. (d)   normally open
2. (d)   parallel, series
3. (a)   interlock
4. (d)   inching
5. (c)   toggle switch
6. (d)   wiring
7. (c)   the holding circuit interlock was welded
8. (a)   plugging

CHAPTER 3A   TEST 2   MOTOR CONTROLS

1. **(b)**   The stop button is normally opened.
2. **(d)**   all of the above would happen.
3. **(a)**   normally open UV closes. UV stands for undervoltage.
4. **(c)**   normally open M opens.
5. **(c)**   The UV coil is energized.

CHAPTER 3A   TEST 3   MOTOR CONTROLS

1. **(d)**   resistor starter.
2. **(d)**   The resistors are in parallel with the CR contacts.
3. **(a)**   At full speed all normally open CR contacts are closed.
4. **(c)**   When CR coil is energized the motor will go to full run position.
5. **(c)**   Parallel.

CHAPTER 3A   TEST 4   MOTOR CONTROLS

1. **(d)**   Full voltage starter.
2. **(b)**   The overloads are in series with the M coil.
3. **(c)**   The heaters are in parallel with the motor.
4. **(c)**
5. **(b)**   Start is pushed, energizing M coil, normally open M locks in.

CHAPTER 3-A   TEST 5   MOTOR CONTROLS

1. **(a)**   Full voltage starter.
2. **(c)**   Pump would only function when container is empty.
3. **(a)**   I only. Line one.

CHAPTER 3B   TEST 1   MOTOR TAPS

1.   Motor #1 = Table 430.250 F.L.C. **143 amps**
        Motor #2 = Table 430.250 F.L.C. **59.4 amps**
        Motor #3 = Table 430.250 F.L.C. **30.8 amps**

2.   Motor #1 = 143 x 115% (430.32A1) = **164.45 amps**
        Motor #2 = 59.4 x 115% (430.32A1) = **68.31 amps**
        Motor #3 = 30.8 x 115% (430.32A1) = **35.42 amps**

3.   Motor #1 = 143 x 125% (430.22) = 178.75 required ampacity T.310.16 = **#3/0 THW**
        Motor #2 = 59.4 x 125% (430.22) = 74.25 required ampacity T.310.16 = **#4 THW**
        Motor #3 = 30.8 x 125% (430.22) = 38.5 required ampacity T.310.16 = **#8 THW**

4.   Motor #1 = 143 x 175% (T.430.52 dual-element) = 250.25   240.6 = **250 amp**
        Motor #2 = 59.4 x 175% (T.430.52 dual-element) = 103.95   240.6 = **110 amp**
        Motor #3 = 30.8 x 175% (T.430.52 dual-element) = 53.9   240.6 = **60 amp**

5.   Motor #1 = 143 x 115% (430.110A) = 164.45 amps minimum = 200 amp **non-fusible** or
        a **400 amp fuseable disconnect** for a 250 amp branch circuit fuse
        Motor #2 = 59.4 x 115% (430.110A) = 68.31 amps minimum = 100 amp **non-fusible** or
        a **200 amp fuseable disconnect** for a 110 amp branch circuit fuse
        Motor #3 = 30.8 x 115% (430.110A) = 35.42 amps minimum = 60 amp **non-fusible** or
        a **60 amp fuseable disconnect** for a 60 amp branch circuit fuse

6.   21 foot taps in conduit cannot be smaller than 1/3 of the feeder conductor ampacity #400
        kcmil = 335 ampacity/3 = 111.6 ampacity required for feeder taps = #2 tap conductors
        Motor #1 = **#3/0 THW tap conductor**
        Motor #2 = **#2 THW tap conductor**
        Motor #3 = **#2 THW tap conductor**

7.   143 x 125% (430.24) = 178.75 + 59.4 + 30.8 = 268.95 required ampacity + 65.92 amps (19
        kw Continuous Lighting Load) = 334.87 amps = **#400 kcmil**

8.   250 amp fuse + 59.4 + 30.8 = 340.2 amps + 65.92 (52.74 x 125%) =406.12 amps
        240.6 = **400 feeder fuse**

9.   143+ 59.4 + 30.8 + 52.74 = x 115% (430.110C2) = 328.83 amps minimum = **400 amp**

10.   19,000w/208v x 1.732 = 52.74 amps actual lighting load. The fuse size to the continuous
        lighting load would be 52.74 x 125 (215.2A1) = 65.9 = 70 amp fuses. The ampacity of the
        tap conductors cannot be less than 1/3 of the rating of the feeder O.C.P. device(240.21C2).
        400 amp fuse/3 = 133 ampacity required = **#1/0 THW tap conductors to lighting load.**

CHAPTER 4   TEST 1   BOX & RACEWAY FILL

1. 314.16(B1) count seven #12 wires x 2.25 cubic inches (Table 314.16B) = **15.75 cubic inches.**

2. Table 5A #1/0 THHN = .1590 sq.in. x 4 = .636 sq.in. #250 THHN = .3525 sq.in. x 3 = 1.0575 .636 sq.in. + 1.0575 sq.in. = 1.6935 sq.in. area required Table 4 = **2 1/2" rigid metal**

3. 314.16(B)   #12 wires: count 1 black, 1 white, 1 grounding, 1 clamps, 2 duplex receptacle = 6
       6 wires x 2.25 cu.in. (Table 314.16B) = 13.5 cu.in.
       #14 wires: count 1 black, 1 white, 2 switch = 4
       4 wires x 2 cu.in. (Table 314.16B) = 8 cu.in. + 13.5 cu.in. = **21.5 cubic inch**

4. Table 4 Total Area 100% = **7.922 sq.in.**

5. 314.16(B)   #12 wires: count 1 black, 1 white, 1 grounding, 1 clamps = 4 wires
       4 x 2.25 cu.in. (Table 314.16B) = 9 cu.in.
       #14 wires: count 2 black and 2 white = 4 wires
       4 x 2 cu.in. (Table 314.16B) = 8 cu.in. + 9 cu.in. = **17 cu.in.**

CHAPTER 4   TEST 2   BOX FILL

1. 314.16(B5) count one #12 grounding and 314.16(B1) count two #12 conductors for a total of three #12 conductors x 2.25 cubic inches (Table 314.16B) = **6.75 cubic inches.**

2. 314.16(B1) count two black wires and two white wires, 314.16(B5) count one grounding wire, 314.16(B2) count one for clamps, 314.16(B4) count two for duplex for a total of eight #12 wires. Table 314.16(B) #12 wire = 2.25 cu.in. x 8 wires = **18 cubic inch box.**

3. Table 314.16(B) #12 wires 4 x 2.25 cu.in = 9 cu.in. and #14 wires 3 x 2 cu.in. = 6 cu.in. for a total of 9 + 6 = 15 cubic inches required. Table 314.16(A) would require a **1 1/2" x 4" octagonal box.**

4. 314.16(B1) count three black wires and three white wires, 314.16(B5) count one grounding wire, 314.16(B2) count one for clamps, 314.16(B4) count two for duplex and two for switch for a total of twelve #12 wires x 2.25 cu.in. (Table 314.16B) = **27 cubic inches.**

CHAPTER 4   TEST 3   BOX FILL

1. Table 314.16(B) #12 = 2.25 cu.in. x 9 conductors = **20.25 cu.in. box required.**
2. 314.16(A1) **one**
3. Table 314.16(A) **3**
4. Table 314.16(B) #14 = 2 cu.in. x 5 conductors = **10 cu.in. box required.**
5. Table 314.16(B) #10 = 2.5 cu.in. x 9 conductors = **22.5 cu.in. box required.**
6. Table 314.16(A) **2**

CHAPTER 4 TEST 4 RACEWAY FILL

1. X = 6 x 2" = **12"**
2. X = 6 x 3" = 18" + 2" + 1" = **21"**
   Y = 6 x 3" = **18"**
   Z = 6 x 3" = **18"**
3. 6 x 3" = 18" + 2 1/2" + 1 1/2" = **22" x 22"**

CHAPTER 4 TEST 5 RACEWAY FILL

1. Table 4 **3.630"**
2. **Table 8, Chapter 9**
3. Table 5 **0.0209"**
4. Table 4 60% nipple fill = **.916**
5. 10 - #12 THW   .0181 x 10 =   .181
    12 - #10 TW   .0243 x 12 =   .2916
     6 - #8 THHN .0366 x 6 =   .2196
     8 - #6 THWN .0507 x 8 =   .4056
                          1.0978 sq.in.   Table 4 requires a **2" conduit 40% fill**.

6. Table 5   6 - #14 TW   .0139 x 6 =   .0834
               8 - #8 THWN .0366 x 8 =   .2928
                                       .3762 sq.in.

18" is a nipple 60% fill, the answer is a **1" nipple at .413 sq.in. fill**.

CHAPTER 4 TEST 6 RACEWAY FILL

1. Table 4 - 2" @ 40% = 1.342 Table 5 - #6 XHHW = .059 1.342/.059 = 22.7 or **22 conductors.**
2. Table 4 **1.020 inch**
3. Table 4   2" conduit = 1.363" 40% fill   Table 5 #8 THHN = .0366" x 10 = .366"
   1.363 - .366 = .997 area left to fill. #8 XHHW = .0437". .997/.0437 = 22.8 or **23 conductors**.
4. Table 4 1 1/2" conduit 40% fill = .794"   Table 5 #12 THW = .0181"
   .794/.0181 = **43.8 or 44 conductors**.
5. 4 - #14 THW   .0139 x 4 =   .0556
    2 - #12 RHW (without outer cover)   .026 x 2 =   .052
    2 - #14 RHH (with outer cover)   .0293 x 2 =   .0586
    6 - #14 THHN   .0097 x 6 =   .0582
    3 - #12 stranded bare conductors   .006 x 3 =   .018
                                                           .2424 sq.in.

   Table 4 40% fill, the answer is a **1" conduit** at .384" fill.
6. Table 4 1 1/4" (nipple) = .916/half filled = .458 area left to fill.
   Table 5 #14 THHN = .0097. .458/.0097 = 47.2 or **47 conductors**.

CHAPTER 4   TEST 7   RACEWAY FILL

1. Table 4 - 1 1/2" = .792   Table 5 - #6 XHHW = .0590   .792/.0590 = **13 conductors.**

2. Table 1   **53%**

3. Table 4   1/2" nipple 60% fill = .130   Table 5 #14 TW = .0139
   .130/.0139 = 9.3 = **9 conductors.**

4. Chapter 9 Tables   Note (4) **24"**

5. Table 4   100% = **1.084**

6. Section 310.3   #8 and larger **shall be stranded**. Table 8   #8 stranded = **0.017.**

7. Table 4 - 2" nipple = 2.013   Table 5 - #12 THHN = .0133   2.013/.0133 = 151 **151 conductors.**

8. Table 4 - 1" @ 40% = .355   Table 5 - #12 RHW (with) = .0353   .355/.0353 = **10 conductors.**

CHAPTER 4   TEST 8   RACEWAY FILL

1. Table 4 - 1 1/2" nipple 60% fill = 1.243   Table 5 - #10 RHW with cover = .0437
   1.243/.0437 = 28.4   **28 conductors.**

2. Table 4 - 3/4" flex = .213   Table 5 - #14 FEP = .010   .213/.010 = 21.3 or   **21 conductors.**

3. Table 5   #500 kcmil THW   =   .7901   x 6   = 4.7406
                 #750 kcmil THW   =   1.1652 x 4   = 4.6608
                 #1000 kcmil THW =   1.372 (Diameter)   x 6 = 8.232
       Table 318-10 Col. 2   8.232 x 1.1 = 9.0552 sq.in. + 4.7406 + 4.6608 = 18.4566 sq. in.
       Table 318-10 requires a Cable Tray **18" wide.**

4. Wireway   Section 376.22   20% fill = 4" x 4" = 16" x 20% fill = 3.2" can be filled.
       Table 5   #2/0 THW = .2624   3.2"/.2624 = 12.1   **12 conductors permitted.**

5. Table 4 - 1 1/2" LFNC-B 40% = **.792**

6. Table 4 - 1" nipple 60% fill = .4128   Table 5 - #12 RHW without cover = .026
   .4128/.026 = 15.8   **16 conductors.**

7. Table 5 - #8 THW = .0437 x 8 = **.3496.**

8. Table 4 - 3/4" nipple 60% fill = .3048   Table 5 - #14 THHN = .0097
   .3048/.0097 = 31.4 = **31 conductors.**

CHAPTER 4   TEST 9   RACEWAY FILL

1. Gutter   Section 366.22   20% fill.   6" x 6" = 36" x 20% = 7.2" can be filled.
       Table 5 - #500 kcmil THHN = .7073.   7.2"/.7073 = 10.17   **10 conductors.**

2. Table 4 - 3/8" flex = .046   Table 5 - #14 THHN = .0097   .046/.0097 = 4.74 or **4 conductors**

3. Section 372.11   40% fill.   10 sq.in. x 40% = 4" can be filled.
       Table 5 - #1/0 XHHW = .1825   4"/.1825 = 21.9 or   **22 conductors.**

4. Table 4 - 2" conduit 40% fill = 1.363   Table 5 - #8 RHW with cover = .0835 x 10 = .835.
       1.363 - .835 = .528 area left to fill.   Table 5 - #8 XHHW = .0437
       .528/.0437 = **12 conductors.**

5. Table 4 Type A rigid PVC = **1.459.**

6. Table 5   #12 RHW without outer cover =   .026 x 6 =   .156
                    #14 RHH with outer cover =   .0293 x 4 =   .1172
                    #12 THW =   .0181 x 8 =   .1448
                    #6   XHHW =   .059 x 4 =   .236
                    #8 bare copper (Table 8) =   .017   =   .017 (310-3 stranded)
                                                              .671 sq.in. required.

CHAPTER 5 TEST 1   COMMERCIAL & HOUSEHOLD COOKING

---

1. 4.5 kw + 9kw + 4.6 kw + 12 kw + 30 kw = 60.1 kw x 65% (Table 220.56) = 39.065 or **39.07kw**

2. 4 - 14 kw - 12 kw = 2 kw x 5% = 10%   T.220.55 Column C four appliances = 17 kw
    17 kw x 110% = **18.7 kw**

3. Table 220.55 Note 1 = 20 kw - 12 kw = 8 kw x 5% = 40%
    Column C = 8 kw x 140% = 11.2 kw or 11, 200w/240v = **46.7 amps**

4. Table 220.55 Note 5   Column C = 35kw x 70% (220.61B1 neutral) = **24.5 kw**

5. 8 kw + 6 kw + 3.5 kw + 6 kw + 3.5 kw = 27 kw x 45% (T. 220.55 Col. B) = 12.15 or **12.2 kw**

6. T. 220.55 Note 2: 12 kw + 28 kw + 17 kw = 57 kw   57 kw/4 ranges = 14.25 kw average
    4 - 14 kw ranges Note 1 = 14kw - 12 kw = 2 kw x 5% = 10%
    Column C: 4 ranges = 17 kw x 110% = **18.7 kw**

CHAPTER 5   TEST 2 HOUSEHOLD COOKING EQUIPMENT

---

1. 15kw - 12kw = 3kw x 5% = 15%. Column C = 8kw x 1.15 = **9.2 kw.**
2. Note 4: For one oven = nameplate rating = **5kw.**
3. Column B 43% x 24kw = **10.32 kw.**
4. 16kw - 12kw = 4kw x 5% = 20%. Column C = 20kw x 1.20 = **24kw.**
5. Column C = 15 kw + 30 kw = **45 kw.**
6. Column C for 2 appliances = **11 kw.**
7. Column C = 21 kw x 70% (220.61B1) = **14.7 kw neutral demand.**
8. Section 210.19 ex. 2 **#10.**

CHAPTER 5   TEST 3 HOUSEHOLD COOKING EQUIPMENT

---

1. Column C = 8kw.   8000w/230v = 34.78 or **34.8 amps.**
2. Column B 65% x 10kw = **6.5 kw.**
3. 13.55 = 14kw range. 14kw - 12kw = 2kw x 5% = 10%. Column C = 8kw x 1.10 = 8.8kw
    8800w/220v = **40 amps.**
4. Column B 55% x 13kw = **7.15 kw.**

5.
    6 - $\not{8}$ kw = 72kw
    4 - 12kw = 48kw
    10 - 15kw = 150kw
    ──────────────
    20   270kw   270kw/20 = 13.5 or 14kw average

    Column C for 20 ranges = 35kw demand.   14kw - 12kw = 2kw x 5% = 10%.
    Column C   35kw x 1.10 = **38.5 kw.**

6. Column C = 50kw (15+35). 50,000w/240v = 208 amps x 70% = 145.8 or **146 amps.**

CHAPTER 5   TEST 4   HOUSEHOLD COOKING EQUIPMENT

1. Column B 55% x 14kw = 7.7kw x 70% neutral = **5.39 kw.**
2. 2 - 14 kw = 28 kw
    <u>3 - 15 kw = 45 kw</u>
    5   73 kw   73/5 = 14.6 or 15 kw average.

   Column C 5 appliances = 20kw demand. 15kw - 12kw = 3kw x 5% = 15%. 20kw x 1.15 = **23kw.**

3. Column C = 25kw + 37.5 (.75 x 50) = 62.5 demand. 14kw - 12kw = 2kw x 5% = 10%.
   Column C 62.5kw x 1.10 = **68.75 kw.**
4. 15 x 3.5kw = 52.5kw x 32% (Column B) = **16.8 kw.**
5. Note 4. 5kw + 8kw = 13kw. 1 - 13kw range. Note 1 13kw - 12kw = 1kw x 5% = 5%.
   Column C = 8kw x 1.05 = 8.4 kw or 8400w/240v = **35 amps.**
6. 4 x 3kw = 12 kw x 66% (Column A) = 7.92 kw.
   4 x 5kw = 20 kw x 50% (Column B) = 10 kw.
   7.92kw + 10kw = **17.92 kw.**

CHAPTER 5   TEST 5   COMMERCIAL & HOUSEHOLD COOKING EQUIPMENT

1. Column C 25kw + 41.25kw (.75 x 55) = 66.25kw.   14kw - 12kw = 2kw x 5% = 10%.
   Column C 66.25kw x 1.10 = **72.875 kw.**
2. Column C = **35 kw maximum demand.**
3. 16kw - 12kw = 4kw x 5% = 20%. Column C = 8kw x 1.20 = 9.6kw.
   9600w/230v = **41.7 AMPS.**
4. Column C = 25kw + 33.75kw (.75 x 45) = **58.75 kw.**
5. Column C = 43kw (15 + 28). 14kw - 12kw = 2kw x 5% = 10%.
   Column C 43kw x 1.10 = **47.3 kw.**
6. 4 - ~~9~~ 12 kw = 48 kw
    5 - 14 kw = 70 kw
    <u>6 - 16 kw = 96 kw</u>
    15   214 kw   214kw/15 = 14.26 or 14 kw average value.
   Now we have 15 - 14 kw ranges. Column C for 15 ranges = 30 kw.
   14kw - 12kw = 2kw x 5% = 10%. Column C 30kw x 1.10 = **33 kw.**

CHAPTER 5   TEST 6   COMMERCIAL & HOUSEHOLD COOKING EQUIPMENT

1. Total connected load of 32kw x 65% (T. 220.56) = **20.8 kw**.
2. Note 5.   Use Table 220.55   Column C for 6 ranges = **21 kw**.
3.   A Phase   B Phase   C Phase
    16 ranges   15 ranges   15 ranges   16 ranges x 2 = 32 appliances.
   Column C for 32 appliances = 47kw (15 + 32). 15kw - 12kw = 3kw x 5% = 15%.
   Column C   47kw x 1.15 = **54.05 kw**.

4. Total connected load 27kw x 80% (T.220.56) = **21.6 kw**.

5.   5 - ~~9~~ 12 kw ranges = 60kw
      4 - 12kw ranges = 48kw
      7 - 16kw ranges = 112kw
     ‾‾‾   ‾‾‾‾‾‾
      16   220kw   220kw/16 = 13.75 or 14 kw average value.
   Column C for 16 appliances = 31 kw.   14kw - 12kw = 2kw x 5% = 10%.
   Column C   31kw x 1.10 = **34.1 kw**.

6. Column C for 2 appliances = 11 kw.   15kw - 12kw = 3kw x 5% = 15%.
   Column C   11kw x 1.15 = **12.65 kw**.

CHAPTER 5   TEST 7   COMMERCIAL & HOUSEHOLD COOKING

1. Total connected load 40kw x 65% (T.220.56) = **26 kw**.
2.   A Phase   B Phase   C Phase
    17 ranges   17 ranges   16 ranges   17 ranges x 2 = 34 appliances.
   Column C = 49kw (15 + 34).   14kw - 12kw = 2kw x 5% = 10%.
   Column C   49kw x 1.10 = **53.9 kw**.

3. Note 4.   6kw + 8kw = 14kw.   One 14kw range.   14kw - 12kw = 2kw x 5% = 10%.
   Column C for one appliance = 8kw x 1.10 = **8.8 kw**.
4. 16kw + 3 kw + 2kw = 21kw x 90% (T.220.56) = 18.9kw, **BUT** the two largest loads =
   16kw + 3 kw = **19 kw demand**.
5. Note 5.   Table 220.55   Column C for 15 appliances = 30kw x 70% neutral = **21 kw**.
6. 30 x 4kw = 120kw x 24% (Column B) = 28.8kw x 70% neutral = **20.16 kw**.

CHAPTER 6 TEST 1 DWELLINGS

---

1. **4** 210.11(C1,2,3)
2. **4200va** 1400sq.ft. x 3va = 4200va
3. **4** 2200 sq.ft. x 3va = 6600va/120v = 55 amps. Need 4 - 15 amp circuits. **Use 120v**
4. **15 amps** 5000w/230v = 21.7a x 70% (neutral) = 15 amps
5. **100%** 220.82(C1)
6. **5400va** 60' x 30' = 1800 sq.ft. x 3va = 5400va

CHAPTER 6 TEST 2 DWELLINGS

	LINE	NEUTRAL
1452 sq.ft. x 3va	4356va	4356va
Small appliance 2 x 1500va	3000	3000
Laundry 1 x 1500va	1500	1500
	8856va	8856va
Table 220.42 Lighting Demand:		
First 3000va @ 100%	3000	3000
Remaining 5856va @ 35%	2050	2050
	5050va	5050va
9.6kw heat	9600	0
5 hp A/C 28a x 230v = 6440va (omit A/C)		
1200va dishwasher	1200	1200
1/2 hp disposal 9.8a x 115v = 1127va	1127	1127
4.5kw water heater	4500	0
4.0 kw dryer	5000	3500
15 kw range	9200	6440
Largest motor 1/2 hp 9.8a x 115v = 1127va x 25%	282	282
	35,959va	17,599va

Line = 35,959va/230v = 156 amps   T.310.15(B6)   175 amp service #1/0 copper

Neutral = 17, 599va/230v = 77 amps

Table 250.66   #6 copper electrode conductor

CHAPTER 6   TEST 3   DWELLINGS

1. **6440va**   28a x 230v = 6440va   220.60 omit the smaller load
2. **6600va**   2400 sq.ft - 200 sq.ft. (not living area) = 2200 sq.ft x 3va = 6600va
3. **5**   2500 sq.ft. x 3va = 7500va/120v = 62.5 amps.   Need five 15 amp circuits minimum
4. **3900va**   220.82(C4)   6kw x 65% = 3900.   220.60 omit the smaller
5. **14.58 amps**   5000w/240v = 20.83 amps x 70% (neutral) = 14.58 amps
6. **#2/0**   T. 310.15(B6)

CHAPTER 6   TEST 4   DWELLINGS

	LINE
2500 sq.ft. x 3va	7500
Small appliance 2 x 1500va	3000
Laundry 1 x 1500va	1500
12 kw heat 220.82(C6) 12kw x 40% = 4800w	
5 hp A/C 28a x 230v = 6440va (omit heat)	
14 kw range	14000
4.5 kw dryer	4500
5kw water heater	5000
1/3 hp compactor 7.2a x 115v	828
750va blender	750
3/4 hp pool pump 6.9a x 230v	1587
1200va dishwasher	1200
	39,865va total "General Load"

220.82(B) Demand:	
First 10 kva "General Load" @ 100%	10000va
Remaining 29,865va "General Load" @ 40%	11946va
5 hp A/C load	6440
	28,386 va total demand

Line = 28,386va/230v = 123 amps   T. 310.15(B6)   125 amp service   #2 copper.

CHAPTER 6   TEST 5   DWELLINGS

1. **75 kw**   60 x 5kw = 300kw x 25% (T.220.54) = 75kw.
2. **135 kw**   40 x 4.5kw = 180kw x 75% (220.53) = 135kw.
3. **65 kw**   House load is nameplate.   10 x 1500w = 15kw + 10 x 5kw = 65 kw.
4. **A/C**   17a x 230v = 3910va   6kw x 65% (220.82C4) = 3900va.   Omit heat.
5. **15.7 kw**   6 x 5kw = 30kw x 75% (T.220.54) = 22.5kw x 70% (220.61B1) = 15.7kw.
6. **6.45 kw**   10 x 1.5 kw = 15kw x 43% (T. 220.84) = 6.45kw.

CHAPTER 6   TEST 6   DWELLINGS

	LINE	NEUTRAL
850 sq.ft. x 3va x 20 units	51000va	51000va
Small appliance 2 x 1500va x 20 units	60000	60000
Laundry 1 x 1500va x 20 units	30000	30000
	141000va	141000va
Table 220.42 Lighting Demand:		
First 3000va @ 100%	3000	3000
Next 117,000va @ 35%	40950	40950
Remaining 21,000va @ 25%	5250	5250
	49200va	49200va
3 hp A/C 17a x 230v = 3910va x 20 units	78200	0
(omit heat @ 3kw)		
4.5kw dryer 5kw x 20 units = 100kw x 38% (T.220.54)		
20 dryers - 11 = 9 - 47 = 38%	38000	26600
1.5kw dishwasher 1.5kw x 20 units = 30kw x 75% (220.53)	22500	22500
1/4 hp compactor 5.8a x 115v = 667va x 20 units = 13340 x 75%	10005	10005
10 kw range T. 220.55 Column C = 35kw	35000	24500
Largest motor 17a x 230v = 3910va x 25%	978	0
	233,883va	132,805va

LINE = 233,883va/230v = 1017 amp demand.

Neutral = 132,805va/230v = 577 amps•
•220.61(B2)   First 200a @ 100% =   200a
Next 377a @ 70% =   264a
464 amp neutral demand

CHAPTER 6   TEST 7   DWELLINGS

1. **30.4 kw**   20 x 4kw = 80kw x 38% (T.220.84) = 30.4kw.
2. **33.75 kw**   30 x 1.5kw = 45kw x 75% (220.53) = 33.75kw.
3. **27 kw   Connected Load** not demand load!   6 x 4.5kw = 27kw.
4. **238 amps**   NEUTRAL
15 x 750 sq.ft. x 3va   33750va
Small appliance 30 x 1500va   45000
Laundry 15 x 1500va   22500
                                                         101,250va

Table 220.42 Lighting Demand:
First 3000va @ 100%   3000va
Remaining 98,250va @ 35%   34388
                                                         37388va
15 - 12kw ranges   T.220.55 Col. C = 30kw x 70%   21000
                                                         58,388

Neutral = 58,388va/230v = 253.8 or 254 amps   (220.61B2) First 200a @ 100% = 200a
                                                          Next 54a @ 70%   = 38
                                                                             238a

5. **52.5kw**   35 x 5kw = 175kw x 30% (T.220.84) = 52.5kw.
6. **129.6 kw**   60 x 4kw = 240kw + 60 x 5kw = 300kw.   540kw x 24% (T.220.84) = 129.6.

CHAPTER 6   TEST 8   DWELLINGS

	LINE
900 sq.ft. x 3va x 24 units	64800va
Small appliance 2 x 1500va x 24 units	72000
6kw heat 6kw x 24 units	144000
(omit A/C load)	
4 kw cooktop 4kw x 24 units	96000
3 kw oven 3kw x 24 units	72000
4.5kw water heater 4.5kw x 24 units	108000
1.2kw dishwasher 1.2kw x 24 units	28800
	585,600va

Table 220.84 Demand:
24 units = 35%   585,600va x 35% =   204,960va
Laundry on premises 1500 x 24 units =   36,000
                                            240,960va total demand

LINE = 240,960va   = 669 amps.
        208v x 1.732

CHAPTER 6   TEST 9   DWELLINGS

1. (b)   110 amps

2200 sq.ft. x 3va =	6600 va	**Optional Method 220.82**
Small appliance =	3000va	
Laundry =	1500va	
6 kw range =	6000	
2 - 4kw ovens =	8000	
4.5 kw WH =	4500	
5 kw dryer =	5000	
1.2 kw DW =	1200	

35,800va "general loads"

220.82(B) = First 10,00va = 10,000 + 10,320va (25,800va x 40%) + heat
15kw x 40% (220.82C6) = 6000 = 26,320va/240v = 109.6 amps

2. (b)   106 amps

1850 sq.ft. x 3va	= 5550va	**Standard Method of Calculation**
small appliance	= 3000	
laundry	= 1500	
	10,050va	

T. 220.42 demand:
1st 3000va @ 100%	= 3000va
next 7050va @ 35%	= 2468va
10kw range	= 8000
4.5kw dryer	= **5000**
fan 9.8a x 120v	= 1176
largest motor @25%	= **294**
AC 23a x 240v	= 5520
	25,458va/240v = 106 amps

3. (a)   859 amps

1640 sq.ft. x 3va x 12 units	= 59,040va	**Optional Method 220.84**
sm. appl. 3000va x 12 units	= 36,000	
laundry 1500va x 12 units	= 18,000	
12 range x 12 units	= 144,000	
water heater 5kw x 12 units	= 60,000	
dryer 5 kw x 12 units	= 60,000	
heat 10.5kw x 12 units	= 126,000	
	503,040va total	

503,040va x 41% demand Table 220.84 = 206,246va/240v = 859 amps

CHAPTER 6   TEST 9   DWELLINGS

4. **(c)   150 - 200kw**

1000 sq.ft. x 3va x 20 units	= 60,000va	**Optional Method 220.84**
Sm. appl. 3000va x 20 units	= 60,000	
20 - 8kw ranges	= 160,000	
A/C 17a x 240v x 20 units	= 81,600	
	361,600va	

361,600va x 38% (T.220.84) = 137, 408va + 30,000 laundry = 167,408va

5. **(c)   123 amps**

2000 sq.ft. x 3va	= 6000va
Sm. appliance	= 3000
Laundry	= 1500
12.5kw range	= 12500
4.5kw water heater	= 4500
1.2kw dishwasher	= 1200
5 kw clothes dryer	= 5000
	33,700va

220.82(B) 1st 10kva @ 100% = 10,000va
remaining 23,700va @ 40% = 9,480va
A/C @ 100%   = 10,000va
                          29,480va/240v = 122.8a

6. **(b)   92.67 amps**

1800 sq.ft. x 3va	= 5400va
Sm. appliance	= 3000
Laundry	= 1500
10kw range	= 10000
4.5kw water heater	= 4500
1.2kw dishwasher	= 1200
5 kw clothes dryer	= 5000
	30,600va

220.82(B) 1st 10kva @ 100% = 10,000va
remaining 20,600va @ 40% = 8,240va
10kw Heat @ 40%   = 4,000va
                          22,240va/240v = 92.67 amps

CHAPTER 7   TEST 1   COMMERCIAL

1. **16 kva** T.220.42   First 20,000va @ 50% =   10,000va
    Next 15,000va @ 40% =   6,000va
    16,000va/1000 = 16 kva.

2. **2500va**   T.220.12   4000 sq.ft. x .5va x 125% = 2500va

3. **10 - 25 kva** Section 220.44 states "you can use Table 220.42" 300 x 180va = 54000va
    T.220.42 First 20,000va @ 50% =   10,000va
    Next 34,000va @ 40% =   13,600va
    23,600va/1000 = 23.6 kva.

4. **8 - 8.4 kva**   1500 sq.ft. x 3.5va x 125% = 6563va
    1500 sq.ft. x 1va =   1500
    8063va/1000 = 8.063 kva.

5. **#6** 250.66(A)

6. **210 kva**   300,000va/12,500 sq.ft. = 24va
    T.220.86:   First 3va @ 100% = 3va
    Next 17va @ 75% = 12.75va
    Next 4va @ 25% = 1
    16.75va x 12,500 sq.ft. = 209,375va = 210 kva.
    1000

CHAPTER 7   TEST 2   COMMERCIAL

	LINE
3750 sq.ft. x 3va x 125%	14063va
50' show window x 200va x 125%	12500
20 receptacles x 180va	3600
1500va parking lot lights x 125%	1875
10kw heat	10000
Sign 1200va x 125%	1500
	43,538va

LINE: 43,538va/240v = **181 amp demand**.

CHAPTER 7   TEST 3   COMMERCIAL

1. **51 - 80**   40,000 sq.ft. x 4.5va (noncontinuous) = $\dfrac{180,000va}{2400va}$ = 75 circuits

    20 amp CB x 120v   = 2400va

2. **190 amps**   Neutral is **not** continuous: 45,600va/240v = 190 amps.

3. **#4**   Table 310.16 requires a #3/0 service conductor for 200a. Table 250.66 = #4

4. **385 kva**   680,000va/20,000 sq.ft. = 34va

    Table 220.86:   First 3va @ 100% =   3va

                      Next 17va @ 75% =   12.75va

                      Next 14va @ 25% =   3.5va

                           19.25va x 20,000 sq.ft. = 385,000va/1000 = 385

5. **#6**   Table 250.122

6. **12 amps**   220.14(H1)   40 feet/5' = 8 x 180va = 1440va/120v = 12 amps.

CHAPTER 7   TEST 4   COMMERCIAL

	LINE
15,000 sq.ft. x 2va x 125%	37500va
2 - 35kw ranges 70kw x 70% (T.220.56)	49000
1 - 15kw heater 15kw x 70% (T.220.56)	10500
1 - 20kw heater 20kw x 70% (T.220.56)	14000
1 - 6kw dishwasher 6kw x 70% (T.220.56)	4200
10 heavy-duty lamps 10 x 600va	6000
65 receptacles 65 x 180va = 11,700va	
Table 220.44: First 10 kva @ 100%	10000
Next 1700va @ 50%	850
20 kva parking lot lights 20,000va x 125%	25000
4 - 5 hp A/C units 16.7a x 208v x 1.732 = 6016va x 4	24064
20 kw electric heat (omit)	
Largest motor 6016va x 25%	1504
	182, 618va

LINE: $\dfrac{182,618va}{208v \times 1.732}$ = **507 amp demand**.

CHAPTER 7   TEST 5   COMMERCIAL

1. **#3/0**   Table 310.16

2. **28 kva**   Section 220.44 states "you can use Table 220.42"
   Table 220.42:   First 50,000va @ 40% =   20,000va
                   Next 40,000va @ 20% =   8,000va
                   28,000va/1000 = 28 kva.

3. **six #250 kcmil THW cu**   #250 kcmil THW = 255 ampacity x 2 = 510 ampacity parallel,
   T.310.15(B2a) = 510a x 80% = 408 ampacity in parallel.

4. **26,719 va**

20,000 sq.ft. x 2va	40000va
Table 220.42 demand:	
First 20000va @ 50%	10000va
Next 20000va @ 40%	8000
750 sq.ft. x 3.5va x 125%	3281
750 sq.ft. x 1va	750
5000 sq.ft. x .5va x 125%	3125
2500 sq.ft. x .5va x 125%	1563
	26,719va

5. **15.8 kva**   120 receptacles x 180va = 21,600va   Table 220.44:
   First 10 kva @ 100% =   10 kva
   Next 11.6 kva @ 50% =   5.8 kva
   15.8 kva

6. **#3/0 AL**   Table 250.66

CHAPTER 7   TEST 6   COMMERCIAL

	LINE
10,000 sq.ft. x 3.5va x 125%	43750va
12,000va x 125%	15000
200 receptacles x 180va = 36,000va	
100 feet multioutlet 100'/5' = 20 x 180va = 3600	
Table 220.44: First 10 kva @ 100%	10000
Next 29.6 kva @ 50%	14800
Sign 1200va x 125%	1500
	85,050va

LINE: $\dfrac{85,050va}{208v \times 1.732}$ = **236 amp demand**.

CHAPTER 7   TEST 7   COMMERCIAL

1. **19**   10,000 sq.ft. x 4.5va (noncontinuous) = $\dfrac{45,000va}{2400va}$ = 18.75 or 19 circuits.

   20 amps x 120v

2. **250 kcmil**   #250 kcmil = 255 ampacity x 2 = 510a x 80% (T.310.15B2a) = 408 ampacity

3. **25 kva**   150,000 sq.ft. x .25va (noncontinuous)   =   37500va

   Table 220.42 demand: First 12,500va @ 100% =   12500va

   Next 25,000va @ 50% =   12500va

   25,000/1000 = 25 kva.

4. **456,250 va**   750,000va/25,000 sq.ft. = 30 va

   Table 220.86: First 3va @ 100% =   3va

   Next 17va @ 75% =   12.75va

   Next 10va @ 25% =   2.5va

   18.25va x 25,000 sq.ft. = 456,250va.

5. **161,250 va**   30,000 sq.ft. x 3.5va x 125% =   131,250va

   30,000 sq.ft. x 1va   =   30,000va

   161,250va

6. **11,750 va**   75 x 180va = 13,500va   Table 220.44 is the minimum in this case:

   First 10 kva @ 100% =   10,000va

   Next 3.5 kva @ 50% =   1,750 va

   11,750va

CHAPTER 7   TEST 8   COMMERCIAL

	LINE
Motel 100 units x 12' x 20' x 2va	48000va
Table 220.42 Demand:	
First 20,000va @ 50%	10000va
Next 28,000va @ 40%	11200
Hallways 4000 sq.ft. x .5va x 125%	2500
Beauty shop 625 sq.ft. x 3va x 125%	2344
Office 1500 sq.ft. x 3.5va x 125%	6563
Office 1500 sq.ft. x 1va (unknown receptacles)	1500
Garage 12,000 sq.ft. x .5va x 125%	7500
Bank 1200 sq.ft. x 3.5va x 125%	5250
Bank 1200 sq.ft. x 1va (unknown receptacles)	1200
	48,057va

The demand is 48,057 va.

CHAPTER 7 TEST 9 COMMERCIAL

1. (d) 98 amps   2300 sq.ft. x 3v (T. 220.12) x 125% (230.42A1)   = 8625va
70 recpts. 180va (220.14L) = 12,600va
Receptacle Demand (T. 220.44):
First 10 kva @ 100%   = 10,000va
Remaining 2,600va @ 50%   = 1300va
15' show window @ 200va (220.14G2)   = 3000va
3ø AC 24a x 208v x 1.732   = 8646va
Largest motor 8646va x 25%   = 2162va
Water heater   = 1500
                                                                                    35,233va total

35,233va/208vx1.732 = 97.7 amps

2. (c) 171.12 amps   3755 sq.ft. x 3.5va x 125% (continous load) = 16,428va
29 receptacles @ 180va (220.14G2)   = 5,220va
40kw heat   = 40,000
                                                          61,648va total

61,648va/208v x 1.732 = 171.12 amps

3. (b) 245 amps   25 sites x 3600va (551.73)   = 90,000va
Table 551.73 demand @ 42% = 90,000 x 42% = 37,800va
37,800va/240v = 157.5a or 158a + 87a service load = 245 amps

4. (c)   #1/0 THW   Table 220.56 Dishwasher   = 2500
Booster water heater   = 2000
Water heater   = 6000
2-12kw ranges   = 24000
2 - 5kw deep fryers   = 10000
2 - 2kw toasters   = 4000
Warming oven   = 2000
                                    50,500va x 65% = 32,825va
Table 220.44 Receptacles   = 12000
1st 10kva @ 100%   = 10,000
Next 2000va @ 50% = 1,000
Lighting 3200 x 125% = 4,000
                            15,000 + 32,825 = 47,825
47,825va/208v x 1.732 = 132.7 amps Table 310.16 = #1/0 THW

5. (b) 572 amps   26 sites x 22,000va (550.31) = 572,000va x 24% (T.550.31) = 137,280va
137,280va/240v = 572 amps

CHAPTER 8   JOURNEYMAN EXAM 1   30 CALCULATIONS

1. **(a) 30 amps**   Table 310.16 Footnote *

2. **(b) 38.5 cubic inch**   T. 314.16(B)   8 wires x 2 cu.in. and 10 wires x 2.25 cu.in. = 38.5

3. **(b) .1831 sq.in.**   Table 4 - 1" EMT = .346   Table 5 #12 XHHW = .0181 x 9 = .1629
   $$.346 - .1629 = .1831$$

4. **(d) 2 1/8"**   Table 314.16(B)   5 x 2.25 cu.in. = 11.25 and 4 x 2 cu.in. = 8
   $$11.25 + 8 = 19.25 \text{ cu.in.   Table 314.16(A)} = 2\ 1/8"$$

5. **(a) 20 amp**   13.2a (T.430.248) x 175% (T.430.52) = 23.1 a   430.52 ex.1 permits going up
   to the **next higher** standard size. The next higher per 240.6 is a 25 amp not 30.

6. **(b)**   Table 4 - 1" EMT = .346 area

7. **(a) 11.52 kw**   32 kw x 36% (Col. B) = 11.52

8. **(d) 16 amps**   #14 THW = 20a x 80% (T.310.15B2a) = 16

9. **(a) zero**   310.4 #1/0 and larger

10. **(a) 11 kw**   Col.C = 11 kw for two appliances which is the smallest value

11. **(a) 6000va**   220.12 living area   2000 sq.ft. x 3va (T.220.12) = 6000

12. **(c) 20.5 amps**   #12 TW = 25a x .82 (correction factor) = 20.5

13. **(b) 17.25 amps**   13.8a (T.430.248) x 125% (430.22) = 17.25a

14. **(b) 6.75 cu.in.**   314.16(B1,5)   3 x 2.25 cu.in. (T.314.16B) = 6.75

15. **(c) 15.48 kw**   36 kw x 43% (Col.B) = 15.48

16. **(c) #8**   Table 250.122

17. **(d) None of these**   40 kw x 36% (Col.B) = 14.4

18. **(c) 4500 va**   220.52(A,B)   3000 va + 1500 va = 4500

19. **(d) 6**   Example D1A and 210.11(C)   1500 sq.ft x 3va = 4500/120v = 37.5a = 2 - 20 amp circuits
    small appliance = 2   laundry = 1   bathroom = 1 for a total of six 20 amp circuits

20. **(c) 17.16a**   13.2a (T.430.248) x 130% (430.32(C) maximum) = 17.16

21. **(b) #4**   Table 250.66

22. **(c) 22.5 amps**   10a (T.430.248) x 125% (430.24) = 12.5a + 10a = 22.5

23. **(c) 27 amps**   #12 TW = 25a x 1.08 (correction factor) = 27

24. **(c) 60 amps**   34a (T.430.248) x 175% (T.430.52) = 59.5 = 60 (430.52 ex.1) (240.6)

25. **(c) 24,100**   1500 sq.ft. x 3va =   4500
                      small appl.   =   3000
                      laundry   =   1500
                                              9000
Table 220.42   1st 3000 @ 100% =   3000
               next 6000 @ 35% =   2100
               12 kw range   =   8000
               dryer (minimum) =   5000
               water heater   =   6000
(omit washer- it's in laundry)   24,100

26. **(d) 16 amps**   #14 THW = 20a x 80% (T.310.15B2a) = 16

27. **(d) meets the Code**   20a x 120v = 2400va   1600 + 600 = 2200   2400 - 2200 = 200 left

28. **(a) 10 amps**   1100 + 100 = 1200w/120v = 10

29. **(c) 22.1 amps**   17a (T.430.248) x 130% (430.32(C) maximum) = 22.1

30. **(b) .82**   Table 310.16 correction factors

CHAPTER 8   JOURNEYMAN EXAM 2   30 CALCULATIONS

1. **(a) 6 kw**   Note 4 Branch Circuit - Nameplate rating for **one**

2. **(d) 33.6 amps**   24a (T.430.248) x 140% (430.32(C) maximum) = 33.6

3. **(d) 200 watts**   the unbalance   1200 - 1000 = 200

4. **(d) .3802 sq.in.**   Table 5 - #8 XHHW = .0437   x 6 = .2622
   #6 XHHW = .0590   x 2 = .118
   .3802

5. **(c) 4 amps**   the unbalance   7 - 3 = 4

6. **(c) 79 amps**   the maximum on the neutral would be if line one is off   9500/120v = 79

7. **(d) 18 cu.in.**   314.16(B)   2-white, 2-black, 1-bare, 1-clamps, 2-duplex = 8 wires
   Table 314.16(B)   8 wires x 2.25 cubic inch = 18

8. **(c) .1921 sq.in.**   Table 4 - 1" rigid metal = .355   Table 5 - #12 XHHW = .0181 x 9 = .1629
   .355 - .1629 = .1921

9. **(c) 35 amps**   28a (T.430.250) x 125% (430.22) = 35

10. **(d) 13**   Table 4 - 1" IMC = .959 (100% csa) x 60% (nipple fill) = .575
    Table 5 - #8 TW = .0437   .575/.0437 = 13

11. **(d) 15.65 amps**   1800/115v = 15.65

12. **(a) 21 amps**   #12 THHN = 30a x 70% (T.310.15B2a) = 21

13. **(d) 7**   Example D1A and 210.11(C)   1800 sq.ft. x 3va = 5400/120v = 45 amp = 3 - 20a circuits
    small appliance = 2   laundry = 1   bathroom = 1 for a total of seven

14. **(d) .0209**   Table 5

15. **(c) .6141**   #14 TW = .0139 x4   =   .0556
    #12 THW = .0181 x 3   =   .0543
    #14 RHW (without) .0209 x 12   =   .2508
    #12 TW = .0181 x 14   =   .2534
    .6141

16. **(b) 25 amps**   no derating required in circuit

17. **(c) 33.75 kw**   10 x 4.5 kw = 45 kw x 75% (220.53) = 33.75

18. **(c) 150%**   Table 430.52

19. **(a) 30 amps**   Table 310.16 footnotes * overcurrent protection

20. **(b) 80 amps**   42a (T.430.250) x 175% (T.430.52) = 73.5a (430.52 ex.1) (240.6) = 80

21. **(b) 40 amps**   24a (T.430.248) x 175% (T.430.52) = 42a (430.52 ex.1) (240.6) = 40

22. **(c) 19**   Table 4 - 2" PVC 80 = 1.150   Table 5 - #6 XHHW = .0590   1.150/.0590 = 19

23. **(a) 2880 va**   24a (T.430.248) x 120v (design voltage) = 2880

24. **(b) full load**   220.82(C1)

25. **(c) 11 kva**

1800 sq.ft. x 3va	=	5400va
small appliance	=	3000
laundry	=	1500
		9900
T.220.42 Demand 1st 3000 @ 100%	=	3000
next 6900 @ 35%	=	2415
12kw range = 8000 x 70% neutral	=	5600
		11,015

26. **(c) 6.5 kw**   10 kw x 65% (Col.B) = 6.5 **service demand**

27. **(b) 16.8 kw**   15 x 3.5 kw = 52.5 kw x 32% (Col.B) = 16.8

28. **(d) none of these**   12a (T.430.248) x 125% (430.24) = 15a + 12a = 27

29. **(b) 15.225 amps** #14 RHH = 25a x 70% (T.310.15B2a) = 17.5a x .87 (correction factor) = 15.225

30. **(b) 15.7 kw**   6 x 5 kw (minimum) = 30 kw x 75% (T.220.54) = 21 kw x 70% (neutral) = 15.7

CHAPTER 8   JOURNEYMAN EXAM 3   30 CALCULATIONS

---

1. **(b) 0.053**   Table 8

2. **(c) 35**   3 hp 208v = 18.7a F.L.C. x 175% (T.430.52) = 32.7a   240.6 = 35a

3. **(a) 20**   Table 310.16 *Maximum is 20 amps.

4. **(a) .0353**   Table 5

5. **(a) 24.64**   #10 RHW = 35 ampacity x 80% (T.310.15B2a) x .88 (corr. factor) = 24.64a.

6. **(d) 4500va**   1800 sq.ft. - 300 sq.ft. = 1500 sq.ft. living area x 3va = 4500va.

7. **(b) 40**   14kw - 12kw = 2kw x 5% = 10%   Col. C = 8kw x 1.10 = 8.8 kw or 8800w
   8800w/220v = 40 amps.

8. **(d) 1.221**   Table 4   2.036 x 60% = 1.221

9. **(c) 14.25 cu.in.**   Table 314.16(B)   #12 = 2.25 cu.in. x 3 = 6.75 cu.in.
                                              #10 = 2.5 cu.in. x 3 = 7.5 cu.in.
                                              $\overline{\qquad\qquad\quad 14.25\ \text{cu.in.}}$

10. **(c) 200 amps**   Table 430.250   25 hp = 74.8a x 125% =   93.5a
                                         25 hp =   74.8a
                                         10 hp = $\underline{30.8a}$
                                                                  199.1a

11. **(a) 2"**   Table 5   #3 THWN   .0973 x 6 =   .5838
                            #8 THW   .0437 x 3 =   .1311
                            #10 THW   .0243 x 2 = $\underline{.0486}$
                                                       .7635

12. **(a) 65a**   T.310.15(B2a) does **NOT** apply to a nipple.

13. **(b) 7.15**   Table 220.55   5kw + 8kw = 13kw x 55% (Col.B feeder) = 7.15.

14. **(d) 15.7 kw**   6 x 5kw = 30kw x 75% (T.220.54) = 22.5kw x 70% (220.61B1) = 15.7.

15. **(d) 5**   2500 sq.ft. x 3va = $\dfrac{7500\text{va}}{1800\text{va}}$ = 4.16 or 5 circuits
                15 a x 120v   = 1800va

16. **(a) 12**   Table 4   1" nipple 60% fill = $\dfrac{.532}{.0437}$ = 12.1 or 12 conductors
    Table 5 #8 THW =

17. **(b) 18.38a**   T.310.16   #10 THW = 35a x .75 (cor. factor) x 70% (T.310.15B2a) = 18.38a

18. **(b) #8**   Table 250.122

19. **(d) none of these**   180va does **NOT** apply to a residence (dwelling).

20. **(b) 16.72 amps**   Table 430.250   15.2a x 1.10 = 16.72a.

21. **(b) 16.8**   15 x 3.5kw = 52.5kw x 32% (Col.B) = 16.8kw

22. **(a) 0.0209**   Table 5

23. **(c) 58.75**   Col.C = 25kw + 33.75kw (.75kw x 45) = 58.75kw.

24. **(d) 45 amps**   17a F.L.C. x 250% (T.430.52) = 42.5a   240.6 = 45a.

25. **(b) .0209**   Table 5

26. **(d) 31%**   Table 4   Two conductors.

27. **(c) 30**   24a F.L.C. x 125% (430.32 S.F.) = 30.

28. **(c) 15**   Table 4   1 1/2" IMC = .889/.0590   Table 5   #6 XHHW = 15

29. **(d) 100%**   220.82(C1).

30. **(c) 6.4 kw**   Column B 8kw x 80% = 6.4.

CHAPTER 8   JOURNEYMAN EXAM 4   30 CALCULATIONS

1. **(c) 35a**   Table 310.16   #8 THW = 50a x 70% (T.310.15B2a) = 35a.

2. **(d) 0.134**   Table 5A.

3. **(b) 2000a**   Section 366.23(A):   .5" x 4" = 2 sq.in. x 1000a (366.23A) = 2000a.

4. **(c) 55kw**   Col.C = 15kw + 40kw = 55kw.

5. **(d) 140%**   430.32(C) maximum 140% for 1.15 S.F.

6. **(d) 133,100**   Table 8 cma

7. **(b) 1 1/4"**
#14 RHH with cover .0293 x 5 =	.1465
#10 THW .0243 x 6 =	.1458
#12 RHW without cover .0260 x 5 =	.13
#6 XHHW .0590 x 2 =	.118
#8 bare Table 8 (310.3 stranded) =	.017
	.5573 sq.in. Table 4 = 1 1/4"

8. **(a) 43 kw**   T.220.55 Column C = 15kw + 28kw = 43 kw.

9. **(d) 17,000va**   T.430.250   46.2a F.L.C. x 208v x 1.732 = 16,644va.

10. **(c) 77.9 amps**   T.310.16   #4 @ 90°C = 95a x .82 (correction factor) = 77.9a

11. **(b) #10**   Section 210.19(A3) ex. 2

12. **(b) #8**   T.430.250 F.L.C. 28a x 125% (430.22) = 35 required ampacity   T.310.16 = #8 TW.

13. **(a) 38.3a**   14kw - 12kw = 2kw x 5% = 10%   Column C = 8 kw x 1.10 = 8.8kw or 8800w
        8800w/230v = 38.3 amperes.

14. **(c) 16**   Table 4   1 1/2" = .794 @ 40% fill   Table 5 #12 THW = .0181" x 5 = .0905"
        .794 - .0905 = .7035" left to fill   Table 5 #10 RHW with cover = .0437"
        .7035"/.0437" = 16.

15. **(c) 18**   Section 374.5 40% fill   Article 374.4 special permission
        10 sq.in. x 40% = 4 sq.in. can be filled
        Table 5   #2/0 THHN = .2223"   4"/.2223" = 17.99 or 18.

16. **(a) 6.5**   10kw x 65% (Col.B) = 6.5kw on feeder.

17. **(c) 4500va**   1500 sq.ft. x 3va = 4500va.

18. **(b) 43.48a**   4.5kw = 5kw minimum x 2 = 10kw   10,000w/230v = 43.47 or 43.48a.

19. **(b) .0260**   Table 5

20. **(d) 8.8 kw**   14kw - 12kw = 2kw x 5% = 10%   Column C = 8kw x 1.10 = 8.8kw.

21. **(b) 36a**   T.430.248 F.L.C. 16a x 125% (430.24) = 20a + 16a = 36a.

22. **(a) 20a**   T.430.248 F.L.C. 17a x 115% (430.110) = 19.55 or 20a.

23. **(a) 19**   Table 4 - 1" = .275   Table 5 - #14 THW = .0139   .275/.0139 = 19

24. **(a) 34.8a**   T.220.55 Column C = 8kw   8000w/230v = 34.78a.

25. **(d) #6**   Table 250.122.

26. **(c) 4**   T.314.16(A)   two types of fittings   6 - 2 = 4 conductors.

27. **(c) 3**   Table 4 3/8" flex. metal = .046/.0133 (#12 THWN) = 3

28. **(a) 20 amps**   Table 210.24

29. **(d) 5400va**   Section 220.12 outside dimensions 1800 sq.ft. x 3va = 5400va.

30. **(c) 16 amps**   Table 210.21(B2)

| CHAPTER 8 | JOURNEYMAN EXAM 5 | 30 CALCULATIONS |

---

1. **(c) 32 amps**   32amp continuous load x 125% = 40a   Branch Circuit   210.20(A)

2. **(c) 130 amp**

1500 sq.ft. x 3va	= 4500va	**Standard Method of Calculation**
small appliance	= 3000	
laundry	= 1500	
	9000va	

T. 220.42 demand:
1st 3000va @ 100%	= 3000va
next 6000va @ 35%	= 2100va
12kw range	= 8000
5.5kw dryer	= 5500
water heater	= 2500
dishwasher	= 1200
AC 6a x 240v	= 1440 omitt
9kw heat	= 9000
	31,300va/240v = 130 amps

3. **(d) 720 va**   220.14(I)   180va x 4 straps = 720va

4. **(b) A = 22"; B = 19 3/4"**
Solution: Side A: Largest raceway = 3". 6 x 3" =   18"
                    Sum of others = 2" + 2"   =   4'
                                        Total   22"
              Side B: Largest raceway = 3". 6 x 3" =   18"
                          Sum of others = 1" + 3/4"   =   1 3/4"
                                              Total   19 3/4"
•Note: Raceways entering side B determine dimension A, and raceways entering side A determine dimension B.

5. **(c) #250 kcmil**
SOLUTION: 250.102(C)   T. 310.16 Equivalent ampacity: #750 THW AL = 385 amps
#600 THW CU = 420 amps. #600 kcmil x 3 phase conductors (neutral not counted) = 1800 kcmil
x 12.5% = 225 kcmil required. Table 8 = #250 kcmil.

6. **(b) 37 amps**   #6 XHHW = 65a x 70% (9 cond.) = 45.5 x .82 (110°F) = 37.31a

7. **(c) 30 conductors**   T.314.16(B) #14 = 2 cubic inch   60 cu.in./2 cu.in. = 30 conductors

8. **(b) 50 amps** 430.62(A) Largest O.C.D. 40a + F.L.C. of other motor 10a = 50A feeder O.C.D.

9. **(d) 90 amp**   T.430.250 F.L.C. = 40a x 225% (430.52(C1) ex.2b maximum) = 90a

10. **(c) the light is good but the switch does not make contact**

11. **(c) 16.8 amperes**   20a x .84 T.630.11(A) = 16.8

12. **(c) 3"**
SOLUTION: Table 5:   #500 THHN = .7073 x 2 =   1.4146 sq.in.
                        # 4/0 THHN = .3237 x 2 =   .6474
                        # 2/0 THHN = .2223   =   .2223
                                                  2.2843 sq.in. area required
          Table 4:   3" conduit required

13. **(b) two (2) single pole circuit breakers, tied together**   210.4(B)

14. **(b) Figure B**   200.7(C2)

15. **(c) 19 fixture wires**   Chapter 9 Note 1 Annex C1

16. **(b) 3/4"**   SOLUTION: Table 5   #10 THW =   .0243 x 2 =   .0486 sq.in.
                                         #8 THHN =   .0366 x 3 =   .1098
                                                        Total .1584 sq.in. required
                            Table 4:   3/4" = .216 sq.in.

17. **(d) The 20 amp receptacles are too large for the circuit rating of 15 amps**
     210.21(B3) T.210.21(B3)

18. **(b) It should be buried 6" deeper**   250.83(C2,3)

19. **(c) the full load running current at each of the three supply line terminals**   430.6(A)

20. **(d) 272 amps**   50,000va x 125% = 62,500va/230v= 271.7a

21. **(a) the light is open (bulb burned out)**

22. **(d) D**

23. **(c) #1/0**
SOLUTION: 240.21(B2)(1)   T. 310.16   240.4(B3)
   #500 kcmil THW cu = 380 ampacity next higher size overcurrent = 400 amps
   400a/3 = 133 amps is one-third of overcurrent device. 133a requires a #1/0 THW cu.

24. **(b) 38.5 amps**   T.310.16   #8 THHN = 55a x 70% (9 cond.) = 38.5a

25. **(b) 4" x 1 1/2"**
SOLUTION: 314.16(B1) each spliced conductor counts as one. T.314.16(A) Six #12 = 4" x 1 1/2"

26. **(c) 56 amps**   T.430.250   F.L.C. = 40a x 140% 430.32(C) MAXIMUM = 56a

27. **(a) #8**
SOLUTION: T.430.250 F.L.C. = 28a x 400% = 112a use 110 amp standard size.
            T.250.122 110a (200a) = #6 grounding conductor
    Wire size: 28a x 125% 430.22(A) = 35a   T.310.16 = #8 TW copper
            250.122(A) equipment grounding conductor is NOT required to be larger than the
            circuit conductors supplying the equipment = #8 grounding conductor.

28. **(d) THWN**
SOLUTION: Table 5   #3 TW or THW = .1134 x 12 =   1.3608 sq.in.
                          #3 RHW =   .1521 x 12 =   1.8252
                          #3 THWN =   .0973 x 12 =   1.1676
            Table 4   2" schedule 40 PVC = 1.316 sq.in. area
            (or) Annex C10 you can put 13 #3 THWN conductors in a 2" PVC schedule 40

29. **(b) 3"**
SOLUTION: Table 5   #350 THW = .5958 x 2 =   1.1916 sq.in.
                          #500 THW = .7901 x 2 =   1.5802
                                                       ‾‾‾‾‾‾‾‾‾‾
                                                       2.7718 sq.in. required
            Table 4   IMC = 3" @ 3.169 sq.in.

30. **(b) Does NOT meet the Code**
Solution: This run is a violation of the 360° total. 180° + 90° + 60° + 60° = 390° total.

CHAPTER 8   MASTER   EXAM 1   30 CALCULATIONS

1. **(c) 26.45 kw**   4 - 12kw = 48kw
            8 - 16.5kw = 132kw
         12   180kw   180kw/12 = 15kw average
15kw - 12kw = 3kw x 5% = 15% Column C increase, single-phase ranges on a three-phase system=
A Phase   B Phase   C Phase
4   4   4   4 x 2 = 8 appliances Col.C = 23kw x 1.15 = 26.45kw.

2. **(a) 1 hp** hp = $\dfrac{E \times I \times \text{Efficiency}}{746 \text{ watt}}$ $\dfrac{230v \times 8a \times 40.5\%}{746w}$ = .998 or 1 hp.

3. **(a) 20.8 kva** Table 220.42 Demand: First 50,000va @ 40% = 20,000va
                        Next 4,000va @ 20% =   800va
                                 20,800va/1000 = 20.8 kva.

4. **(a) 66.88** Efficiency = $\dfrac{\text{output}}{\text{input}}$ $\dfrac{15 \text{ hp} \times 746}{230v \times 42a \times 1.732} =$ $\dfrac{11,190}{16,731.12}$ = 66.88%

5. **(c) 9** Table 4 1 1/2" = .814 40% fill, half of .814 = .407/.0437 (#8 XHHW) = 9.3 or 9.
6. **(c) 5.16** 10 x 1200va = 12,000va x 43% (T.220.84) = 5160va/1000 = 5.16 kva.
7. **(a) 70** T.430.250 F.L.C. = 40a x 175% (T.430.52) = 70.

8. **(c) 41.7 amps** 16kw - 12kw = 4 kw x 5% = 20% Column C = 8kw x 1.20 = 9.6kw or 9600w
            9600w/230v = 41.7 amperes.

9. **(b) 250** 200 x 5kw (minimum 5kw) = 1000kw x 25% (T.220.54) = 250kw.

10. **(a) 150** First step find branch circuit CB size: Largest motor 59.4a x 250% = 148.5 or 150 amp
            B.C. breaker size. Feeder CB = 150a CB + 24a F.L.C. = 174 amp ca**nnot** go up = 150a.

11. **(d) 57.6 kw** 60 x 4kw = 240kw x 24% (T.220.84) = 57.6kw.

12. **(b) 79.5 kw** T.220.55 Column C = 25kw + 41.25kw (55 x .75kw) = 66.25kw
            16kw - 12kw = 4kw x 5% = 20% Column C = 66.25kw x 1.20 = 79.5 kw.

13. **(b) 14** Table 4 - 1 1/2" ENT = .774 Table 5 - #8 RHH (without) = .0556 .774/.0556 = 14

14. **(a) 21** T.430.250 3 hp = 10.6a x 125% (430.24) = 13.25a + 7.5a = 20.75 or 21 amps.

15. **(c) 25.3 kw** 14kw - 12kw = 2kw x 5% = 10% single-phase ranges on a three-phase system =
            A Phase   B Phase   C Phase
            4   3   3   4 x 2 = 8 appl. Col.C = 23kw x 1.10 = 25.3kw.

16. **(a) 28**   T.310.16   #10 RHW = 35a x 80% (T.310.15B2a) = 28 ampacity.
17. **(d) 6000 - 7000**   T.430.250 5 hp = 16.7a x 208v x 1.732 = 6016va.
18. **(a) 0.0209**   Table 5
19. **(b) #8**   T.430.250 28a x 125% (430.22) = 35 required ampacity. Table 310.16 = #8 TW.
20. **(c) 1 1/2"**   #3 THWN   .0973 x 6 = .5838
                     #8 THW   .0437 x 3 = .1311
                     #10 THW   .0243 x 2 = .0486
                                             .7635   Table 4   40% fill = 1 1/2" conduit.

21. **(d) 9.7875a** T.310.16 #14 RHH = 25a x 45% (T.310.15B2a) = 11.25a x .87 (corr.factor) = 9.7875
22. **(c) 170**   T.430.250 25 hp = 74.8a x 125% (430.24) = 93.5a + 74.8a = 168.3a required.
23. **(d) 27 kw**   6 x 4.5kw = 27kw **CONNECTED LOAD** not demand.
24. **(a) 5.005 kw**   8kw + 5kw = 13kw x 55% (Column B feeder) = 7.15kw x 70% (220.61) = 5.005.
25. **(c) 270 kw**   60 x 6kw = 360kw x 75% (220.53) = 270kw.
26. **(b) 418,750va**   600,000va/25,000 sq.ft = 24va
                     Table 220.86 Demand: First 3va x 100% =   3va
                                           Next 17va x 75% =   12.75va
                                           Next 4va x 25%   =   1va
                                                              16.75va x 25,000 sq.ft. =
                                                              418,750va

27. **(b) 3.269**   Table 4 Total 100%
28. **(c) 182 kw**   50 x 14kw = 700kw x 26% (T.220.84) = 182kw.
29. **(c) 7**   Table 4: 2" PVC 80 = 1.15" 40% fill
                     Table 5: #8 RHH with cover .0835 x 10 = .835"   1.15 - .835 = .315 left to fill
                     Table 5: #8 XHHW = .0437   .315/.0437 = 7.2 or 7

30. **(b) 38.5**   6 x 12kw = 72kw (change the 9kw to 12kw)
                     4 x 12kw = 48kw
                    10 x 15kw = 150kw
                    ‾‾20‾‾   270kw   270kw/20 = 13.5 or 14kw average

                    14kw - 12kw = 2kw x 5% = 10%   Column C = 35kw x 1.10 = 38.5kw.

CHAPTER 8   MASTER EXAM 2   30 CALCULATIONS

1. **(c) 9.45 kva**   Section 630.31   15 kva x .63 (40% duty cycle) = 9.45.
2. **(b) 24"**   Table 5   #500 kcmil THW   .7901 x 4 = 3.1604"

   #750 kcmil THW   1.1652 x 6 = 6.9912"

   #1000 kcmil THW   1.372 x 8 = 10.976"

   Table 392.10 Col.2   10.976 x 1.1 = 12.0736 + 3.1604 + 6.9912 = 22.2252

   Table 392.10 requires a tray 24" wide

3. **(b) 73.3**   T.430.248 F.L.C. 3 hp = 34a x 125% (430.24 & 430.17) =   42.5a

   T.430.250 F.L.C. 10 hp   =   30.8a

   73.3a

4. **(d) 47**   T.220.55 Column C = 15kw + 32kw (1kw x 32) = 47kw.
5. **(b) 1"**   Table 5   #14 TW   .0139 x 8 =   .1112

   #8 THWN   .0366 x 6 =   .2196

   .3308   Table 4 = 1" nipple @ .5328 fill.

6. **(b) 110a**   T.430.250 F.L.C. 59.4a x 175% (T.430.52) = 103.95a   240.6 = 110a.
7. **(b) 75**   T.310.16   #3 THWN = 100a x .75 (corr. factor) = 75a.

8. **(c) 46.325 kva**   150 rooms x 15' x 20' x 2va   90000va

   Table 220.42 Demand:

   First 20000va @ 50%   10000va

   Next 70000va @ 40%   28000

   3000 sq.ft. halls x .5va x 125%   1875

   Office 1200 sq.ft. x 3.5va x 125%   5250

   Office 1200 sq.ft. x 1va (recpts.)   1200

   46,325va

9. **(b) 25.3 kw**   T.220.55   14kw - 12kw = 2kw x 5% = 10%   Single-phase ranges on a three-phase system:

Phase A	Phase B	Phase C	
4	4	4	4 x 2 = 8 appliances

   Column C = 23kw x 1.10 = 25.3kw

10. **(d) 44a**   T.310.16   #8 XHHW (wet) = 75°C   50a x .88 (corr. factor) = 44a.
11. **(b) 75 - 90 kva**   40 x 950 sq.ft. x 2va (not a dwelling)   76000va

    Hallways 8 x 130 sq.ft. x .5va   520va

    76,520va **Connected Load**

12. **(c) 18.5 kva**   150 x 180va = 27,000va/1000 = 27 kva

    T.220.44 Demand: First 10kva @ 100% =   10 kva

    Next 17 kva @ 50% =   8.5 kva

    18.5 kva

13. **(b) 18**   220.14(H1)   60'/5 = 12 x 180va = 2160va/120v = 18a.

14. **(a) 525a**   30 x 15a = 450a   20 x 30a = 600a   450a + 600a = 1050a x 50% (555.12) = 525a.

15. **(b) 33750va**   30 x 1500va = 45,000va x 75% (220.53) = 33750va.

16. **(d) 25kw**   T.220.55 Note 5   Column C = 25kw.

17. **(a) 20.25 kw**   20.25kw is **not** less than the two largest loads 16kw + 3.5kw = 19.5kw.

18. **(d) 22**   Table 4   1" IMC = .959 x 60% = .575 can be filled
                   Table 5   #12 RHW without cover = .0260   .575/.0260 = 22.1 or 22

19. **(a) 20**   *#12 = 20a maximum **overcurrent protection**.

20. **(d) 70**   T.430.248 F.L.C. 5 hp = 56a x 125% (430.32A1) = 70.

21. **(b) 60a**   #6 XHHW (dry) = 75a x 80% (T.310.15B2a & 310.15B4c) = 60 ampacity.

22. **(b) 11,250w**   60 x 150w x 125% (215.2A or 230.42A1) = 11,250w.

23. **(d) 17,010va**   45 x 1400va = 63000va x 27% (T.220.84) = 17010va.

24. **(d) 90,000va**   20,000 sq.ft. x 4.5va = 90,000va

25. Motor "A" **30.8a**   Motor "B" **10.6a**

26. Motor "A" 30.8a x 115% = **35.42a**   Motor "B" 10.6a x 125% = **13.25a**

27. Motor "A" 30.8a x 125% = 38.5 required ampacity   T. 310.16 = **#8 TW**
    Motor "B" 10.6a x 125% = 13.25 required ampacity T.310.16 = **#14 TW**

28. Motor "A" 30.8a x 250% = 77a   use **80a CB**
    Motor "B" 10.6a x 150% (wound rotor) = 15.9a   use **20a CB**

29. Feeder size = 30.8a x 125% (430.24) = 38.5a + 10.6a = 49.1 required ampacity = **#6 TW**.

30. Feeder CB = 80a CB + 10.6a = 90.6a   cannot go up on a feeder, down to a **90a CB**.

CHAPTER 8   MASTER EXAM 3   30 CALCULATIONS

1. **(d) 2 - 750 kcmil THW**   T.310.16   750 kcmil THW = 475a x 2 = 950a.
2. **(c) 90 circuits**   40,000 x 3.5va = 140,000va/1920va (continuous lighting 80% of 2400) = 73
   Need 73 circuits for continuous lighting 20a x 120v = 2400va x 80% =1920va
   40,000 x 1va (unknown recpts.) = 40,000va/2400va = 17 circuits for receptacles
   Receptacles 20a x 120v = 2400va per circuit (not continuous) total 90 circuits
3. **(d) 31**   T.220.55   Column C = 31kw.
4. **(d) #6**   Required ampacity = 25a/.58 corr.factor = 43.1a   T.310.16 = #6 TW.
5. **(c) 96kva**   Section 550.31   25 x 16 kva = 400 kva x 24% (T.550.31) = 96 kva.
6. **(b) #2**   Commercial T.220.56   100%   21,850w/240v = 91 amps   T.310.16 = #2 TW.
7. **(d) #4 cu**   Section 250.102(C) use Table 250.66 = #4 copper.
8. **(a) 28.9**   24 x 5kw (220.54) = 120kw x 34.5% (T.220.54) = 41.4kw x 70% (220.61) = 28.9
9. **(d) 189a**   T.310.16   #4/0 THW al = 180a x 1.05 (corr.factor) = 189a.

10. **(b) 40.95 kw**
$$6 - \cancel{9}\overset{12}{}\text{kw} = 72\text{kw}$$
$$8 - 12\text{kw} = 96\text{kw}$$
$$\underline{10 - 15\text{kw} = 150\text{kw}}$$
$$\overline{24} \qquad \overline{318\text{kw}} \quad 318\text{kw}/24 = 13.25 \text{ or } 13\text{kw average}$$
Column C = 39kw x 1.05 = 40.95kw

11. **(c) 1"**

#10 THW	.0243 x 4 =	.0972
#12 RHW without outer cover	.0260 x 2 =	.052
#14 RHH with outer cover	.0293 x 2 =	.0586
#14 THHN	.0097 x 6 =	.0582
#12 bare stranded (Table 8)	.006 x 3 =	.018
		.284 Table 4 = 1"

12. **(a) 150**   Table 430.52

13. **(c) 17.55kw**   T.220.56: 27kw x 65% = 17.55kw.

14. **(b) 510 kva**   750,000va/30,000 sq.ft. = 25va
   Table 220.86 Demand:
   First 3va @ 100% =   3va
   Next 17va @ 75% =   12.75va
   Next 5va @ 25% =   1.25va
   17va x 30,000 sq.ft. = 510,000va/1000 = 510 kva.

15. **(c) 300 kcmil**   T.310.16   #300 = 285a x 2 = 570a x 80% (T.310.15B2a) = 456a parallel.

16. **(c) 14 kw**   T.220.55 Column C = 20kw x 70% (220.61) = 14kw.

17. **(b) 89.1 kw**   30 x 4kw = 120kw + 30 x 5kw = 150kw = total 270kw x 33% (T.220.84) = 89.1.

18. **(d) 33.88**   T.430.250 F.L.C. = 24.2a x 140% (430.32C) = 33.88a.

19. **(a) 25a**   T.310.16 #12 THW = 25a (T.310.15B2a ex.3) **No derating for a nipple**.

20. **(b) 910a**   220.61 Incandescent First 200a @ 100% = 200a
                                         Next 300a @ 70% = 210a
                   Fluorescent   500a @ 100% = 500a
                                                            910a

21. **(c) 1050a**   Section 366.23(A)   .250" x 6" = 1.5" x 700a = 1050a.

22. **(b) 38.2a**   T.220.55 Note 5 14kw - 12kw = 2kw x 5% = 10%
                    Column C = 8kw x 1.10 = 8.8kw or 8800w/230v = 38.2 amps.

23. **(a) 67**   Table 4   2" nipple 60% fill = $\frac{1.975"}{.0293"}$ = 67
                    Table 5 #14 RHH with cover =

24. **(b) 3** Table 314.16(A)

25. **(c) 20"**   314.28   6 x 3" = 18" + 2" = 20".

26. **(c) 8**

27. **(d) 2**

28. **(a) 4**

29. **(b) 3**

30. **(b) 5**

CHAPTER 8   MASTER EXAM 4   30 CALCULATIONS

1. **(c) 50a** T.430.248 F.L.C. 40a x 115% (430.110) = 46a.
2. **(c) #4** Required ampacity = $\dfrac{42a}{.70\ (T.310\text{-}15b2a)\ x\ .75\ (corr.\ factor)}$ = 80a   T.310.16 = #4 THW cu.

3. **(c) 45a** T.430.250 F.L.C. = 16.7a x 250% (T.430.52) = 41.75   240.6 = 45a.
4. **(d) 83**   Annex Table C1
5. **(c) 2.8%** 630.31 FPN 300 x 20 = 6000/216,000 = .0277777 x 100 = 2.77 or 2.8%.
6. **(b) .7938** Table 4   1 1/2" 100% = 1.986 x 60% (nipple) = 1.191"
   1.986" x 20% fill = .3972" filled.   1.191" - .3972" = .7938" left to fill.

7. **(c) #6**   Required ampacity = $\dfrac{34\ amp\ load}{.75\ correction\ factor}$ = 45.3a x 125% (430.22) = 56.6a

8. **(c) 80%** Do **not** count neutrals or equipment grounding conductors per 310.15B4a & 310.15B5.
Count the **two** sets of three-phase = 6 current-carrying conductors. T.310.15B2a = 80%.

9. **(b) 30a** T.430.247 F.L.C. 17a x 150% (T.430.52) = 25.5a   240.6 = 30 amps.
10. **(a) 81.125 kw**   T.220.55 Column C = 25kw + 48.75kw (.75kw x 65) = 73.75kw
    14kw - 12kw = 2kw x 5% = 10% Column C = 73.75kw x 1.10 = 81.125 kw.

11. **(c) 4** $\dfrac{2200\ sq.ft.\ x\ 3va = 6600va}{15a\ x\ 120v\ \ \ \ \ = 1800va}$ = 3.6 or 4.

12. **(a) 282a**
20 x 800 sq.ft. x 3va	=	48000va
Small appliance 40 x 1500va	=	60000va
Laundry 20 x 1500va	=	30000va
		138000va

Table 220.42 Demand:
First 3000va @ 100%	=	3000va
Next 117000va @ 35%	=	40950va
Remaining 18000va @ 25%	=	4500va
		48,450va
T.220.55 Column C = 35kw x 70%	=	24,500
		72,950va

72,950va/230v = 317 amps 220.61: First 200a @ 100% = 200a
Next 117a @ 70% = 82a
282 amp on neutral

13. **(a) 193.5 kva**
36,000 sq.ft. x 3.5va x 125% =	157,500va
36,000 sq.ft. x 1va (recepts) =	36,000va
	193,500va/1000 = 193.5 kva.

14. **(c) 44.85 kw**   Single-phase ranges on a three-phase system:
A Phase   B Phase   C Phase
12   11   11   12 x 2 = 24 appliances
15kw - 12kw = 3kw x 5% = 15% Column C = 39kw x 1.15 = 44.85kw.

15. **(b) .3496**   Table 5   #8 THW = .0437 x 8 = .3496"
16. **(c) 43.2 kw**   24 x 4kw = 96kw + 24 x 5kw = 120kw   216kw total x 20% (Column B) = 43.2
17. **(c) 17.5 kva**   T.220.44   First 10 kva @ 100% =   10 kva
                                                    Next 15 kva @ 50% =   7.5 kva
                                                                                          17.5 kva

18. **(a) 21.55 kva**   50 x 280 sq.ft. x 2va =   28,000va
Table 220.42 Demand:
First 20000va @ 50% =   10000
Next 8000va @ 40% =   3200
3200 sq.ft. x .5va x 125% =   2000
600 sq.ft. x 3.5va x 125% =   2625
600 sq.ft. x 1va (recpts) =   600
5000 sq.ft. x .5va x 125% =   3125
                                                        21,550va/1000 = 21.55 kva

19. **(c) 241.5 kw**   75 x 14kw = 1050kw x 23% (T.220.84) = 241.5kw.
20. **(a) 15a** T.430.248 F.L.C. 1 hp 8a x 150% (T.430.52) = 12a   240.6 = 15a.
21. **(c) 0.027**   Table 8
22. **(d) 36.96**   Table 610.14(A) notes   33a x 1.12 = 36.96a.
23. **(a) 66.25a**   T.430.250   53a x 125% (T.430.250 80% PF) = 66.25a.
24. **(d) 3819va**   T.430.250 10.6a x 208v x 1.732 = 3819va.
25. **(c) 116.2a**   T.430.250 F.L.C. 15 hp = 46.2a   T.430.248 F.L.C. 5 hp = 56a
                56a x 125% (430.24) = 70a + 46.2a = 116.2 amps.

26. **(b)**

27. **(a)**

28. **(c)**

29. **(d)**

30. **(d)**

CHAPTER 8   MASTER EXAM 5   30 CALCULATIONS

---

1. **(d) 110,500 va**
•SOLUTION: Table 220.12 230.42(A1,2)

Store	25,000 sq.ft. x 3va x 125% =	93,750va
Restaurant	5,500 sq.ft. x 2va x 125% =	13,750va
Auditorium	3,000 sq.ft. x 1va =	3,000va
		110,500va total

2. **(a) 27 kw**
SOLUTION: 1ø ranges on a 3ø system. 18 ranges/3 phases = 6 x 2 connections = 12 ranges.
Table 220.55 Col. C = 27kw.

3. **(d) 447 amps**   #500 kcmil THHN = 430a x 1.04 (70°F) = 447 amps.

4. **(a) #2/0**
SOLUTION: 250.102(C)   T. 310.16 Equivalent ampacity: #500 THW AL = 310 amps
#350 THW CU = 310 amps. #350 kcmil x 3 phase conductors (neutral not counted) = 1050 kcmil
x 12.5% = 131.25 kcmil required. Table 8 = #2/0 kcmil.

5. **(d) #4/0**
SOLUTION: 3/16" thick = 3/16 = .1875 x 4" sides x 2 = 1.5 sq.in. T.392.7(B) = 1600 amp O.C.D.
T.250.122 = #4/0 copper

6. **(b) 5 conductors**
SOLUTION: T.314.16(B) #12 = 2.25 cu.in x 6 = 13.5 cu.in.   Box 27 cu.in. - 13.5 left to fill.
#10 conductor = 2.5 cu.in.   13.5/2.5 = 5.4 or 5 conductors

7. **(c) 1 1/4"**
SOLUTION: T.430.250 3-phase F.L.C. = 52a/80% (5 cond.) = 65a x 125% 430.22(A) = 81.25a
          T.430.248 1-phase F.L.C. = 40a/80% (5 cond.) = 50a x 125% 430.22(A) = 62.5a
Wire size: 3-phase motor T.310.16 for 81.25a = #3 TW copper
          1-phase motor T.310.16 for 62.5a   = #4 TW copper
Conduit size: Table 5:   #3 TW = .1134 x 3 = .3402 sq.in.
                                #4 TW = .0973 x 2 = .1946 sq.in
                                        Total   .5346 sq.in.
          Table 4: = 1 1/4" IMC

8. **(b) 55.6 amps**
SOLUTION: T.430.250 F.L.C. = 124a x 125% 430.22(A) = 155 ampacity required.
460.8 155a/3 = 51.7 ampacity required for capacitor conductors, but 460.8 also states the conductors shall not be less than 135% of the rared current of the capacitor. 34,250va/480v x 1.732 = 41.2a x 135% = 55.6 required ampacity. Take the largest.

9. **(b) B**

10. **(c) 690 amperes**
SOLUTION: 550.31(1) 16,000va x 45 lots = 720,000va x 23% T.550.31 = 165,600va/240v = 690a

11. **(d) 3 1/2"**
SOLUTION: Table 5:

#300 kcmil	= .5281 sq.in.	
#400 kcmil	= .6619	
#500 kcmil .7901 x 2	= 1.5802	
	2.7702 sq.in. required	

Table 4: 3 1/2" required area of 3.475 sq.in.

12. **(b) reversing the terminal connections of any two supply wires**

13. **(c) 83%**
SOLUTION: EFF = OUTPUT/INPUT   6.5 hp x 746w = 4849w/220v = $\dfrac{22 \text{ amps output}}{26.6 \text{ amps input}}$ = .83 or 83% efficiency

14. **(d) 12**   514.9; 501.15 (A4); 501.15(B2)

15. **(a) 7 breakers**
SOLUTION: Table 220.12   210.20(A)   220.14(E)   220.14(I)

Auditorium 9,500 sq.ft. x 1va x 125%	= 11875va
Corridor 500 sq.ft. x .5va x 125%	= 312.5va
Lampholders 20 x 600va x 125%	= 15000va
Receptacles 5 x 180va x 125%	= 1125va
Sign 1800va x 125%	= 2250va
	30562.5va/240v = 127.3a/20a = 6.36 breakers

16. **(a) 249 amps**   #500 kcmil THHN = 430a x .58 (70°C) = 249 amps.

17. **(b) 14 sq.in.**   392.9(A2) T.392.9 Col. 1

18. **(c) 800 ohms**

19. (c) 10,556 va

SOLUTION: T.220.55 Col. B 2 x 3.5kw = 7,000 x 65%   = 4,550

                       Col. A 2 x 2500 = 5000 + 2,300 + 1,800 = 9,100 x 66% = 6,006

                                                                     10,556va

20. (c) 40 and 400

SOLUTION: T.430.250 F.L.C. = 32a x 125% 430.22(A) = 40 ampacity.

                430.52(C1) ex.2c = 400% maximum inverse time circuit breaker rating

21. (c) 500 amps

SOLUTION: 550.18(A1,2,3)   12' x 35' x 3va =   1260va

                              2 small appl. & laundry =   4500va

                                                5760va

  550.31(1) requires a minimum per lot of 16,000va x 30 lots = 480,000va x 24% = 115,200va

115,200va/240v = 480 amperes.

22. (c) 4,500,000 ohms

23. (b) 1 1/2"

SOLUTION: Table 5A: #3/0 THHN = .2290 x 2 =   .458 sq.in.

                          #2/0 THHN =   .1924

                                     Total   .6504 sq.in. required

                Table 4:   1 1/2" = .814 sq.in.

24. (d) #6

SOLUTION: 32,500va/480v x 1.732 = 39.09 amperes x 135% (460.8A) = 52.7 amperes

                Table 310.16 = #6 THW copper

25. (b) 45.3 amperes

SOLUTION: T.220.56   2 x 3000   = 6,000

                                             5,000

                                           3,000

                    2 x 7500   = 15,000

                                    29,000va x 65% demand = 18,850

18,850va/240v x 1.732 = 45.34a

26. (d) time-delay on de-energizing

27. (a) line contacts supply power to the motor

28. (d)

29. (b)

30. (d)